Kim Johnson

A Journey to and Beyond the Blackboard

Memories of a Boy Who Became a Maverick Headteacher

novum ◢ pro

This book is also
available as
e-book.

www.novum-publishing.co.uk

© 2021 novum publishing

ISBN 978-3-99107-543-1
Editing: Caroline Lawson
Cover photos: Steve Ball, Libux77, Martinmark | Dreamstime.com, Kim Johnson
Cover design, layout & typesetting: novum publishing

www.novum-publishing.co.uk

Dedication

*This book is dedicated
to my three wonderful children
Kara, Allan and Tony.*

During their lifetime I have toiled hard at my craft in education often neglecting them without fully realising. Now retired and having written this book I have the chance to give them something back and explain what I have been up to.

Contents

Prologue

'This book charts the fascinating journey of an inspirational leader of education, both at a local and national level. Full of wit and wisdom, it is a timely, and much needed reminder, of what draws us into teaching. A timeless story of someone who wanted (and succeeded!) in making a difference. An inspiring read.'

James Hilton (Author, Speaker & ex-school leader)

James is the acclaimed author of three books on teacher wellbeing and resilience: 'Leading From the Edge' (Bloomsbury 2016), 'Ten Traits of Resilience' (Bloomsbury 2018) and 'Riding the Waves' (Bloomsbury 2020)

'Kim's experience is as deep as it is wide. There is so much for teachers and leaders here in all settings.

Kim reveals the roots of his practice through his own story. This book drips with experience, understanding and integrity.

Kim shows us how great leaders are made. His experience is striking, relevant and inspiring.'

Paul Dix (nationally known educationalist)

Paul is the acclaimed author of two books: 'When the Adults Change Everything Changes' (Crowne House 2017) and 'After the Adults Change Achievable Behaviour Nirvana' (Crowne House 2021). Paul is an internationally acclaimed leader and speaker on Behaviour in Schools.

Introduction

As a child I had many dreams about what I would like to do on reaching adulthood. Just like many children then and now there were times spent watching and listening to grandparents, parents, uncles and family friends. Their adventures in life and working roles being the fuel to my imagination. The very inspiration that would set my own mind thinking of what possibilities life might present.

Although I started school as a five-year-old in the then West Germany, my first real recollection of school was a few years later in Middlesex. It was not a particularly happy time. The adults I met then seemed at odds with the philosophical notion that education was about learning and the enjoyment of discovery. It was a poor starting point for me when retrieving the very memories of childhood ... which are supposed to be joyful.

With my father's job in the RAF causing us to move regularly, it was such an opportunity that caused things to change. In moving 2,500 miles a single teaching figure literally altered everything and had a huge impact on me. This person being my wonderful Primary Class Teacher, the young Miss Kirkpatrick. One of the few people I will actually name. She was an inspiration and lit in me a spark of enjoyment, interest and enthusiasm that was undoubtedly the foundation of my personal and professional future.

Thereafter moving to boarding school and being there for six years meant some of that enthusiasm was sometimes lost. Certainly, a great deal of what many would consider to be formative years were spent away at school. Yet there were also gains and fun to be had. As I grew up, I began to question and at times to rebel. That journey through three schools and university is tracked in Part One where I undoubtedly learned a great deal about myself and what I wanted from life.

The prospect of ever working in education seemed a million miles from being likely. Unknown to me Teachers, Lecturers and other Educational Professionals lay in wait for me … and in time they were to help me focus and determine the very route of my life. Their wise words, professional insight and enduring encouragement kept me going and believing in the power of education to shape lives. It may seem an unlikely addition to a story of becoming a Headteacher and then Principal, but it explains how adults and teachers can unlock our potential and set us off on our life journey. As you read of my interactions you will see how those relationships can impact on a child and young adult to help shape who we are and how we are. I believe this is something often lost when we speak of the importance of education and its meaning in the widest sense. Take from this part of my journey how at times I was close to coming off the rails and how those in education helped to guide me. The position such teachers had sometimes assisted with my journey as a child and young adult and helped take me beyond a sense of being lost in those tricky times of a teenager. It could have broken me … but there were good adults around and they saw something in me. In the end … they certainly helped take me to a place where I felt being a teacher was the right career pathway.

Part Two unpicks the experiences had as a teacher in five quite different settings. All the children I met and taught, along with my many teaching colleagues, opened my eyes to the varying challenges of those in mainstream and specialist provisions. As I ventured into teaching, my stories show how I navigated that journey. They also reveal how I gained an insight into the potential I had and the opportunities that presented to develop life-changing skills. The switch from being the one being influenced to that of being the one who influences was immense for me. In that time, I actually 'grew up' with those I taught as I developed my craft in a teaching role.

Parts Three and Four reveal many mixed experiences as a school leader of four vastly different schools in Special and International settings. The hard toil involved in breaking mediocrity in school performance in order to motivate all to want to embrace excitement, challenge, discovery and excellence in their practice. No easy feat and one that had its own personal toll, eventually working through such hurdles and achieving success and outstanding practices. These stories reveal the reality of a relentless pursuit of excellence which many will be able to relate to in their own time in education, both present and historic. They may also enlighten those aspiring to venture forth.

Forty-four years after leaving school as a pupil I retired as the Principal of a Special Academy for children and young adults with complex needs and as the former National President of a School Leader's Association. The highs and lows of that journey were many and often intertwined. So many people and places each with their own tale of happiness, sadness, harsh lessons learned, and opportunities taken to try and make a difference.

As you read, I trust that you will consider that all of us can be a leader ... but not everyone is quite ready. The key point I look to make being the importance of learning at every stage of my journey towards becoming a school leader. This often meant asking the question of myself 'What did I learn? Did I make sure I stopped from time to time to listen and think?'

If my story and the actions I took throughout inspire others to ... dream more ... learn more ... do more ... and become more ... then it may help them to be a future leader. The attitude of one's mind being crucial in this ... as portrayed in this simple tale:

'When out at sea ... the pessimist complains about the wind ... the optimist expects it to change ... the leader adjusts the sails.'

Often feeling as if I was one of Education's 'Respectable Revolutionaries' I tried to make my mark. Throughout, my motivation being to overcome the negative half full world of many and replace their thoughts of adversity and difficulty with a sense of challenge and opportunity. It was no easy task. I was paid by my employers in brass ... and rewarded by all the children and young adults I taught ... with memories made of gold. All this warranted a story being told ... and once retired I collected my stories together ... to share with you.

If you are after some sort of academic expose on leadership or an A-Z manual on being successful as a school leader then this is not my intention. I am trying to take you away with me for fifty-five years of travel through a variety of educational settings to give you an insight into the many roles held in this most unlikely of expeditions.

I was once told that as a school leader 'everyone sees what you appear to be ... few experience what you really are'.

Do read on ... make your mind up about my journey and take from it what you wish to help you with yours.

Part One

Learning My Future Craft

In 2015 a Minister addressed an Education Summit in London and when speaking about the purpose of education he said:

"Education is the engine of our economy, it is the foundation of our culture, and it's an essential preparation for adult life."

He went on to say,

"We all have a responsibility to educate the next generation of informed citizens, introducing them to the best that has been thought and said, and instilling in them a love of knowledge and culture for their own sake. But education is also about the practical business of ensuring that young people receive the preparation they need to secure a good job and a fulfilling career, and have the resilience and moral character to overcome challenges and succeed."

My earliest memories of the journey you are about to travel with me should have mirrored his words. Surely that would have been the very basis of why I was turning up at school each morning from 1960. Yet you will see that from 1963 such great words could not have been further from the reality I experienced.

Thank goodness for one young Primary Teacher in 1965 who typified the words of Albert Einstein:

"It is the supreme art of the teacher to awaken joy in creative expression and knowledge."

She loved teaching and as a result I began to love learning. This was a significant discovery for me. At that time I had a positive grasp of what my educational experience could be ... and how the school I was in should be. My life was touched by this teacher.

Secondary school had its moments where such experiences grew, faded and grew again. It was here that the characters I related to were the difference.

As Andy Rooney is reputed to have said:
"Great teachers are usually a little crazy."

I met such inspiring characters and they cast a spell on me. Are such individuals not the very ones we remember?

In his speech in 2015, the Minister also referenced the disdainful words of Mark Twain:
"I have never let my schooling interfere with my education."

As a teenager, with all that means psychologically, socially and physically we have our heads turned by the distractions and our minds energised by the challenging of boundaries. You may connect to my time away from home at boarding school or indeed spot a similar child or pupil in your life experience to date. I learned so much outside of the classroom and more importantly got the chance to test its efficacy.

Mark Twain would relate to the view that it provided me with an insight into the meaning of the saying:
'The only difference between a good day and a bad day is your attitude.'

This all lead to going to University in 1974 ... with a desire to learn the craft of being a teacher ... not just any teacher ... for as you will find out I wanted to be one who could make a real difference ... to some incredibly special children.

As you read through the five chapters in Part One you may sometimes question my arrival at such a conclusion in my 'Learning'. I trust you will also reflect on the impact that the adults had on me and how I arrived at the point where wanting to become a teacher was a reality. Can you remember such a moment and is it something you are still true to now?

It is important to stop and think as an adult and particularly as a teacher to question in your life journey what your personal trail has left behind. Probably best captured in the discussion between two old friends about their driving. One says to the other "I've had a safe life driving a car and never been involved in an accident." His friend replies "I take it you looked in your rear-view mirror from time to time just to be sure?"

As such, to stop from time to time and think what it is like to be a child or teenager in their home, classroom and school is time well spent. Too often we focus on 'what' they have done rather than 'why' they did it. For sure, if in the case of where there has been a wrong it should be addressed. But in order to understand, so it isn't done again, the 'why' is important. And actually, the 'why' should always be important in all cases. As adults, teachers and school leaders we must take on the responsibility of playing a key role in assisting with this fundamental in education for life. The question is there to be asked ... 'Can you think of times when it worked ... and those when it could have?'

Chapter 1

Memories Start in Middlesex

I had started school as a five-year-old at St Patrick's Primary School at Rheindahlen in the then West Germany. It was a five minutes walk to school and I really have little recollection of teachers, friends and lessons from that time at all. We returned from there to England and my first real abiding memory of schooling was at Juniors in Middlesex. It wasn't a very happy experience in what was a rather Dickensian brick building which even looked unwelcoming on the sunniest of summer days. The adults often added to this sense of foreboding as many of my teachers were clearly of that time in both their interaction with pupils and abrupt delivery of education. I reflect now that it wasn't an inspiring time in my life or one where confidence was encouraged to flourish.

The Arithmetic teacher was from Burma and his steely look though small round-rimmed glasses struck fear into all who sat before him. His snap questions delivered like a coachman's whip across the classroom caused panic to the often unsuspecting and probable daydreaming nine-year-old recipient. Many times, I was overwhelmed with fear of being asked … and amusingly total surprise on giving a correct answer to a question. The rapidity of the bursts of questions on times tables often seemed like the room was being sprayed with machine gun bullets. The carnage of wounded pupils berated or beaten for incorrect answers in what seemed like war trenches between the wooden desks. Such was the imagery of these lessons every day of the week. It all seemed to resemble the stories I often immersed myself in when reading the Victor or Hotspur comics and my developing imagination often saw me drift away into a daydream wondering if I would survive.

The ultimate punishment for poor performance of any sort was by way of the wooden twelve-inch ruler. Held firmly in his hand and with the precision of his mathematical mind it was delivered thin and inked edge across my fingers many times. There were, I am sure, occasions when he smiled. However, I hesitate to suggest this may have been at such a time as my eyes closed in anticipation of the pain yet to be delivered. They were often clouded by my tears at the conclusion of this act of punishment. It would be fair to suggest that all future teachers of arithmetic would find my love and desire for their subject more than an academic challenge.

This teacher was not alone in the use of physical punishment deemed to be so important in assisting learning at this time in the mid-1960s. The P.E. teacher also had the role of teaching basket-weaving. A curious subject clearly deemed important in our preparation for future life. The art of wetting the cane to enable it to bend without splitting or snapping became another great challenge in this chapter of my schooling. Enough to say that my cane, like that of many others in class, would often split as it had dried out when being worked. At such a moment I would have to join the queue to the teacher's desk with my fellow failed weavers. Each and everyone of us with our heads bowed lower and lower as we got closer to the front. The burst of rebuke from the teacher for poor workmanship often added to by being beaten with a plimsoll for repeat offending in the production of weaved baskets. It was never clear why this chubby and not particularly athletic teacher of P.E. was given such a teaching role. Was it his hobby at home? Was it the Headteacher's humorous timetabling retribution for a previous incident in his teaching? Whatever the answer, it was often the case that to walk the three miles home at the end of the day was celebrated with relief if I had not been hit with a ruler or slipper.

Were there any nice teachers at this school? Gosh, I just don't remember any, such is the abiding memory of the two I mentioned. Later in my life a phrase used by my Arithmetic Teacher suddenly reappeared in my thoughts. He used to say on a regular basis in all sorts of contexts, "He who points one finger at you points three at themself!" and then go about modelling his hand to show this physically. He would then explain how when apportioning blame with the pointed finger it was important to realise the contributory facts (the other three fingers) that may have been the accusers responsibility. I didn't really get it at the time but did wonder later if he realised that when he crushed us for our mistakes, he ever thought of applying this philosophy to his own teaching performance.

As to the question 'Were there any happy and fun moments otherwise?' Yes of course, but none were within the school building. As I look back to this time I wonder where those teachers I have referenced had lost their way. What had happened to make them breakers of my spirit and feeling scared of the place where I was supposed to be learning of the richness and excitement of life still to be lived? Undoubtedly on becoming a headteacher thirty years later this experience of mine was not to be allowed as a blight on the life of any child in my school. What can and should we do to ensure such are not in the profession?

There was something in me, as indeed there is in every child, needing to be saved from being lost. For I had something in me that a good teacher should and could help me realise. The problem ... was my problem ... there was nobody who was in that school who played out that role at that time.

As daft as it may seem, break-time epitomises the simplicity of what was there just below the surface. I was at this time one of the five most celebrated members of the school's equivalent of Freddy and the Dreamers, and the Dave Clark Five. I both played the air guitar with the most incredible skill and sang sweetly in unison with my band members delivering tunes such as "You were made for Me" to adoring fans in the playground. The requests for an encore often meaning we were slow back to class at the end of playtime because we were having to fight our way through eight- to ten-year old girls swooning because of our celebratory status in the long Summer months. These fifteen-to-twenty minute breaks from the adults were the only moments I recall as being fun.

Football hadn't gripped my interest yet, which was still influenced heavily by my 'Matt Braddock VC' and 'Alf Tupper of the Track' as well as making and painting Airfix model planes to hang by cotton from my bedroom ceiling. Yet twice a week we went to the recreation ground to play football. I realised years later that I would have been an ideal disinterested player in the making of the film 'Kes' for I could spin on a sixpence with clumsy precision to miss tackling an oncoming eager forward dribbling towards our team's goal. Needless to say, that the basket weaver track-suited teacher would find a moment to insult my interest and ability at the time with his sharp tongue. Thankfully, his black plimsoll was not within reach to seek further retribution if I was one of his team's defenders.

Walking the three miles home enabled me and my younger brother Keith to shrug off the bewilderment of our educational day and return home to smiles and warmth. It didn't matter if it was sunny, snow or rain because walking home was to escape and it was all the quicker achieved.

One winter when the snow and ice was of seemingly glacial proportions to my young mind, it became clear that the toilets were the nerve centre of our beloved school. The work of the caretaker to keep them warm(ish), thereby preventing the pipes from freezing, was integral to the school being open. At this point the musical opportunities of our celebrated group were limited by the adverse weather. Our lead singer realised a great plan for renewed adulation in this barren time of Playground Palladium performances. One afternoon as we left school, we turned on the taps in the toilets and walked away nervously. The following morning on arrival at school the fearsome Headteacher was there announcing that owing to the frozen flood the school could not open and we should all go home. Our thrill and joyous celebration was naturally measured as he scoured the faces of those before him trying to turn happy smiles to guilt with his heavy stare.

The Frozen Five were never discovered as our fan base remained loyal to us throughout the winter and through into the summer. With the warmer days and bright sunshine, we were there again against the playground fence performing many a happy rendition of popular songs to lighten the day before and after the never-ending challenges of arithmetic and basket weaving.

Of course, this was wrong, but it was a silent rebuke of the misery meted out by some teachers. It literally stopped the systematic violence of two adults being the norm ... just for a single day. If only the Headteacher had been as eager to seek out such culprits on his staff.

Can you imagine my excitement in the Summer of 1965 to find that my father was posted with the RAF to Cyprus and we would be leaving to join him in the Summer Holiday? That last day at school in Middlesex was one when relief ran through me at speed. The war that had been waged in my Primary schooling came to an end and I was released from so much unhappiness.

Chapter 2

Happiness in the Mediterranean Sun

On Friday 13th August 1965 we flew from RAF Lyneham by a Britannia propellor plane. Fully laden we charged down the runaway with the engines roaring. We took off with what looked like a final desperate flap of the wings ... goodbye England.

My baby brother Simon in a hammock suspended from the ceiling of the plane's cabin. Excitement was rife throughout the plane but we all fell asleep quickly to begin our dreams of what may be ahead. When we landed, I remember a frightfully posh officer coming on board and welcoming us all. As he did the heat entering the plane was incredible. I knew then that no wooly jumpers would be needed living in the Mediterranean.

It was probably no surprise that on arriving in Cyprus I was initially somewhat hesitant and withdrawn when it came to school. My experience in Middlesex had impacted on me quite profoundly regarding my desire to engage and feel comfortable in the presence of those responsible for teaching and learning. There had been no excitement and certainly none of what I now know as the awe and wonder of true learning. Then I met my Junior Class Teacher Miss Kirkpatrick (I have to name and celebrate her). When she spoke there was kindness, honesty, enthusiasm and a gentleness in her voice. She was inspirational in making everyone in our class realise they had ability and a great deal to offer every learning experience presented to us. If you got it right, you not only began to believe but your classmates acknowledged you were of talent. If you got it wrong, you were praised for your contribution and effort and your classmates encouraged you to try again. This wonderful lady ... this wonderful teacher created this for us all. She set us all alight and I loved every moment in her presence.

Even on a cloudy and overcast day school still had a sparkle about it. On a very sunny day ... or should I say very hot day when one hundred degrees Fahrenheit was reached ... the school closed. We would all then trek home across the scorched ground to get our swimming kit and head off to the RAF Nicosia pool. It was great ... Yes! Yet there was a touch of disappointment as an exciting learning moment was being cut short and we were having to say goodbye to Miss K. No thoughts ever again of acts of junior school terrorism and frozen toilets. It is with teachers such as her that we should fill our schools to make them places where every child's dreams can be set free.

My class had one particular girl in it with blond hair that had a green sheen to it from the chlorine in the pool. Over time I believe the same started to happen to me and my three brothers for at every opportunity we would look to go swimming. My brother Keith proved to be the most incredible swimmer and I still wonder if he has webbed feet and gills for he could swim far ... ever under water. 'Tupper of the Track' was left in his wake and Keith was my hero in water. No wonder he joined the Royal Navy at fifteen!

The Headteacher was the most relaxed individual I had ever met in a school. It's only now that I realise his philosophy was simple ... make learning fun and enjoyable ... create interest and a questioning mind ... be kind, friendly and honest in all you do ... and never give up. He ran the basketball and football team and suddenly the sportsman in me was released on court and in goal. I loved my sport and he made that happen. This man only raised his hands to applaud honest individual and team effort. Middlesex was banished to the back of my mind and schooling was now an absolute joy. I had discovered that teachers were capable of being caring, happy and inspiring individuals.

When I rummage through my attic boxes, I often come across my stamp album which was given as First Prize for a Handwriting Competition and my Observers Book of Architecture, another prize for a school project. These are remnants of good memories from 1965–67 at St Michaels Primary School in RAF Nicosia. This part of my own education was a defining moment in my life. Miss K. had a key in her teaching skills box with which she could unlock potential. Yet at the time I would have had no idea that the day would come when I would seek out those with the very same magical skills and fill my schools with such wonderful teachers. When such teachers are found ... of which there are many ... every Head must do all they can to keep them in their school.

My enduring interest in Politics started here with an introduction to the electoral process in our Junior School Presidential Campaign. I was blessed with some great classmates on my campaign team who canvassed for me and helped create a Pupil Charter for future adoption. We were successful and I was duly elected as Pupil President in assembly. Word had it that my performance in a recent football match and the promise of an escalator to the first-floor classrooms clinched the vote in a closely run campaign. This may have been true, but the stairs were never replaced!

One of my best friends at the time was a classmate called Bob. His father was a medic at the RAF Medical Centre. Sadly, when a Swiss passenger plane crashed trying to land in a terrible storm at the nearby airfield, the Medical Centre was used as the morgue for the one hundred and twenty-six of the one hundred and thirty crew and passengers who perished. Bob's Dad was always a cheerful man. After this he was marked emotionally by the terrible experience. Some twenty years later Bob and I met again during my Gap Year at RAF Rheindahlen in the then West Germany. His dad worked at the RAF Hospital at nearby Wegberg. The crash still hung over him like a dark cloud.

Bob is the only person from my Junior School time that I have ever met again. Such are the challenges of being a 'Forces Brat' that you travel every two to three years and may never be reunited with a classmate or friend. It remains something of a regret when I find myself in conversation with current friends who have sustained their connections and friendships going back to Junior School and earlier. More of Bob later in the book.

Under the educational spell of Miss K. most of our class took and passed the Eleven-Plus. I don't remember extra tutoring or cramming for the exam. It was just something we did as part of our normal everyday learning and I really don't recall feeling under pressure or worried of any potential outcome. When I was told the results were in and that I had passed I recall Miss K. having tears in her eyes and the most wonderful smile on her face. It was as though she knew of my journey and realised what she had unlocked. I was allowed to hug her and say thank you. Then, full of excitement, I ran all the way home to tell my parents. They probably understood more of the implications and possibilities than I did … my mum cried; she was so proud.

The rest of that first school year in Cyprus continued to be a great adventure. Through listening to Miss K. read aloud magical and often complicated stories I discovered the joy of reading books. This act of reading pleasure took place in the siesta period each hot summer afternoon as I lay on my bed with the ceiling fan whirring above me. Some of the books related to the lives of young boys at boarding school and all the 'Jolly Japes' they got up to. I didn't realise at the time how this was to influence my next learning experience beyond Cyprus.

The next school year saw Defence Cuts bite on the island and the Secondary School section at St Michaels was faced with closure as the military presence on camp was reduced. The prospect for my second year was that I may have to travel seventy miles to the Sovereign Base Area at Dhekelia or Akrotiri for my schooling.

Miss K. remained my teacher throughout the year. Her influence further inspiring me to love every moment of school in her magical presence. Something that has stayed with me and been motivational regarding schools ever since.

As the Secondary School faced closure my parents asked me if I would be prepared to go back to England to attend boarding school in Sussex not far from Gran Johnson. At this point the stories of boarding school dormitories, tuck boxes, teachers in gowns with wisdom in their lessons and the fun of young boys away from home ... all that I had buried my nose in ... suddenly were real in their possibility. I said 'Yes!'

The end of the school year was sad in that I had to say goodbye to Miss K. and so many school friends and teachers. What a difference in my life from Middlesex to this point. I was the same person ... but so much happier and confident in my eleven years of age.

About this time my parents suddenly became gripped with the idea that Sunday School in the Military Church would be a good thing for me to take two of my brothers to. We would be dressed up in best clothes and sent across the scrubland to attend. The first occasion was pure torture for us, and we wondered afterwards why so many angry adults gathered otherwise happy children together to batter them with 'Thou shall not' in so many ways. If God spoke to us that morning it was to advise us to see the light ... the light of outside. Every Sunday thereafter we would take ourselves off to church with a convincing smile. We would walk past the church door and go to the NAAFI to buy a bottle of Seven Up then sit up the tree drinking our pop waiting for Sunday School to be over. We would then return home and between us we had enough stories about religion from R.E. lessons to weave a convincing tale of our morning. It took twenty years for this story to be released to our parents from our classified memories. Such was the ingrained military mind.

The Summer Holiday passed fairly quickly with frequent visits to the beaches on the north coast of Cyprus, east and west of Kyrenia. The adventure of the journey each Saturday and Sunday through the Greek Checkpoint, across 'No-Man's Land' and on to the Turkish checkpoint in the foothills of the Kyrenia Mountains. Then through the Pass at St Hilarion Castle, once a Crusader Stronghold, and past the Canadian Soldiers UN Base before driving down through the checkpoints again into Greek Kyrenia. This was definitely a boy-excitement-thing for me as a Victor and Hotspur comic reader. My three younger brothers and myself hanging on every word of explanation by my knowledgeable father of all things military. There was probably a touch of added drama and intrigue thrown in to suggest John Wayne or Richard Attenborough were somewhere to be seen en route. But then ... Hey what was there we didn't want to believe!

The beaches were empty of all civilisation until we arrived. No hotels to be seen outside of Kyrenia and each beach was known by the mile distance east or west of the port. Sometimes a Greek National Guardsman would appear with binoculars looking out to sea. But nobody startled him on the horizon while we were ever there. We would swim and snorkel in the clear blue and warm sea finding ancient pottery remnants by rocks. My imagination about such findings being another example of Miss K.'s impact.

Before leaving the island in the Summer to travel back to England the last haircut had to take place in the city of Nicosia. The barber was a jolly Greek and Ex-EOKA freedom fighter (once deemed a terrorist during British Rule before Independence). After each haircut we would always be given a small white ceramic bottle of Tabac aftershave. I duly had mine to take to boarding school.

With some mixed emotions and probably a great deal of naivety I said goodbye to my Mum and two youngest brothers, Chris and Simon. My Dad, brother Keith and I flew back to England by RAF Transport Command via RAF Luqa in Malta.

Life was about to change again ... because of school.

Chapter 3

Secondary Years in Sussex

Having been fitted for the full school uniform in a prestigious outfitter in Brighton under the close supervision of my dear Gran, it was time to journey to the country town that was to be more than just school for it was to be my home for most of the next six years.

We travelled in a very old car borrowed from the dear elderly couple in Burgess Hill where my father had been evacuated to during the war. It was a classic from the thirties which had flip-out indicators and a wiper operated manually. My trunk was tied to the rack on its rear and my brother Keith and I took it in turns to sit in the front next to my father who drove cautiously in this relic of the road. Periodically at junctions the engine would decide it needed a brief rest and would have to be cranked back to life using a heavy handle.

On arrival in the school car park, our car was surrounded by many a sporty car and large modern saloon. It later transpired that initial impressions of other new boys arriving was that we were loaded and quite eccentric thus the car of our choice. In this early stage of establishing myself in the school I felt it wise neither to agree nor dismiss the view but just smile and then change the subject. With another boy announcing bravely he was called William Alexander Van Tromp it seemed attention would not stay with me over such a car ... one that many years on would rival the children's stories of Mr Gumdrop!

The rigorously enforced routine soon became entrenched in my mind as I settled into the old Grammar School. The softer and friendlier boundaries of my Cyprus experience would both be challenged and gradually unpicked as I tried to fit the model instilled by this traditional setting.

The school was founded in 1614 and many of the original Elizabethan frontage remained. The rest being a mixture of buildings from the 18th century through to the 1950's. It was, and still is, situated in the centre of a small Sussex town with a public pathway through the sprawling site. At the time there were four hundred pupils of which three hundred were day boys coming from nearby coastal towns and rural inland towns and villages. The Headteacher was a formidable and frightening character rarely seen without his gown flowing in a trail behind him as he moved around the school creating a silence and respectful bow from staff and students alike. The Housemaster was an ex-army officer and very brave man with the nickname 'Shocker' saying all about his manner if crossed or not listened to. It's only through the passage of time that I have realised they both had a softer and kinder side. Many years later I have read just so in the 'Old Boy's Newsletters' I still receive.

As a boarder it was instilled in us that we were the best in the school and as such loyalty to our Holland House (red in colour) was deemed paramount in all we were to do. The first few months in the midst of this setting ... which was almost more military than the life I had led to that day ... was quite challenging. It soon became evident that the term attributed to me and all others in the first three years of the school identified our true status. We were the 'Grots'!

My first dormitory was on the second floor of the most recent of buildings. The room was large with sinks in the middle and then divided into bays with two or three beds in each. We would have a small locker by our beds with personal effects at a minimum. Whatever we did have, it had to conform to the manifest given prior to arriving and then packed in our large trunk. This was then checked on arrival. It truly was regimented and there was no grey in anything at all … for all was very black or white in more than our clothing.

We had a common room and a T.V. room for recreational use. Most activities being dictated by older boys … not those necessarily with the best ideas. The T.V. was for all, but the Dorm Captains or Prefects decided on what was to be watched and whether some or all of us newly anointed Grots could sit and watch too. On every Saturday morning we lined up to be given our pocket money which in my first term was 1/6d in three silver sixpenny pieces. We were then allowed to venture a few yards into the town to the Tuck Shop to buy sweets or the local bakery to buy bags of broken biscuits. For the first time in my life, I noted older boys skulking in the shadows nervously smoking cigarettes for fear of being caught by a boarding house master. An act I was to gravitate to in a few years' time as a respite from the rigour … or was it a moment of rebellious challenge to be enjoyed?

On every Sunday morning we sat for an hour writing letters home. I enjoyed this as it was my way of staying in touch with my parents so far away. I understand that some of my letters revealed a great deal of heartache and upset at being away from home, which impacted particularly on my mother. However, the magical tales I had read as I lay on my bed in Cyprus were no longer just so and there were times when a hug or a smile were sorely missed, and homesickness went through my heart and soul in big waves. At its worse gently crying into my pillow eased the speed at which I fell asleep many a time through that first term. The gift was not to be heard in my sadness for the resultant bullying would be relentless, as I had witnessed with the emotional crushing of lesser boys suffering from the same heartbreak.

The whole experience was like that of being a newly-born lamb in a field with many a sheep dog as senior pupils running the show for a farmer like teacher gazing on. The difference being there was no parent to rush to for support, comfort or explanation on what to do. The dormitory routine was enforced rigorously by a member of the Lower Sixth who would be the Dorm. Captain. His performance would be further scrutinised by one of the Upper Sixth Prefects. Lights out was initially at eight fifteen p.m. and talking or going to the bathroom was dealt with by reference to what seemed a compendium of dubious punishments initially including anything from being screamed at, to physically struck. This would, in the years that followed, be refined by senior boys who clearly enjoyed the privilege of their position and meted out punishments with a worrying sense of power and enjoyment. I was recently amused to read that the year before my arrival that the use of physical punishment by staff and prefects had been forbidden with the exception of the Headmaster and Boarding Housemaster. I recall the hook in the Elizabethan Long Dorm. from one of the cross beams where it was said that boys had once been beaten when suspended from it. True or false it did not matter for the very thought was enough to ensure most pupils may pause and reconsider before doing anything deemed wrong.

I did mostly manage to avoid capture by those seemingly demonic wardens of the night but sometimes my enthusiasm to catch up on the day after lights out resulted in what was in my mind a very public arrest. The trouble for me was that in having three brothers it had always been common practice and very normal to talk with them for a while after saying good night to our parents. Seeing darkness in the same way after lights out was clearly a mistake and often ended in tears accompanying the physical or mental pain.

On being caught ... which sometimes meant being given up by other pupils to avoid mass punishment ... the Dorm. Captain would decide on the consequence. If a repeat offence, then the

Prefects would be called upon. Their rebuke, which was often littered with swear words and poking of the finger in my chest, could be followed by a detention or immediate return to bed after some other punishment. I recall such as having to stand with my arms outstretched sideways making circles with my fingers the size of a sixpence for an hour … holding an Encyclopaedia Britannica in each outstretched arm for fifteen minutes at a time … having a page of The Times and having to cross out all the vowels … and being used as the replacement to a ball by four Hockey-playing Dorm. Captains and beaten around the ankles and shins as they 'passed' me around the corridor for sport. I often wonder what sort of adult, parent and co-worker they went on to be in their future life. Is this what I've heard over the last twenty years as what some men say is 'character building' and includes the often accompanying and qualifying remark "It never did me any harm!" Undoubtedly my latter interest in playing in goal at hockey to shelter behind pads and body armour may have had its subconscious roots in this particular run-in.

My dear Gran lived not far away by the coast and requested several times in my first year for me to be allowed out for a visit on a Saturday. I caught the bus, and she was there to meet me at the other end. I had to wear my full school uniform and that included my cap perched on my head. She would walk with her head held proudly high as indeed I'm sure she did for most of her life. I found her to be such an incredibly interesting lady and so rich in experiences to make the day a treasure trove of tales. We would take tea in the most splendid cafes and retire back to her modest flat where I was taught to play cards and pretend bet on the T.V. horse racing. Throughout, the tales were delivered so eloquently about her knowing royalty and statesmen from abroad such as Seretse Khama and his wife Ruth in Bechuanaland (now Botswana) and Eamon de Valera in Eire. I was shocked to hear how at the time the Afrikaans would spit at my Gran for her liaison with Seretse and Ruth. Another defining moment when racism became apparent to me and left me feeling disgusted. This lady had fought a crocodile, helped pull teeth from a poorly hippopotamus and ridden on an ostrich in a race. She most certainly was not your 'everyday grandmother'. At the time, as a young impressionable boy, I was convinced she should have had her own part in the Victor or Hotspur comic ... for she was really a most amazing woman. Another adult who helped me realise the importance of 'dreaming big'.

That first Christmas saw my brother Keith and I meet up in London under the escort of a SSAFA Social Worker who took us to Heathrow Airport. From there we flew unaccompanied to Athens where we had to change flights for one to Nicosia. All this as tender twelve and eleven year olds performed without a thought of risk and danger. Unknown to us, the life in Cyprus had changed quite dramatically with the expected threat of the Turkish mainland forces invading. My mother had recently returned from the Sovereign Base Area of Dhekelia to our home at Nicosia where my father and other British Military personnel were stood beneath Union Flags indicating to any potential invaders that they were not the enemy. As my father said years later it was the first time he had been told that our national flag was a bullet-proof shield. Thankfully he never had it put to the test. In my child's eye he would have been ready though with his tin helmet and machine gun. The two weeks at home on a military base were a refreshing relief after the greater regimented life at boarding school. Our return flight required changes in Athens and Rome. No adult posed a single question on our independent adult-free status. How times have changed since.

I never quite conformed to all the expectations and routines at boarding school and maybe all too often failed to see the true error of my ways. Yet there was a growing desire to fight back in some way and as such it did emerge that I was becoming a bit of a rebel. It seemed only right to me at the time as very quickly I realised for bullies and wrongdoing to exist, all you have to do is nothing. So, I promised myself that when I became a Sixth

Former I would 'try to be different'. Following on from being squashed into conforming in Middlesex and then freed in Cyprus it felt right not to give up on my new-found confidence. The maverick beginning to show his ways and shaping my own philosophy on how life could be.

As a teacher and Headteacher years later I often took an interest in such pupil behaviour. I saw it as a challenge ... not always to the authority and routine but also as to the reasons such structures were in place and whether they actually worked. Is this something we need to do more often so as to check that our organisation is right for the time we are in ... and fits those within it?

The dorm. routine required mathematical precision in folding hospital corners on my bed with the travel rug folded three times at its base. I can still do this instinctively with a sheet before twitching and realising what I am doing. As a new boy we were all timetabled to a bath on two nights of the week irrespective of our state of full cleanliness. Water and soap were no stranger to me at twelve years of age so I would sneak a bath whenever I could and even take the place of another who preferred to stay in his self-professed respectable grubby state. We had to wear our school clothes and remain pristine in outward presentation throughout the day unless changed for sport or allowed to go for a walk in civvies. As such, in blazer with cap (with boarders special v-bend in the peak) perched on my head we would carry out all aspects of eating meals, attending morning prayers, going to lessons and doing prep in the evening so attired.

Meals were simple and never quite filling with us all sat at long tables with benches down each side. We would be called to every meal by the brass wall bell being rung by one of us being sent by a master to the main playground. On arrival in the dining room we would stand with our backs to the table whereupon at a silent signal, the prefect at the head of our table would walk slowly along our line ensuring our polished shoes, combed hair and clean hands were of a standard befitting being fed. If we were not up to it then we were dismissed to improve our performance. It was known to take several attempts particularly if the prefect had taken a dislike to you. The meal always started with grace in Latin.

There would be a roll call at the evening meal and if there was any post from home it would be eagerly pocketed to be read later. Receiving mail was a great moment for us all as contact with the outside world was soul-lifting. With my parents being over two thousand miles away it was my only contact and has still to this day an importance to me. Outdated I may be, but sending cards, letters and postcards is something I continue to enjoy .... and of course receiving them too.

Each Wednesday evening meal was quite special and a worry for all the boarders. It was during this time that the Housemaster would walk around with the designated Prefect to decide who needed a haircut. Woe betides you if your hair touched your collar or ears. If it did then a haircut would have to follow irrespective of whether you had received one the week before. After that the routine was just work through the one hundred names on the boarder's list for the hour the barber was present. The barber was a strange, gruff and oldish fellow with one leg shorter than the other made good with an extended heel. Before coming into school, he would be in the public house across the road for a couple or more pints of beer and then be heard banging his heavy shoe on the wooden steps to the room in the Elizabethan frontage of school. Here he would work his hour of boarder shearing with little regard for ears consequently often drawing blood. His breath barely enough of an anaesthetic to his craft. I recall one rebel fifth former having his hair completely shaved off at home and then being banned from having a haircut for a term. I found that quite funny but didn't want to pursue such a line as skin heads were something I'd become weary of when out in my cap and blazer. We were seen as fair game for any such locals in villages and towns nearby.

For years afterwards having a haircut was only marginally more enjoyable than a trip to the dentist. Make no mistake about how what happens in a school can have such an effect. How ironic it is that still in the present day some headteachers have made hairstyles such a point of conflict. We portray a need to draw the individual out in each pupil but some of us insist they must all be almost clone-like in their appearance.

Every Sunday we would have a visit to the Parish Church which saw us travel the short distance in our Sunday suits and then listen to the Vicar dutifully instil all manner of his reputed wisdom into our less interested minds. Yet one Sunday I did listen and to my confoundment heard him make openly racist remarks about those with a darker skin. Sat next to me was my Indian friend Paul and it was all I could do as a fourteen-year-old to stay sat down for the voice in my head was saying "Stand up and shout shame on you!" at the vicar. From that day forward I was deaf to this man and lost to any thought of the Church. The exception being about once a month when we would all travel the short walk to the Methodist Church, and it was less of a bible bash but more of a conversation. The fact that a wonderful array of sandwiches, cake and numerous cups of tea would also be available was not important, but it was welcome. The kind minister and dear old ladies actively encouraged us to eat and drink as much as we could. To make it even better, there was no getting in a queue behind older and senior pupils.

Once a year we would go on what was deemed a Pilgrimage down a long single-track lane at the bottom of our town to a country house and its own church. It never rained and the sun made the walk an enjoyable excursion despite the true purpose. In my third year, myself and two other boys fell short in our godliness when in the church. A younger and irritating boy sat in front of us kept making rude and disingenuous remarks. When we all knelt on the prayer cushions, he momentarily disappeared from view to the congregation as we rearranged his manner with a couple of thumps from the pupil next to me. It was our belief that all but the Lord had seen us ... but we were mistaken. On return to school the Housemaster requested our presence in his study. We received three strikes of the cane on our backsides with the proviso that God knew too and would judge us later. All well and good to this newly signed up non-believer but the true pain was to follow. 'Shocker' had his study on the first floor and the steps from it were narrow, short and steep. On leaving his study with our backsides literally on fire the pain increased as our footing was unstable and we slipped down the steps adding a further dozen or so strikes to our buttocks as they caught each step. Clearly God got us quicker than I had initially thought.

I was only caned one other time when at the school. This was by the Headteacher for being on the lawn in front of his courtyard study. I'd been sent by grinning Prefects to collect a ball they had kicked there. I was their bait to fuel the Headteacher's anger and promised retribution for stepping on this hallowed turf. Now I had seen and heard of other boys being caned by him coming out from his study holding their backsides and back of the head. This misadventure of mine enabled me to feel and see why this mystery was just so. He would require you to bend in front of his study door. As the strike of the cane cracked against my backside my head instinctively came up and hit the large brass door handle. Thereby presenting my backside for the second stroke of the cane as I lowered my head in pain. So with two of the cane and a sore head I was the wiser and thereafter avoided that lawn for the remainder of my time at the school ... bar my last day as an eighteen-year-old when I walked across it with a smile on my face.

My initial academic performance in Sussex was, in my mind, on a par with the successes enjoyed thanks to Miss Kirkpatrick. However, by the third year I had found that school was not very motivating, interesting or enjoyable in too many cases. It really had not completely captivated me as had been the case at St

Michaels in Cyprus. As and when I was engaged, what seemed to spur me on was teaching performed with passion and enthusiasm by younger staff. Consequently Geography, Physics and History captured my full attention and sustained it throughout. I wondered at the time if other teachers realised how some of their contemporaries were gifted in this way.

Maths, despite its more seemingly grown-up name from Arithmetic weighed heavy until a quirky teacher performer was assigned to my class. He was an ex-Royal Marine Commando from WW2 with a pronounced limp owing to an active service injury. I'm not sure that my ability with numbers was particularly enhanced … albeit that I just could not get enough of quadratic equations … but the performance of his teaching was quite simply best described as awesome. His semaphore like use of his arms to express numbers, angles, the use of a slide rule and search out answers from his audience was positively theatrical.

None more so than when performing the wizardry of drawing a circle. He would pull a handkerchief from his breast pocket and with a flick and twist turn it into a long white extended linen line to which with the speed of hand he would attach a piece of chalk. Then placing one end in the centre of the blackboard he would create the most perfect circle on the board. At this point he would momentarily turn his back on us all. He knew we were sat open mouthed gazing at him in amazement. Then he would conclude this piece of precision showmanship as he looked at us over his glasses. He would remove the piece of chalk then flick the handkerchief back to life as a square of linen and replace it in his top pocket with a movement akin to waving a wand. Pure theatre performed with such effortless skill.

Now, do I remember the language and use of trigonometry thereafter? Sadly, not a lot. Yet his circle making art has stayed with me to this day. No wonder quirky teachers with mind capturing performances were central to my craft in later years. I should add I did get my 'O' Level Maths and all other subjects with my best grades in the subjects where I had been more inspired by the teachers.

When it came to A Levels, my Economics Teacher was of a 'New Teaching World' compared to his peers in the Senior Common Room. With the classroom door closed we would call him by his Christian name (Ron), take tea at the mid-point of a double lesson, read the Economist, do share trading completions using the Daily Telegraph and be captivated by his knowledge and the genuine excited passion with which he delivered the subject. He had a hole in one of his shoes made good with a cigarette packet folded inside to keep the damp from his socks. This troubled me for why was it that this academic economist who could spout such means to develop wealth could not sort out his own finances enough to get his shoes a new sole? When his car finally gave up the ghost and died of part old age and part neglect, all Sixth Formers studying with him were invited to its funeral. The lines "Rust to Rust" and "Going to the Car Park in the Sky" trotted out at its memorable bon voyage. Under this man's academic spell every student got an A in their exams at the end of our Upper Sixth. This is what can happen when you are inspired by the very best of teachers. As indeed 'Ron' undoubtedly was, for he made the subject come alive.

A few years ago I returned to the four hundredth Anniversary of the School being founded and met an elderly ex-pupil. He had come along to the celebration with his Geography Exercise book from his third year in the late 1940s. It was similar in every detail to how mine had been lovingly used to write and draw notes of learning enjoyed because of how the teacher had taught. He spoke of his heartfelt enjoyment of being in such a class and relishing every moment in that teacher's presence. Such men and women who create learning in that way are truly stars in their own right. They are remembered by us all from such days long passed.

The rear of his exercise book had the top right card cover torn away. True authenticity of the book as one that had been fully used and not a page removed. For the way in which I recall receiving a new exercise book in all subjects was to line up in the top corridor by the store cupboard awaiting my turn in front of the Senior Master. He would flick the pages to his ear ... balance it in one hand and judge its weight and then if satisfied that no ill deed had been performed to its entirety, he would give you a new book and signify the fact with a tear to the rear cover of the old one. Such hearing and balance of hand being another curious and quirky memory and one I engaged this elderly former pupil in ... and we chuckled and sighed with a smile at the tale.

When allowed out in Years Four through to the Sixth Form I enjoyed the opportunity to wander the Downs and side-streams of the river. Enjoying anything from panoramic views north, collecting blackberries and chasing Small Blue butterflies across the chalk lands to just laying on my back watching clouds scuttle across the sky above. I had often wondered what my parents and brothers would be up to. A family I was part of but for the main, apart from.

Down by the river I'd enjoy catching dozens of gorging eels, the most beautiful rudd, voracious perch and shoals of eager-to-be-caught roach in the side stream in what seemed like beautiful long sunny summer days. I would be lost in a tranquillity of nature with butterflies, dragonflies, kingfishers and water-voles putting in numerous visits to the stream. They encouraged my mind to slip away into a calmness and sense of momentary happiness. I used to go there mostly with Roger (another boarder) and Graham (a day boy from the town) our exploits with rod and line memorable to this day.

Such moments allowing me time to think more deeply about my present day and consider what I would like for my future. That's the thing about fishing, it creates such moments as you wait for a bite and gaze into the surroundings. It is only years on that I can reassemble such time and make sense of where life took me.

In the Fifth Form I discovered 'Number 6' cigarettes and began the clandestine art of smoking. It just seemed a natural thing to do and its impact on health was not a significant agenda item in those days. I was rarely caught at first and then one day being too bravado, I was seen with one alight when walking back from the Downs. My punishment being to weed the Housemaster's garden where fruit and flowers were growing. At first this seemed a pretty easy detention on a Sunday afternoon until I realised the soil was quite hard and the weeds stubbornly well rooted. 'Shocker' and his wife announced they were going out for a drive and I was to continue alone for the two hours they'd be gone.

I sat amongst the weeds and decided on a cunning plan. To be ruthless with the hoe and spade would be to endanger the growth of the strawberries so it would be best to lift them and then blitz the weeds. Afterwards I could then return the strawberries and achieve all within time. In an hour the task was complete, and the strawberries were now nestling in well tilled soil and the flowerbeds were equally clear. I leant on my spade feeling very clever and actually quite pleased with the horticultural skills I had developed in such quick time. 'Shocker' and his wife returned to see their new landscaped plot. He looked at me part confused and part pleased ... as he'd always had the measure of me. I was dismissed with the reminder of no smoking.

The rest of the week was very warm with no rain. On the Friday I saw 'Shocker' coming towards me looking very cross. He took me to his garden where dozens of strawberry plants were dry and dying. He was not a happy man. If only I had replaced each plant with its full root system and a great deal of water how things would have been so different!

The following day my resultant detention was to help him with his wine-making hobby and bottle some of his finest homemade fruit wines. He growled that one of his favourites ... a strawberry-flavoured speciality would not feature that year ... because of me. On completion of my task, he insisted that my name be written on the bottle as a 'bottler' in his wide-ranging cellar.

In the Summer holidays of 1971 we were living in West London while my father was at the Ministry for Defence, in Whitehall. As I was waiting for my 'O' Level results I looked for a job locally. When out I walked past a pub and thought I would try my hand there. Perhaps they would have something for me washing glasses and clearing tables as a general dogsbody. The landlord seemed to like me and invited me to return that evening saying he would then run through responsibilities and prices. I was a touch puzzled at the reference to prices but asked for no clarification. That evening I found myself as the new barman in the public bar where the clientele were very engaging and quite mixed in their backgrounds. Clearly my sixteen-year-old looks had been mistaken for an older age so I then had to respond to questions on what I was doing by replying I was awaiting my A-Level results before going to University. Nobody questioned me otherwise. Well, until a friend two months older than me came into the pub early one evening for a pint and a chat. As he walked towards the bar the landlord whispered in my ear, "Don't serve him, he's not old enough!" The initial conversation with my friend resulting in denial of his pint was a little embarrassing but then over a lemonade we caught up on our hopes for sixth form studies. I worked in the Fox and Geese pub for the rest of the Summer and got on particularly well with a group of menacing-looking bikers who were actually Hell Angels. They turned out to be quite a laugh to talk with and I learnt so much about motorbikes and certainly broadened my understanding of their art in swearing. Anxious about such customers at closing time my father picked me up by car each end of my night shift. Needless to say, their only anger was at my departure for as they saw it I did not judge them. Not surprising really because even if I foolishly wanted to I certainly would not dare!

Smoking continued to be quite prevalent amongst the older pupils particularly in the Upper Sixth. A semi-official understanding was reached with 'Shocker' that he would not come looking for us if we could sort out what was becoming a problem in other year groups. As such it was open season in catching younger pupils smoking. Still being on Number 6 cigarettes (with the change found inside the cellophane wrapping when bought from a machine) I was at the cheap end of smokers. The younger pupils would be smoking the likes of Peter Stuyvesant and Marlboro. These were much more the top end. So when caught they would plead not to be given up to 'Shocker' and the prospect of facing a detention or loss of visit home for the weekend. The deal was therefore that we had their cigarettes, they were not in trouble, 'Shocker' saw a drop in younger pupils smoking and everyone was happy.

As for the development of punishment ... No Encyclopaedia Britannica, no Times Newspaper, no Hockey Sticks and no swearing or physical brutality. Just let me smoke those for you and we will forget this incident ever happened. How pleased they were to be relieved of these forbidden cigarettes and there be no other consequence.

Smoking each evening before a cup of tea and some toast or a watch of Monty Python continued to be a regular activity. Needless to say, some of the boarding house staff were not impressed with 'Shocker's' approach and relished the chance to catch a member of the Upper Sixth enjoying a smoke. The back of the boiler house venue albeit predictable in most school settings was not an easy place to get to for smoker or stalking staff member. As such, smoking Gauloises was a bit daft as the easily detectable smell was a giveaway. Nevertheless, having caught some smaller pupils with them it was part of the deal to smoke the French variety. One evening I was sat on the wall enjoying my cigarette with a classmate who rolled his own. Suddenly a torch flickered as a staff member came in search. As he turned left and lifted his torch to light up the end of the pathway we both rolled backwards over the wall into the graveyard of the Methodist Church. Behind and below us were all the grass cuttings piled high so our landing was cushioned. As we rolled backwards we tried to stub out our cigarettes to remove the glowing giveaway.

The teacher was confounded as his beam of searchlight just lit up the empty area ahead of him. We heard him mutter but he did not walk the five yards to where we had moments earlier been sat. He turned and went off. The relief in us was significant or at least so I initially thought, for I was fine. My smoking classmate was covered in glowing embers from his homemade rolled cigarette. His latest version was to add tea leaves and these continued to burn all over his jacket and school tie. Eventually he stopped smouldering but 'Shocker' remained puzzled by the burn holes in his tie for weeks.

This same sixth former was the master of disguise when it came to Saturdays and we were allowed out to the nearby coastal towns. We had to wear school uniform and look smart. Before leaving to catch the bus (which we never did as hitching a ride was cheaper) we were subjected to a cursory inspection. He would present himself wearing a greatcoat beneath which he had his tie-dye t-shirt and jeans. These were concealed by two calf-length sections of trousers with elasticated tops and v-shaped section of shirt and collar with tie worn below the bottom of the coat and in the visible neckline. When off-site these were easily removed and stuffed into his pocket … a true escape of Hollywood proportions. Clearly, I wasn't the only one who had read war comics in my younger days and then related all manner of escapades to such texts.

On one such Saturday three of us were hitching a lift and were picked up by a butcher's van. I got the front seat and the other two were told to get into the back where the driver said he had some birds to deliver. During the journey I chatted to the driver who was only a few years older than us. When we got to our destination, he dropped us off and I let the other two out of the back. Their faces were a picture. One looked quite shaken up, the other quite embarrassed. The latter just said "Run!"

It transpired, as we sat in a pub sipping a beer, that the butchers van had ten geese in it. All but two were dead and hung from hooks. The two were very alive and one became aggressive towards my two classmates. By the time we had been dropped off there were now nine hanging from hooks. We laughed as we drank our beer and I wonder to this day what happened when the young driver got to his delivery point.

A much earlier 'Great Escape'-like encounter saw my brother Keith and I get a much longer weekend break away from the school than we were entitled. Keith joined the school at the start of his second year at Secondary. He had spent his first year staying at our mum's parents in Worcestershire and attended school from there. He was with me at the school for three years before he joined the Navy at fifteen. In my fourth year (curiously termed 'Remove') and his third, our parents lived in Cambridgeshire just north of Royston. We were housed at RAF Bassingbourn while my father was on an unaccompanied year's posting to Bahrain in the Middle East.

Our rational for getting out early was quite simple. If the weekend did not start until the end of the normal school day it was likely we would not be home until very late in the evening because of the long journey by train and tube. So we hatched a plan to be executed in our minds with the precision of Steve McQueen et al. Our overnight bags were placed after breakfast at the bottom of the grassy slope where we would be playing football at morning break. When kicking a ball around, a skilful mis-hoof ensured it rolled down the slope into the bushes. We duly went after it not to be seen to return and certainly not missed. We collected our bags and walked the lane to the next village where we caught the bus to the coast and the train to London.

On our return back to school on the Sunday night there was no inquisition or reprimand. The remaining five hours of the school day had passed without a soul realising our absence and seeking out where we were. Our secret remained safe and variations on it were used several times thereafter with similar discreet success. Our distance from home was eventually recognised and departure at lunch time was conceded to us and other such pupils. I do wonder if 'Shocker' had found out and just made the change to re-establish his position ... but without a fuss. Keith remembers this tale well and it is in fact a rare piece of this part of his life that he will reference even to this day as he was not happy during his time as a boarder.

I had enjoyed sport when in Cyprus because the coaching had been a positive experience drawing out a level of skill and the ability to use it with confidence. Boarding school made additional demands to my physical ability as we would have a cross-country run one afternoon after school to 'keep us busy'. Many a freezing Autumn or Spring late afternoon we would have to run up the scarp face of the South Downs and on to a WW2 pillbox facing south, to be checked off by a teacher sat in the warmth of his car. Then we would turn back and run even faster back to school. At the time it was plimsolls, shorts and running vest ... no underclothes as an additional barrier against the cold. We all found that a bit weird, but clearly to voice any question would be to possibly incur much worse. We also had sport every Saturday morning for the whole school when football on an icy-coated muddy pitch with the old laced house brick of a ball posed a danger to all parts of your anatomy not least of all your head. Now that sounds like I was beginning to wane in my interest and enthusiasm for sport, but it was not quite true. I actually enjoyed the representative football, cricket and athletics and although no outstanding star I do believe my reliability and 'do or die' approach was noted in my selection.

House matches within school were no-holds-barred events with so much at stake in the bragging rights. An example of my commitment to the challenge being in a football match when I both headed the ball and an opponent. Suddenly a rich runny red curtain enveloped my face and reduced my sight. Confused and naturally a bit bewildered I was surrounded by players from both sides staring at me with concern etched in their faces. I had split open my eyebrow and blood had poured out. Naturally, the red Holland House shirt soaked up a great deal and made it all look a lot less dramatic. On the way to the Surgery for a stitch it became clear that 'Shocker' had us all in red as we were expected to give our blood if called upon in battle against our foes in Cuthman, Chancton and Cissa Houses. This was after all the same reason British Soldiers wore red tunics in battle … 'Shocker' definitely knew his stuff!

One sporting activity I really took to and did in fact excel at was Triple Jump. Additional technique and sprint coaching added to my success. After many a training session the group of us hop, step and jump astronauts were to be found laid out cloud-gazing listening to our song of the time 'Hey Jude'. Albeit the lyrics espouse a positive look on a sad situation, we were indeed a happy gathering of athletes.

With there being no girls at the school on arrival, there were few moments when we saw the like. One of the activities on offer after school was Judo, which I had briefly done in Cyprus. There were girls there who were boarders from the local convent. This physical interaction was quite revealing as the girls would often allow a judo move to result in them being thrown to the mat. At this point their seemingly-less Judo experience would often disappear and they became very strong in ground moves. It became clear that they enjoyed taking charge and I do believe that I was often given a full and quite unexpected and intimate body check out at the early age of thirteen. The club activity ended after a year, so any interest aroused was unable to flourish.

By the time of the Sixth Form, meeting girls was clearly on the agenda and gaining access to them often quite difficult. At eighteen I had met one girl from a neighbouring village who had recently moved to the area. We had seen each other a few times in the village and one summer's evening arranged to go for a walk by the river. I planned to jump over the fence and then run to the nearby trees so I could slip away. The fence was at the bottom of a short bank where it was possible to leap forward and clear it safely. Well, that was the plan, but I had not bargained that as I ran and went mid-flight that one of the young boarding housemasters would come around the corner of the building. He shouted my name out as I was about to clear the fence. Startled, I dropped my right leg a fraction clipped the top of the fence and landed in a heap beyond it. I thought my evening liaison was going to be over there and then.

In a brief discussion I explained what I was up to ... it seemed the best thing to do. He laughed and told me to go and enjoy myself but be back before lights out. He added, "Just use the gate the next time ... it's easier!" He was my P.E. Teacher, a Yorkshireman too. After that when we were doing athletics his jibe to me was always, "Don't do the hurdles lad ... you'll never make it to the finish!" Anyway, the girl wanted to see me to say the family were moving away ... but the "Goodbye" was very worthwhile and I got back into school via the gate without being caught.

I spent the Summer half term with my Granddad and Nan in Worcestershire and used the time to try and revise for the exams which were coming closer. Sat in their rose garden on a sunny day was enjoyable while trying to battle through the voluminous content of historical notes on Peter the Great of Russia and the Tudors. I caught the sun on several occasions, but the eighteenth-century European facts were not to be captured as success-fully. One day I was encouraged to take a break by my Nan and walk through the town to meet my Granddad. He was work-ing as a gardener and I met him as he finished for the day. As of the era he had a jacket, shirt and tie on to perform this strenuous but much-loved work. As we walked home, he rolled a cigarette and smoked it. Every now and then taking a loose bit of tobac-co from his lips and flicking it away without a pause in his sto-ry-telling. As he came towards the end of the 'rolly' he docked the end and put the butt in his pocket. He carried on talking and I suddenly noticed smoke coming from the same pocket. Several times I tried to interrupt to alert him to this … but he kept on talking. In the end I had to shout, "Granddad you are on fire!" He stopped and beat his pocket furiously to end the prospect of flames and worse. As we got to the end of the road we were sup-posed to turn right and walk one hundred yards directly home. He chose to turn left to his local pub 'The Squirrel' for a pint and treat me to one too. My first taste of Mild beer was not greeted with wholehearted gratitude and he tried to make good by add-ing a bottle of brown ale to it. I bought the next drink and had a pint of bitter. There was a 'note to self' moment on drinking with him in the future.

I was amused by one of his old tales of when he would go to the pub on a Sunday while Nan was preparing dinner. His dog would accompany him and sit under his chair. Granddad would take an empty ashtray and pour some of his beer into it and place it next to his dog with a bag of crisps. The dog would slap his paw on the crisps to pop the bag open, then lap the beer and eat the crisps. A man's best friend indeed and also a drinking com-panion. There was something about the importance of the sim-plicity of life that I learned that holiday from a man who I nev-er got to properly thank.

Naturally the school climate got very serious as the A Level exams grew ever closer and the isolation required to really immerse in revision meant finding spaces in the oldest part of school where few were likely to roam. I had never been much of a fan of exams throughout my secondary schooling as they seemed to be a greater test of my revision methodology than my exact knowledge and passion for my chosen subjects. It was at this point that developing extended acronyms as keys to topic knowledge started to work. I found that my new-found system of mnemonics meant I could write down my key nonsensical words at the start of my practice exams and they could then be unpicked as a sort of menu to the wider detail. Well, it worked, and I would write them across a sheet of paper on being told to start the actual final exams. Once banked there I would read the exam questions and after the usual nervous 'Gulp!' realise that my ability to confidently address the exam challenges was much improved.

The group of fellow sixth formers in the boarding house and a few day boys would retreat into the High Street after each final exam to a charming Coffee Shop run by a delightful Irishman and his son. There we would drink coffee, have a smoke and relax our minds from the pressure of these key exams. The understanding being no mention of the exam just completed. No post-mortem whatsoever was countenanced in our gathering for it was recognised that it was potentially unhealthy to one or all of our group. It was a good time to catch up on what and where such friends were going on to when leaving school. All of us having secured a place at University with future careers in Banking, Marine Biology, Scientific Research and Commerce featuring highly. We would sit for a couple of hours and share aspirations with some incisive humour often being thrown at some of those present. The experiences we had shared so closely over the years having given us a good insight into the journey taken by all present to set such a target for future work and life. My mind still somewhat muddled about what to do next for I had secured my University place but wasn't completely convinced in my degree choice and doubt was beginning to set in.

My deep reflections at this time being around the whole school experience which had certainly been mixed in so many ways. The sadness of my early years at the school had been lost in the distractions that latter teenage life had presented. The many escapades and adventures probably clouding my thoughts and removing those early day memories. As my A Level exams came to an end, and the place secured at University to do a BSc Hons in Quantity Surveying many thought the die was cast for me. However, I began to think it all through and soon realised that I didn't really want to take up the offer and so I began preparing the case for taking a Gap Year, but with a difference. Once again, the thought of following the family tradition of joining the Armed Forces reappeared, but it was very brief. This being based on a previous and very disappointing visit to the Forces Career's Office in Brighton.

I had been thinking for a number of years of joining the Royal Navy like my brother Keith, and in my early Upper Sixth had an interview with a Naval Officer in recruitment. The Forces connection within the family goes back to beyond my Great Grandfather who had been in the military in Victorian times. My Granddad had been in the Royal Air Force in and beyond WW2. Both my father and mother were also in the RAF from the early 1950s and met in the then West Germany where they were married, and I was born. Two of my three Uncles likewise, with one in the Parachute Regiment and the other in the King's Royal Horse Artillery. It had been a life I had grown up in and therefore one I was both very aware of and fairly comfortable with. My thoughts were of being a Helicopter Pilot and on mentioning this in the interview my aspirations were immediately dashed. The interviewer merely responded, "But you wear glasses!" That literally shot down my aviation career hopes, and he then did not even try and encourage thoughts otherwise of alternative Officer Entry. I left the office a touch crestfallen and the thoughts of the military never crossed my mind again.

I reflect that by the age of eighteen I had developed an enforced independence due to the separation from home life. Maybe that was another undetected reason why the military may have not been the right course for me since I had also acquired a sense of rebelliousness to challenge many things ... and had recently sought change for the better and fairer ways of doing things.

That Summer of 1973 was the end of my schooling life as a pupil. I had experienced teachers who over that time had taught me both the best and worst of what it can be like. The fact that it was time now to leave seemed to reinforce that I was done with education ... or at least that's what I thought.

I received an invitation from 'Shocker' on my last night at school. It was for both myself and Hugh (the Pupil Pianist and celebrated lead in all Gilbert & Sullivan school plays) ... who was my Upper Sixth roommate. We were invited for supper with Mr and Mrs 'Shocker'. A surprise to us both ... a wonderful meal indeed followed. It was washed down with that very same wine I had bottled in detention with him three years earlier. Needless to say, he said with a grin "I am sorry we have none of my favourite as we had no strawberries that year!" That last night I had an out-of-body alcoholic experience when trying to sleep ... with my feet feeling as though they were lifting from the bed in an attempt to walk across the ceiling. The wine certainly did for me.

As I walked away from the school on my last morning with that dull hangover from 'Shocker's' wine, his final words of, "I will miss you and your mischief!" were still sinking in.

I recall quite clearly not being tempted to look back one last time at Brotherhood Hall, the old school frontage.

My mind was set on what lay ahead and the strong desire to be at home. School had ended ... but it's influence was bubbling inside me.

Chapter 4

Reconnecting and making a Big Decision

On leaving school I travelled home to West Germany where my father was now stationed at JHQ Rheindahlen near to Monchengladbach and very close to the Dutch border. The base with its extensive barracks, offices and varying military support infrastructure was actually akin to a town with two police stations, two cinemas, two churches, a large shopping area, an outdoor swimming pool, expansive sporting facilities, a Secondary School and six Primary Schools. All this serving the multi-national NATO forces and their families, mostly from the UK. Initially we were in a wonderful flat in the German community, eventually moving on to camp and into a married quarter befitting my father's military rank.

When I left school, I already had this place offer to study at a Midlands University but was increasingly aware that my future was not destined to be a Quantity Surveyor. Indeed, I could not for the life of me remember what had interested me in pursuing such a career. My parents were expecting me home for the Summer before departure to University for the four-year sandwich course of study. I was to be the first ever family member to go to University and already my dear mother had developed her bragging rights on this with friends and family. This was about to change. I really needed to say something pretty soon after arrival at the family home in Rheydt. After a few days I plucked up the courage to tell my parents that I wanted to rethink my career pathway and take a Gap Year.

Surprisingly, I don't think it was a difficult decision for them to make in agreeing. After all I had been absent from home since I was twelve apart from most school holidays and certainly not all of them early on. Taking a Gap Year at this time was seen by many as 'dropping out' but for me it was really different and quite simple. I wanted to be part of the family again after six years at boarding school and I wanted to get to know my parents. The agreement was that I would find a job and earn money for myself and contribute to the household. Very quickly I had a pretty mindless mode of employment at the Airmen's Mess at RAF Rheindahlen with all sorts of jobs in the kitchen and dining rooms. Although I met some interesting characters and peeled a mountain of potatoes, it really was not for me.

Thankfully, I then got a job in the admin section of the Central Registry. I had my own office where I had to go through all the mail coming in to ensure it was delivered to the right section as well as sourcing posting addresses to make sure mail got to those who had moved to other bases around the world. It was not a dynamic role or very taxing but the people in the office were great fun to work with.

After a month, my job increased in responsibility as I had security clearance and signed the Official Secrets Act paperwork. My additional role was to deliver/return signals and files of varying classification between HQ Rheindahlen and HQ RAF Germany (known by all as 'The Big House'). I had a black leather briefcase with EiiR embossed in gold on it for these documents to be locked in and then carried from one building to the other. As and when such a task was required to be completed, a WRAF driver would collect me in a car and then drive me to the 'Big House' where I would pass through the rigorous security to deliver the documents and/or collect those to come back.

Most of the WRAF female drivers were only a few years older than me and some became good friends during my year there. Our topics of conversation on the short journeys together often related to music, life and humorous tales of social activities. I also got on well with many of the RAF Police guards on the entry point into the 'Big House'. I think they enjoyed giving me quick access to this high security building while making senior officers queue to be processed because they had not got the level of access clearance I had. Many a time these visitors would look puzzled at the speed of my entry as I was a young long haired teenage 'civvy'.

During my spare time, I enjoyed meeting others of the same age who had been educated at the Service Schools run by SCEA on the base. It struck me how their father's rank signified a status that ensured they were mostly segregated from each other. I soon came to realise that because my father was a Flight Sergeant (as such a senior non-commissioned rank ... but not an officer) I was not supposed to attend the Youth Club held in the United Services Officer's Mess. Needless to say that my varying exploits at boarding school and perhaps a degree of developing charm was enough to secure access.

The engagement with these teenagers enabled me to settle into a regular pattern of meeting up to discuss all manner of topics and access some great events. For a couple of months about ten of us would meet at least once a week in the Blue Pool Bar and the discussions must have seemed to onlookers and listeners as being similar to that regularly convened at the Philosophical Society of most 'Red Brick Universities'. One such evening resulted in me being made aware of a forthcoming Field Trip away by the Sixth Form of the Secondary School on camp. Ultimately, this resulted in me having the opportunity to further my interest in canoeing as an 'Assistant Instructor' to the P.E. department. What followed was a great week to the lakes in the Eiffel Mountains further south. I was the instigator of chasing the paddle steamers across the lake to ride their white-water wake which was great fun. I realised in this time that I enjoyed teaching and training these students and maybe there was a career for me in that type of work.

This was quite a moment after my varying school experiences but nevertheless it did seem a way forward beyond my year off. On return home I pondered as to how to proceed, then I recalled having been to a Geography seminar at a College in Sussex and how I had enjoyed both the evening away from school and the presentation. It was the only place I knew of that trained teachers, so I duly wrote an application letter and waited for a reply.

At my place of work, one of the civilian workers at the Central Registry was an elderly German man called Hans. He was over six foot tall, very fit for his age and had a really sharp mind. He had a most charming disposition and was a delight to talk with when we took morning coffee breaks and discussed all manner of things. He furthered my ability to both speak and read German, not least of all when we discussed football and the local Bundesliga team Borussia Monchengladbach. At the time the likes of Berti Vogts and Jupp Heynckes were regular players and playing at a very successful time for 'Gladbach'. Hans and I would unpick each match and talk of the other famous names that I also had the pleasure of seeing at the Bokelberg Stadion such as Frank Beckenbauer and Gerd Muller. Each week he would buy me the sports magazine 'Kicker' to help further my language development. It would always be at my office desk to break the boredom of the routine of work.

Hans spoke of the Second World War and his training to become a member of the 'Fallschirmjager' (the paratroop branch of the Luftwaffe). His stories were enthralling and evidenced his sense of duty to his country and certainly never any Nazi ideology. He spoke with a soft voice and was always so calm and kind in his manner. The General Office along the corridor had some Dutch airmen in it who sometimes would push too far with their ill-placed humour and banter. One such time occurred when the monthly test of the Early Warning sirens was taking place. One of the Dutch said rather nervously, "Hey Hans, does that remind you of when the Allies bombed here during the war?" Hans walked towards him and with his outstretched right arm and no discernible effort lifted the airman by his throat up into the air. As the Dutchman was held his legs wriggling and his face reflecting the remark may have been an error, the rest of us looked on wondering what was about to unfold. Hans looked him in the eye and said quietly, "Now listen here young man, during the war it took us five days to beat you … and we spent three looking for you!" At this he eased the airman's feet to the ground, grinned knowingly at him, patted him sympathetically on the head and then walked away. As he left the office, he turned to me, smiled and winked. Never again was a silly remark made about Hans, Germans or the war … and rightly so.

Here was another adult who influenced my thinking, my actions and my sense of place. The unimaginable experiences in his young life not lost but also not hindering his ability to be a good man. I ask you … can you recall such as him in your time when growing up as someone who started to shape your own values and beliefs?

My mother's parents came to visit us at Christmas that year and one day we took them to Arnhem in Holland. My Granddad wanted to visit the town and the military cemetery at Oosterbeek where many of the young British and Polish paratroopers were buried. Granddad Wilkie was ex-military and one of his sons, my Uncle David, was in Two Para Regiment so there was a link for him. That day he was very quiet, and quite shaken to see the average age of the dead was eighteen to twenty-five years of age and that there were so many of them. It was a memory that has stayed with me, for he was ashen for several days thereafter.

Early into the New Year they left to return to England via coach and ferry. He was still quite subdued. About fifteen minutes before the ferry was about to dock at Dover he went to get himself a whisky and my Nan a brandy. On returning and sitting down next to her he died quite suddenly. I wonder now if at Oosterbeek he'd had some sort of premonition.

A week later it was his funeral but sadly I missed it as the day before I attended interview at College and then got stranded in Sussex by a rail strike. Wilkie had been in the RAF and served in Burma alongside the Gurkhas fighting the Japanese. His previous time as a Docker in Liverpool and the jobs after the war had literally worn him out. His death was before his time with many rich memories preserved and passed down to my own children over the years. He was buried near to his home in Worcestershire and not, as he wanted, by having his ashes sprinkled on the Kop at Liverpool FC. My Nan would not allow that. Their house was called 'Anfield' and of course the woodwork on the windows and doors were red and white. His grave has the inscription 'You'll Never Walk Alone' and indeed I am sure to this day he is not and the pub he will be going to in heaven will be a short walk and serve a good pint of Brown and Mild ... his preference.

On returning to Germany, a letter soon arrived stating I had a place from September to train to be a teacher at College in Chichester. The die was cast and the future career in education now ever closer. Wherever Miss Kirkpatrick was at this time I am sure she would have smiled at the prospect. Indeed, good old 'Shocker' would have too and probably said 'the poacher is to be a gamekeeper'. Both of them key influential characters in my decision. As for those at the Middlesex Primary School who had once told my Mother I would not end up doing much with my life ... who knows? An interesting observation by them of someone about to follow their career pathway ... albeit with a touch more humanity.

A few months later news arrived from the UK that my Nan had experienced something quite surreal. She had already informed my mum that there had been many nights when she had been restless and unable to sleep properly. Then came the news that she claimed that one night she woke to be confronted by my Granddad at the end of her bed. She claimed that he had spoken to her and said, "Now I've found you m'duck and know you are okay, I can Rest In Peace." After some discussion within the house, we concluded that Nan may or may not have been dreaming ... but clearly as she had moved from their home my Granddad had been looking for her and tracked her down to her new sheltered accommodation. Interestingly, she was forceful in saying she slept really well every night thereafter. Now whether you believe in ghosts or not ... what a tale. Not to be upstaged, my mother then recounted a story from the early 1950's before she married my father. As a WRAF in Germany returning from a night out with her peers she said a troop of German soldier ghosts marched through the hedge and across the road in front of them before disappearing in a field. She described how the moonlight glistened on their helmets. Now obviously there was some alcohol involved in my Mother's story ... but my Nan? Well, let's just say it's a lovely story so its providence was not questioned.

The rest of the year proved just as I had intended it to be. The simplicity of everyday events such as breakfast with my parents, walking my other two brothers (Chris and Simon) to school, going out to events and visits with my family (with the exception of Keith who was somewhere at sea on board HMS Achilles) and going to the Mess with my mother and father made it special to me. Germany was a great place to live in and the military bubble of JHQ at Rheindahlen very cosmopolitan indeed.

I had got to see both my parents in a different light, and I was indeed better placed to understand the complexity and challenges of my father's work. My mum provided a loving home for my younger brothers. Simon was now eight and Chris thirteen. Their place was secured by all the daily contact be it encouraging, congratulatory or corrective for it framed them. Keith and I had missed this consistency and regularity since the Summer of 1967.

Keith was now the tender age of seventeen yet already he had sailed all four oceans on board a naval frigate. His normality of life now the routine on board his ship. His contact with home was by way of a 'Bluey' whenever in port or during replenishment at sea. Face to face contact rare and dependent on being back in his home port at the end of a deployment. Shattering news was received by my father one day that a sailor named Keith Johnson had died when ashore at a north German port. He was unsure how this terrible news was to be shared with us all when he came home. As he was leaving that evening the news broke that the sailor was not our brother, his son ... but another poor soul with the same name. His voice crackled and faltered as he recounted the unfolding news that day ... and then the relief.

My father's work with the Provost and Security Services was mixed and I was to learn of its variety when we had time to sit and talk over a drink at the Mess. A new dimension to my life and one I enjoyed wanting to know more of, and had all ears for. I became accustomed to taking the snippets which lacked full detail due to its sensitivity. Some of it I found out I had been part of albeit mostly unknowingly.

Some such stories included him being part of the Test Team to assess the security of Bomber bases down the east of England by literally seeing if they could break in and then how long they could go without being caught. The picture he painted of him and others being seen by gamekeepers wandering through woodland at daybreak close to the airfield perimeter with ladders across their shoulders. Amusingly their greeting to the gamekeeper often being no more than "Good morning!" as they continued towards the fence guarded by RAF Policeman armed with live rounds. I also found out that my clothing as a seventeen-year-old had been worn by him as he took part in CND marches incognito clearly gathering intelligence of some sort.

He recounted being part of the security detachment providing protection to the Prime Minister of the day in meetings in war-torn Nigeria and on board HMS Fearless where the Rhodesian issue was being diplomatically resolved. That, at least, explained the vast array of West African fruits that appeared one day on our kitchen table.

The removal of oak panelling from No. 10 Downing Street and its eventual recycling by my father's good woodworking skills into a needle work box, coffee table and two bookends being the best story. Stripped out to be replaced shortly so as to ensure uncompromised security. As such the humorous post-script to this tale being that periodically the phone would ring wherever the bookends were situated and a voice at the other end would be suggested as saying "Good day Mr Johnson ... it's GCHQ here can you speak up please as we can't quite hear what you are saying!" I've recounted this elaborate tale my-self several times since. It adds providence to the one bookend I still have and indeed the listeners remain captivated through-out and thoughtfully staring at me as I speak. Just as I did when my father spoke.

During my time in the Central Registry the IRA were busy with their bombing campaign both on the mainland and in West Germany because of the British bases present. On one oc-casion as the office staff were being ushered out of the building because of a bomb scare my father was entering with other ci-vilian-looking individuals and the bomb disposal team. As we passed in the corridor he just said quietly "Don't tell your moth-er I was going in what she would consider to be the wrong di-rection!" Of course, my lips were sealed at home that evening.

On another occasion I was with my parents at a formal 'dining-in event' at the Mess when there was a loud explosion nearby. All wives, other dependents and most RAF members left and went home. My father and some of his team went to the scene. That occasion was where a bomb had been placed by the gas canisters of caravans parked by an adjacent cinema. Fortunately, the exploding bomb and resultant shrapnel harmed nobody as it went off before the end of the film being shown, thus sparing the lives of those inside. It was suggested that a female sleeping in her Barrack block never heard the explosion but woke in the morning to find a piece of shrapnel embedded in the wall above her bed.

The worst one I recall being where a young girl had been murdered by her father and my Dad was one of the first on the scene and had to go to her post-mortem. That one drained his otherwise ever-present smile and tanned complexion. All in all, his work in Special Investigations and Counter-Intelligence was riveting to listen to. It was over thirty years before he spoke again about his work and then only in a hushed tone. His reservation being as if the notable oak book end was on the table between the pints of beer we were drinking together at the time. I should add the phone still never rang!

I met up with Bob in the Summer just before going off to University. Some seven years had passed since we had been together in Cyprus and every day disappeared quickly as we struck up our friendship again. We developed a great thirst for the 'dunkel bier' an altbier brewed locally in Monchengladbach. The journey from the bar back to camp was through a wooded area with lakes either side of the rough pathway. The influence of our well-consumed favourite Hannen Alt had a most extraordinary impact on the trees according to our alcoholically impaired vision. It was always the case that the trees would now and again jump out into our cycled pathway without warning and cause us to crash to the ground in fits of laughter. Fortunately, our falls were never so dramatic to end up in one of the lakes. Happy days as our teenage years came to end and the alleged serious time of being twenty-years-old approached. We parted company in the August, each to go off to University and unfortunately, we have never seen each other since.

My gap year may seem to have been shrouded at times in a slight alcoholic haze, but it had most certainly served me well in helping me reconnect. When I left home to return to England and start University, I felt I was a full member of the family once again and I knew my parents so much better.

I was now very ready for the promised academic challenge that was waiting for me in Sussex. I was about to go off to College and learn how to become a teacher. Not just a teacher of a subject discipline ... but a teacher of children ... about what life can be.

Chapter 5

University Challenge

The leafy small campus at College was a welcome sight when I arrived. Existing students were allocated to us as our 'parent' to enable us to settle in and become accustomed with the routines of the day both academic and social. This was most helpful and certainly beneficial to those who had never been away from home before. On our second day the Principal gave a stirring speech revealing his passion for teaching, laced with a refreshing humour. One couldn't help but feel the real sense of joining a 'new family'.

The College had around six hundred students in the four course years with the second year being significantly larger. My peers in Year One were mostly eighteen-year-olds straight from schools in the South and Home Counties, with a few from abroad and some much older and life experienced known as 'mature students'. Everyone was very friendly, and this was undoubtedly helped by the fact that females outnumbered males by eight to one ... so there was a gentler demeanour ever present.

The induction was pretty varied and the contact timetable rather brief at first to allow us to get to know the wonderful city of Chichester and what was on offer regarding clubs and other activities. I initially joined the football and mixed lacrosse teams and started to dabble in the Student Union representative work.

Within a few weeks my enthusiasm and seemingly organisational skills saw me become the College Football Captain. That year we weren't the most gifted of representative sides, but certainly had great fun in our matches against teams across Sussex and Hampshire. I found myself back in goal and enjoyed the position albeit the defence in front of me was rather leaky at times and apt to miss vital tackles. One evening I was invited across to the City's Club to train with the first team on a barely-lit and very muddy pitch. It went well and I had a trial match during which I injured my arm and thus ended such a team role. Thereafter I played outfield for the Uni and our overall performances strangely seemed to improve.

I had never really heard of lacrosse before but did rather enjoy the Mixed Team and fun we had together. I was pleased not to have been asked to be the goalie as it seemed such a dangerous place to be where wounding by a closely flung ball or clubbed by a netted stick seemed to be a regular occurrence. Our goalkeeper was already blessed with a well-padded body but would be seen removing chair cushions from the Out-Student's Common Room and then stuffing them down his tracksuit bottoms and top. Many a tackle in this game often ended up with profane muttering in response to the resultant hits and scrapes received. At the end of the season the enthusiasm for this sport waned across College and I am sure that the Medical Centre were relieved at the lack of business after matches.

My sporting interest sustained throughout Year One. I played for the Mixed Hockey Team in a number of positions and enjoyed the speed of the game being played on a redgra surface. It was inevitably a surface likely to leave you with scraped elbows and thighs if you went to ground. I had many such a minor wound, like my teammates. One particular close-fought 'derby match' against Winchester College saw an opponent carry through an attempted shot and hit me on my hairline. I remember the moment of impact and then waking up an hour later in bed at the Medical Centre. My concussed brain still struggling to attach itself to my mouth and make intelligible responses to questions posed. One early visitor to my bedside being a Year Four student Ivan who winked as he told me, "Don't worry I got him for you!" I'm not sure what that actually meant and thought it best not to enquire once in full control of my marbles again.

I enjoyed playing some cricket matches for the College Team with the infrequent opportunity to use my bowling skills to undo otherwise stubborn opposition batsmen. The real joy this particular summer was being able to play for the city's Priory Park C.C., a splendid cricket venue within the city walls. The matches away from home being in some equally picturesque settings such as Parham Park C.C. within Parham House and Grounds. When in the deep outfield it was a joy to be offered tea and cucumber sandwiches by a delightful elderly lady spectating on her own. To this day they still play there, and their team is known as the 'Friendly XI' ... just as cricket should be.

I was taken by the organisational structure of the Student Union and became involved as a representative for my Year. It was clear that some members enjoyed their roles in relation to social activities and the bands they booked certainly livened up our Saturday nights. I was mightily impressed with Abre, GT Moore & The Reggae Guitars and Showaddywaddy to name a few. The politically motivated interests of some was interesting to watch unfold. Later in the first term I found myself at a Union gathering at Sussex University where some very forthright political aspirations were being exercised. My presence clearly did not go unnoticed and within that period of my first year I was approached by an ex-colleague of my father who was in Special Branch. 'Trevor' wanted to know if I would consider 'working' for them from within the Union. All a bit too serious for me at this and probably at any time ... so I declined.

The highlight of the initial Induction saw a group of us spend two weeks at the Open Air Weald and Downland Museum. I had visited this new attraction in my Sixth Form when, over a series of weekends, we had helped to cut steps into the hillside and would then sit in an oak tree to shade from the summer sun as we smoked and ate our packed lunches. Our task as new University students was to build a Saxon Charcoal Burner's Hut. We had no plans, just the charred wooden remains of some debris and the post holes cut into the ground as a clue from a previous similar task completed by others before us. The collective brains of twenty budding students who had probably never done anything like this bar making a den in the woods as a child was soon to come up trumps. From the woodland we cut logs for the frame, made wattle and daub-like walls and thatched it from straw in the valley. How pleased we were and how well we got on when working with each other.

The purpose of this exercise being more than our Saxonesque skills but also learning about ourselves and how we could complement each other in our studies to follow. A few days prior to completing the hut we were all dramatically evacuated from the site when an unexploded WW2 German bomb was found in an area where they were making a duck pond. We were sent to the safety of the village pub to the delight of the landlord. While there the Military Ordnance team dealt with the stray bomb which evidently was jettisoned by a Luftwaffe plane scurrying back to Northern France.

Other induction activities to allegedly open our minds to creativity saw us being challenged with the emotional engagement of hugging trees and making electronic music to amaze our student peers and the lecturers. Up until this point I had never smoked or taken any substance resulting in a need to feel tree hugging or painful electronic compilations would be normal and endear me to any other human being. I add, in all honesty, it reinforced a need to remain clean from such acts and I merely smiled appreciatively if my performance resulted in any sort of congratulatory acknowledgement.

Only having to wear leotard-like clothing and take part in a Performing Arts week topped this as the embarrassing and curious introduction into allegedly what I either needed to be able to do, or get others to do, in my future role as a teacher. Whatever the rationale for such tasks I recall steering clear of such lecturers and any optional activities they offered thereafter.

My real joy in the educational studies was driven by the Child Development aspect of our work which fascinated me. Not least of all the Piaget Theory which I felt helped me better understand my own growth in childhood as well as being better placed to understand the schoolchildren I was yet to meet. I also soaked up any options and avenues of study related to psychology particularly around behaviour. Already my career path was beginning to shape because of this developing academic specialism.

This doubtful preparation for our first foray into a school with 'live pupils' was seen by some peers as a test of our resolve to sustain our time through to graduation. Nothing could be further from the truth. To be greeted by eager six-year-olds as if you were their long-lost Uncle was quite a welcome. It stimulated a belief that these children and their eagerness was going to be a great insight into what a career in teaching could and should be like.

Our initial task being to help them make a variety of musical instruments from readily available resources. Naturally beer bottle tops were not so available to them but my continuing visits to the Nags Head Pub ensured I had a good supply which endeared me to the children. In good time we had several workable rattles that brought delight to their faces. The orchestral performances may have sounded off key at times but there was no getting away from the fact that pride in producing the instruments both created a further interest in music and the adults (us) present. Great fun for all involved and probably fuelling my mischievous belief that future headteacher colleagues in Primary felt at home with sticky-back plastic, glue, toilet rolls and other such 'Blue Peter' paraphernalia.

The introduction to teaching in a coastal Primary School was reflected upon once back at College. Lessons learned, ideas shared and anecdotes from pupil interactions revealing real energy amongst us and a desire to be back in a school. When the first full teaching practice of three weeks arrived, I was eager to start. I had been given a Hampshire village Primary School and my selected class of Juniors had an ex-Royal Navy matelot as their class teacher. He was such a star in coaching me to a very successful start and thoroughly enjoyable experience throughout my time there. I travelled in each day on my recently bought Honda CB200 motorbike which seemed to add to my credibility with the pupils and always ensured a crowd at the gate at the start of each day as they waited for me. I realised during my placement that my future in a school needed to be with pupils in Primary and upwards as I often came very close to standing unexpectedly and accidentally on some 'very small people' in younger age groups. Not a good outcome for someone aiming to become a qualified teacher.

On concluding my placement, I was sorry to leave the school and the brilliant motivator of a class teacher. He had reminded me of the equally astounding Miss K. and he said to me, "Never say that someone is just a teacher. Because to many around them they are a true superhero!"

The feedback I received from my Monitoring Tutor was encouraging and I was more than sure now that this was absolutely what I wanted to do.

It wasn't the same for all others. One close friend decided that while teaching was what he wanted, he couldn't cope with being away from home in Bury, Lancashire. I had been tasked by our tutor to try and coax him around but to no avail. A great shame as his northern accent had ensured a full clarity in every word spoken to student peers and many children in leafy rural Sussex. There were others that decided to go. At the time, a shame. Later

I wondered in my career how many stayed on when they were neither enjoying their 'trade' nor inspiring those children before them to enrich their lives with a thirst for learning.

At this time, I took my motorcycle test which required the examiner to ask me to answer various traffic signs and other general riding questions and then be observed doing varying manoeuvres within his sight. All went well and my confidence under his tight scrutiny was growing. To finish he requested I did a circuit from his position on the Roman Wall near the Shippams Paste Factory around East Street and return to him whereupon he would require me to do an emergency stop by stepping out in front of me. He reassured me that he would give me good notice of his intention.

I duly set off and within a few minutes turned back into the road where I was to expect him. Ahead of me I could see a commotion unfolding. He was laying on the road and a small moped was on its side with the rider sat nearby. Members of the public were rushing towards them both. I pulled up and walked across. The examiner stood up dusted himself down and said, "Ah ... Err ... Hello! Right ... Err ... You have passed. Well done!" Dishevelled and embarrassed he thrust the pass paper into my hand and walked away. It transpired he had stepped out in front of an unsuspecting biker mistakenly thinking it was me. I was now in possession of my full bike licence and the story of my test has amused many biker friends since.

An early lesson for the future here about keeping an eye on those making judgements about me and my work. Certainly true in later years about OFSTED Inspectors getting in a muddle and needing to be helped with their view of things. As I went on to say to many colleagues ... 'Keep this in mind when they come knocking at your door!'

My holidays during the year were important to recharge my financial coffers and sustain the amazing social life with fellow students. The Nags Head already had my half litre ceramic mug hanging at the bar and dear old Sid needed to be sure I was a true regular to confirm its privileged space. My Christmas Holiday saw me work for a month in the NAAFI at JHQ in Germany. I was in the freezer and refrigerator section of the huge supermarket and spent day upon day stocking the main freezers from incoming lorries. The chilling experience being worth it as I was able to earn Deutschmarks at a much better exchange rate when returning to College in January.

The Easter month off was spent at my aunties in Wiltshire where I worked as a building labourer on various sites including Porton Down. My knowledge of laying yard upon yard of concrete as well being a bricklayer's mate humping hods of bricks to feed his speed of laying, was quite a challenge. In the Summer I taught English to German Exchange Students in Chichester, did potato picking on Sussex farms and then had two weeks back in Germany unloading beer lorries at the smaller Buschof NAAFI at JHQ. All adding further experiences to my life journey and providing a tremendous top up balance to my grant which was insufficient in seeing me through the year.

The first year had ended with our Rag Week which was great fun after a year where the studies and school placements had filled up increasing amounts of time. It is hard to describe how the average shopper may have viewed three of us carrying out a mountain climbing exercise up the pedestrian zone of North Street fully equipped with ropes, carabiners and all other such kit. Stopping midway in our fully prone positions to take a break drinking coffee and eating sandwiches, we were quite a distraction. The Twenty-Four Hour Le Mans Scalelectrix Race equally gathering great interest in the courtyard of College added to by the shouts from one student precariously climbing the Chapel Bell to shout out invites to others nearby. With these and many other activities both on and off site we raised substantial monies for charity. The most memorable for myself being achieved in partnership with the athletic Mike, when we won the three-legged beer race. This required us to visit six pubs in the city (naturally including the Nags) drinking a pint in each. We were in the lead from the third pub and raced away from our nearest competitors. In the final yards in good spirits and laden equally so with good ale we raced to the steps of College, whereupon Mike embarrassingly discharged his full intake with quite remarkable projectile ease.

Later we were to be found with a dozen or so of fellow male and female students at West Wittering Beach. In the bright moonlight we noisily raced into the sea for my first ever experience of 'skinny dipping'. Thankfully in those days there was no social media or mobile phones, so our act was anonymous, and our careers were not blighted in later years by our unreserved modesty and fun-loving antics being revealed to the on-line world.

The summer holiday started with a group of us renting a small three-bedroomed house in Orchard Street. I shared a large room with the mercurial Paul from the year above me. A humorous fellow with a great philosophy of life ... 'Enjoy!' It is a friendship which has been sustained to this very date. Our mutual interest in motorbikes developed further in this period with the return of my brother Keith to RNAS Yeovilton after a period of him visiting us. Paul had him as pillion on his 500cc Suzuki which was a striking bike in an electric blue colour. I followed behind on my Honda. We still speak of this journey there and back and one day say we will repeat it for memories sake.

Sadly, Paul's bike was soon after squashed beyond repair by a lorry reversing over it. Luckily, Paul noticed the lorry in his mirror and dived to safety as the bike was struck and fell beneath the huge crushing wheels. I had a scare myself as I rounded the road approaching the roundabout by College Lane. The oil slick on the road causing my bike to lose traction and slide from beneath me. I followed, sliding along the road only stopping when I hit my bike which had abruptly stopped when colliding with the kerbside. As I lay there rather dazed an elderly man walked by with his dog. He looked down and said, "Bloody Motorcyclists!" then just walked off. Both my bike and self were okay, and I rode back to our house nearby. This being a lesson in better observing road conditions and that, as a group, motorcyclists were not to everyone's liking.

Year Two saw me share digs in Chichester with one of many bearded friends, Nick. Our landlady would fuss over him and do all she possibly could to ensure he was comfortable and cared for. Should there then be enough time left in the day then I received the same service. This rather surprised me as he would regularly not return to digs as he had secured accommodation at a late hour on campus. It transpired that this was a preferred option, and I took up the same absent tenancy role.

Now as a very seasoned student I was part of the welcoming committee for new arrivals into Year One. Paul and I schemed up an activity with a difference to make the whole experience more welcoming for the likely nervous and apprehensive newcomers. We turned the minibus into an aircraft looking vision. It had clouds stuck on the windows and full BOC Airline insignia along its side. Paul was the pilot and I was the co-pilot, with both of us dressed accordingly. One of our friends was dressed as the air hostess in tight clothing that almost suggested another line of work … a part she played in a flirtatious and amusing way, serving mints to assist the vagaries of take-off.

In very good humour we were parked up at the railway station awaiting inbound trains from London and the South Coast. Two other students were on each platform in white coats with a swimming cap on their heads and flippers on their feet as Airport Porters. There was another similarly dressed airline staff member in the car park with a table tennis bat in each hand to direct us from our point of embarkment to the runway and on to College. Memorable for those collected and flown to their first night at College to the theme tunes of the Dambusters and 633 Squadron. On completion of our flying duties the full aviation team retired to the Nags Head where nobody batted an eyelid at our dress code … but then of course, they knew us well!

Our education studies were enjoyable as they continued to develop my interest in the psychology of behaviour and a new area in multi-cultural education. At this time, my preference for Ska and Reggae music gained momentum and I recall giving a tutorial presentation on the challenges of ensuring inclusivity in multi-cultural education. My delivery accompanied by tracks from Bob Marley 'Get Up Stand Up' and Desmond Decker 'You can get it if you really want'. With Bob Marley's words, "Get up stand up … Stand up for your rights … Get Up stand up … Don't give up the fight" capturing the message I wanted to deliver to my very white audience. This really seemed to liven our discussions and I was thrilled when later in the course we visited The Archway School in North London to immerse ourselves in a brilliant multi-cultural setting.

My Teaching Practice at the end of Year Two was in a Hampshire Secondary School. At the time a real tough setting compared with my previous Primary experience. The school had some great teachers working hard to raise standards and the aspirations of pupils … who were clearly responding. The behavioural challenges at times were quite an eye-opener in both the speed at which they escalated and the fact some of the pupils barely blinked as they accepted it was a strange sort of normal.

I recall one fellow college student teacher being visited by his Tutor who was clearly intimidated by the behaviour displayed in the class. When the tutor had felt he had seen enough (or was it that he no longer felt very safe?) he gave the signal he was 'done' and exited through a door. The lesson finished not so long after and as the class departed one pupil turned to the student teacher and said, "Well done Sir, you are getting better with us …

stick at it!" Then as he got to the door he turned and said with a broad grin, "You had best let your Tutor out of the store cupboard now!" It seemed that the tutor in his hurry to leave had taken the wrong door and being embarrassed or was it fearful, he decided it was best to stay there until the lesson ended hoping nobody had noticed. How wrong he was.

I got the true measure of the pupils in the P.E. lessons I taught. They were a tough bunch but committed to enjoying their sport whenever it presented on the timetable. In fact, some made it clear they were only part-time attenders ... on the days that P.E. appeared. Should this have been true, what was clear was that the quality of football was truly exceptional, and this was proudly spoken of by the P.E. Department. One of the older pupils walked off the pitch with me one afternoon and responded to my admiration of the skill level that had just been so evident, with his own brief story. He told of how the team had been together throughout their secondary schooling and had become winners of everything going in the competitive matches played locally and at County level. He said they had never been beaten for a number of years and then in this particular year it happened. I enquired as to how that had happened and what was the team's response. He quickly replied "Oh it was fine we went into their changing room and had a fight with them ... and we won!" He grinned and ran off to change. That grin and that philosophy permeated through many of the boys. It was a tough area north of Portsmouth and this is how they seemed to survive. I never questioned the validity of his story, there seemed no point.

I won't say that I was sorry to finish my practice there, for it had kept me awake many nights agonising on how to tranquillise my classes with inspirational teaching. I was most certainly pleased to receive confirmation from my own tutor that I had passed. In the debrief tutorials I spoke of how I was quite taken by the experience. I wanted to say how I admired the honesty in so many of the pupils and indeed their never-give-up staff.

78

I stopped smoking in the Spring Term. It seemed that a date I had arranged at a wine bar would be short lived had I not done so. Cigarettes weren't the same escape any more, in fact they were now just a habit. So I broke it. A relationship started that would change the picture frame on how future life would be lived. A very talented member of the P.E. Wing from Newcastle had caught my eye and me hers. So started a relationship with Jan that lasted thirty years. I have never smoked from that first date onwards.

Her parents made the long trek down from the North East to visit her ... and it seems meet me. How disappointing it was that I had family ties with Liverpool, the Forces and Conservative Party. I was faced by her father who saw Christianity and Socialism as inextricably linked. There seemed no point in saying that my parents were tenuously similar with their political and church views. I say this based on the fact mine seemed ever increasingly to believe that the Editorial team at the Daily Mail were so honest that they must also have been responsible for The Bible. I left the matter alone. It was enough that Liverpool had recently beaten Newcastle United in the FA Cup Final. Best not stir the Geordie hornets' nest further.

Despite the misgivings her father seemingly had, her mother took a shine to me and we got on very well. Just as I thought this fact may influence things better, I invited Jan's Dad to watch late night football in the College T.V. Common Room. All went well until the end of the match. Just as I respectfully pushed the swing door open for him it started to close again. I put out my left foot to catch it ... and missed. Well, when I say it missed that's not quite the end of the tale, for it missed the door but not Jan's Dad. He was tripped by my extended foot and he catapulted through the door space into the yard outside landing face down. No manner of kind, apologetic or embarrassed words were enough to convince him of my accidental error. He left the following day with his dear wife to return to the softer safer Geordie life where I felt sure I'd now no longer be welcome.

How wrong I was, as I spent a great deal of the Summer in the North East of England, an area I'd never been to before. The opportunity to help her parents out with their SPCK Shop deliveries to Durham and Carlisle Cathedrals giving me a real insight into this historic part of our country. It also managed to help me retrieve a deal of my credibility after the infamous 'T.V. Room Trip'. To walk parts of Hadrian's Wall and see for miles northwards across beautiful countryside it was easy to drift away and think what the Roman soldiers would have woken up to each day. I'm sure there were times when the locals and indeed the Scots were not so friendly to such foreigners, but I was quite taken by the Geordie smile and "Hello Pet!" greeting of our time. Always a friendly face and a helping manner was my experience that Summer and by the end of it my girlfriend's parents were similar in their manner to me. In fact, her mother particularly so. It later transpired that my personality was not dissimilar to one of her sons who had sadly died in a traffic accident coincidentally a few miles from where I had previously lived in Cambridgeshire.

On return to College the third year started with the academic studies being ramped up considerably. The education aspect being even more enjoyable as my Tutor Jo really was an inspirational man. There it was again ... an individual fuelling the desire to learn by his skilled teaching methodology and genuine intellectual connection with me and my fellow students. At this time, I also became aware of the mercurial Dr. Jock Wilson, a smallish and elderly lecturer who took Education Studies and developed our initial understanding of Psychology. He was so captivating when he spoke and thereafter any opportunity to take his lectures was grabbed by me. Because of him I started a journey in seeking answers to question the 'What' ... the 'Why' ... and the 'How' in teaching. It saw me commence a desire into trying to understand those I would later often call 'the hard to reach and therefore the hard to teach'.

There were many fun and often wild moments with fellow students in a variety of sporting and social activities. Our football team continued to grow in strength and success. I got through the season remarkably uninjured until the last game when I took a pretty innocuous blow to my lower right back. It was only later that I realised that it was tad more serious as I was peeing blood and getting severe cramps in my kidney area. It transpired that I had a bruised kidney and then a 'barium meal' and x-ray showed I had a duplex kidney that side and also an additional urethra. Evidently quite common and the Urologist added with humour, "You will be fine. There is no long-term damage, but you may find you will pee more often as your ability to process is far more efficient due to your additional plumbing!"

My final Teaching Practice was in a secondary school in the Selsey coastal headland of Sussex. Delightful teaching staff in a very friendly school ensured a quick introduction into their routines. Exactly what was needed to further my developing confidence both in teaching Geography and P.E. to well-motivated pupils. Every opportunity afforded me was taken on with enthusiasm and the rapport I developed with students allowed me to experiment a variety of teaching methods with success. Even when it poured down with rain and the football pitch was akin to the trenches of the Somme there was no battle in anything I was asked to teach or the response of the teenagers in my charge. In fact, the joy I felt of such a soggy lesson outside or a dry one in a well-resourced classroom caused some humour in the staff room. On one occasion as I was getting a coffee and biscuit at morning break, I heard one of the teacher tutors tell a colleague not to sit in a particular chair. When I looked over my shoulder, I saw that the fuss was about the chair belonging to the 'new Head of Geography' ... and I was duly invited to sit down. My supposed promoted position causing a great deal of laughter and when I sat down it was added, "You're doing a great job Kim ... well done ... don't mind us!" The practice was a great personal success and once again confirmed in my mind that I really had something to offer when I joined the teaching ranks.

The feedback received from my tutor and the school staff referenced their belief that I had shown a 'never ending determination to make a difference to all pupils irrespective of age or ability'. I recall thinking at the time that such a philosophy and approach was nothing special. But then remembered some of whom I had faced as a pupil. There had been those who clearly disliked the job and the pupils. Such teachers had not grasped the same view of their career ... or had lost it.

On returning to College for the remainder of the Summer Term one Lecturer told me of a teacher from his days at school who had a quote painted on the wall above his blackboard. It read: 'The law says you have to be here. It does not say you have to like it and it does not say I have to like you either!' Evidently he would point to it before peppering those in front of him with ridicule and abuse. The lecturer told me how he had come into teaching and then lecturing in a College of Education to make a difference and help train others to be likewise ... and not like the teacher in his tale. My thinking was further fuelled by this and I wanted to know more of how I could be positive and remain that way about my chosen career.

The college community was always supportive of its members with excellent pastoral care afforded by both Lecturers and the Student Union itself. As is the case within such a vibrant learning setting the pressures could be difficult for anybody and everybody at some time in the academic year. There is no doubt that this was called upon when a fellow student was washed from a cliff face by a freak wave on the Dorset Coast. The climbing group was well equipped and the experience present considerable to support all. By all accounts what was the equivalent of a splash of water in the face to one turned out to be strong enough to literally rip one other male climber off the cliff side and throw him into the sea where he was sadly lost. The service in the chapel was so well attended by the complete staff and student membership. It was one of the most moving celebrations of such a young life that I had experienced to that day. Two artistically talented students performed a beautiful song dedicated to him which furthered the heart-ache and tears present in the congregation. The caring ethos of our College shone through that day.

The year finished with the series of final exams which would go some way in determining the opportunity for me to do a fourth year. The strategies developed at boarding school held good and ensured a confidence in answering all asked of me. This was such a relief as so much was at stake. So ended that year and the news in the Summer was greeted with great merriment when I found I had the grades to return for the greater academic challenge of turning my acquired Certificate in Education into a Bachelor of Education Honours Degree. Actually, that sounded good but the personal determination to return to where my girlfriend was studying and be further inspired by 'Jock' outweighed the end qualification.

The summer was spent in Lincolnshire as my father was now at RAF Waddington to the south of Lincoln. The roar of Vulcan bombers regularly rattling the windows as they took off in twos and threes from the ready alert positions in case of nuclear conflict. The pub in the village was often full of aircrew and the landlady was reputed to bring out a very large snake at closing time to encourage them to leave. I never ventured in there of a night-time, but it always seemed bustling as I walked by.

I secured a summer job at the East Midland Gas Board helping to move the motor vehicle section to a new site and carrying out various delivery jobs. As I had not passed my driving test another fellow student from a Midlands University was the driver. However, I should add that his driving skills and sense of direction required me to be alert throughout any and every journey. The EMGAS mechanics were good company and what some describe as the salt of the earth in their work ethic and family values. Such a philosophy and determination to do their best every day, belying the rather ignorant view of some I had met at University who seemed to think such work was an indication of poor intellect and low aspirations. Their insight into making the best of life and enjoying each day no matter what it threw at them was exactly the same as my dear Granddad had held true. It was a happy summer with them, and the money earned set me up well for the year ahead.

When not at work I was often to be found on the banks of the River Witham with my youngest brother where we would fish until dusk catching plenty. Often our swim would boil as a pike moved in to enjoy its own supper and take a few roach. The best place to fish required a strong constitution as it was by the outlet pipe from the sewage works. All that had been filtered and re-fined before being pumped back into the river was an attractive source of nourishment for the shoals of roach and bream ... and in turn the pike. It often required the skill of breathing through one's mouth and not the nose so as to limit the less-than-pleasing fragrance of the hard-working sewage works. My interest in the pike grew each time I fished this particular spot, and I researched it's etymology, behaviour and habitat to better understand how it lived. This interesting fish with the glorious Latin name of Esox Lucius is often reviled by some anglers, but it truly is a noble fish with prehistoric lineage and the most incredible fast start move-ment to catch its prey. It became a favourite species that summer with every catch carefully returned to the water to live longer.

On return to College the academic requirements increased once again. It beggared the question as to whether the four-year course could actually be done in three and the need to hug trees, wear a leotard and make weird electronic music could have been skipped. After the evening meal on the campus a group of us would sit in one of our rooms and pose such profound questions. Naturally, the views were mixed and by the end we would all agree that the fun filled first year and growing up in year two were im-portant if not at times rather over timetabled. One of our group had the great skill of making a tea bag turn boiling water in four cups into a decent brew as we focussed our thoughts on such topics including the latest essay title. It was always amusing when a late arrival to our group posed the question as to whether a cuppa was available, and the almost exhausted tea bag was retrieved from the wicker waste basket to meet his need.

The essays came thick and fast both on Education Theory and subject specific topics. As such titles related to education policy, selective education, Marxist economics and child development would often have their frontispiece pinned to my bedroom wall. They were a less than subtle reminder of the need for studious late nights drifting into the early hours to be spent bent over my desk. Such working time did prove to be most productive to me and as remarkable as it may seem the contents of each submission became increasingly popular with my two tutors, particularly Jock.

This working practice also fitted into the increased demands of the football team which now had a much larger squad to pick from, with talent levels so much improved. The training sessions were hard work and paid dividends in both our stamina for hard fought matches and our style of play, which was well coached. Throughout the season we were only defeated twice and then by a team of semi-professionals by the odd goal in both matches. Our home games were refereed by the local publican from the end of College Lane. He was well-qualified and as sharp as a razor with his wit in every game ensuring we realised he was right … even when he was wrong. He put on a training course for us to become qualified referees. A great idea for our own careers and match sense. Needless to say, we all passed and thereafter he would take every opportunity to remind anyone committing a foul why they were being pulled up for it and how they should have known better. Some of the female students also did the refereeing course particularly those from the P.E. Wing. My girlfriend was one such and suitably amused by the fact she had done better than me in the exam.

The social scene was equally busy with various groups playing on campus attracting youths from the city for a good night out. If I was not working behind the bar, then I was a bouncer on the door. I preferred the bar work as it entitled me to a free drink every hour, but the door work was often hilarious and rarely confrontational. To be faced by bold sixteen-year-old lads often with fresh faced and scantily dressed fourteen-year-old girls on their arm could be fun. It required suitable wit without destroying the lads' ego as he puffed out his chest and deepened his voice two octaves when trying to gain access claiming he was a young looking eighteen-year-old. It was often helped by a fellow student greeting such a lad with, "Hi … Have you done the homework I set yet when I was in your school last week on teaching practice?" Throughout my life to this time, I had never been in a fight either defending myself or the opposite. The bouncer role was one where brain beat the need for any helping hands and it always worked.

The pranks in this final year warrant mention for the technical skill implicit in their performance. One such case being when one junior year student continually made a big fuss about how 'Mummy and Daddy had bought him a Mini'. The student in question made the mistake of bringing it back to College and paraded himself in it all too often. One tea bag summit after our evening meal unanimously decided that some sort of response was required. The outcome being we pushed his car into the building through the double doors and parked it in the wide corridor outside his room. He was asleep inside his room and oblivious as to what was unfolding feet away from him. It was an easy task for us to complete and we retired to our rooms and essays. The following morning the forlorn-looking student and his tutor were found scratching their heads in bewilderment as to not just how the car had been placed there … but also how on earth it would be extracted.

Very studious and equally innocent looking fourth year peers offered a few ideas but no muscle, as impending deadlines required attending to. Over an hour later the car was back in the car park having been a challenge to remove as the reversing procedure was evidently harder to manoeuvre. The following day we were told the car was taken home and interestingly never seen again for the rest of the year.

Another Year One student liked his music loud … or should I say very loud. This was an irritant to us within the Halls of Residence as it could start at any time of day but seemed to be mostly linked to his drunken return from the pub. Again, the Tea Bag Team conspired a plan and delivered it with impeccable precision. One balmy late summer evening the offending student went off to the pub. On leaving the grounds the removal team set to work and every single item of his room was transported across the adjacent lawn and set up beside the ornamental pond. A long electrical extension lead providing the finishing touch and allowing for his bedside lamp to cast an inviting glow over his relocated room with a view. On his return he found his room completely empty bar an electrical lead going out the window from where he could view the apparition. To his credit he slept there that night and then agreed to moderate his music. His record player was then handed back to him.

Two interesting lessons for new students on life away from home and how to get on with other students. As with everything in College it was done with humour and indeed no malice.

Another tale is that of an ex-student now teaching many miles away who returned one weekend to meet up with his girlfriend in the second year. Because she was in digs, they could not be together, so a friend had given up his room to them for the weekend in the male halls. The mistake made was sharing his impending joy with one of the Tea Baggers. Prior to their arrival to take up amorous residence the cleaner's hoover was set up under the bed and connected to a cable which went out the window and then back into an adjacent room. The set was ready for prankster fun. As the obligatory empty Mateus Rose bottle and lit candle helped establish the re-joining of these two lovers the silent gathering of so-called friends was taking place next door. The walls did not protect every action from being heard and at a point of impending climax the electrical switch was flicked on. The hoover immediately started up causing screams of panic from the pair as their focus was shifted to a "What the F*** was that?" cry of astonishment. The switch then quickly flicked off leaving them none the wiser but certainly less focussed on their previous engagement. Respectful of their absence from each other the same electrical intervention was performed five minutes later at which point the culprit hoover and lead were found. The expected shout of "You bastards!" was our cue to leave be for the night. The following morning no words were said but smiles were aplenty, and their relationship blossomed further with no other similar interruptions when in our halls.

As has always been the way, and indeed in recent years has become more prevalent, economies of scale in education resulted in amalgamations. The historic tradition implicit in our college was somewhat lost when it joined with the Teacher Training College in nearby Bognor Regis. The new acronym of WSIHE, pronounced 'Wishy' seemed to suggest a loss of more than a name. 'GPMcG' our Principal had moved to York (where I caught up with him years later as a Visiting Lecturer) and there became a rivalry between the two campuses and their students. We were the 'Otters' so it became folk law that they must be the 'Rats from the Bog' or the 'Bog Rats'. The logic was in using part of each college name.

A magazine produced at our College with all manner of information, advertisements and witty columns was called 'The Otter'. In the light of some tensions at one Saturday night disco on our campus the next edition of the magazine had a new column. 'The Cyril Turnbull Column' had arrived in print with a regular review of life in college and a somewhat 'Private Eye' view of proceedings. Otters in the main finding the wit and risqué descriptions amusing to the extent that to gain a mention seemed to become for some a 'badge of honour'. Reference to the invasion of 'Bog Rats' at the disco resulted in three burly rugby players, with altered good looks, coming to our campus seeking to find out who was Cyril Turnbull. Naturally, as the person submitted their column inches anonymously nobody was able to answer the question, including myself with innocence portrayed with minimal deceit across my face. The column became even more widely read and discussed thereafter as it referenced this ratty visitation. My anonymity lasting very securely for the rest of the year and was helped by a 'Poll' on 'Who do you think is the Real Cyril Turnbull?' Amusingly, I was not even cited in the possible top three!

My enthusiasm for Jock's seminars and tutorials allowed me to probe further into the various behaviours that may impact from children on my teaching. They equally showed how my teaching would undoubtedly shape the relationships I could establish with my students and how that would impact on their enthusiasm or otherwise to learn. I soaked up his words of wisdom like an enthusiastic sponge and was always keen for more, and was so disappointed when each session came to an end. An interest into 'Education in the Light of Psychology' was being engineered by Jock and it was another piece of my developing life-defining-jig-saw following on from Miss K. and 'Shocker'.

One essay for Jock turned out to be a veritable challenge to construct and it really was not helped by me acquiring a taste for Pernod. For over two years I had avoided shorts after a bad night with whisky (which incidentally I have never drunk since). From then on, I had only really enjoyed beer in varying amounts and naturally this was mostly taken at the Nags Head. It may have been the aniseed smell that was the lure to try something new but what became apparent was the lingering impact of this drink was significant. In a mad moment this new drink served over iced water was quite enticing. The cumulonimbus of a headache and the sloth-like influence on my physical capabilities was pretty quick and long lasting. Even a drink of water seemed to renew the alcoholic effect and send me back to being a recluse in a dark room wearing sunglasses. However, as I embraced the early stages of remission, the words started to flow in my essay and before long I was allegedly moved to such inspiration that I was commended accordingly with an excellent grade. My flirtation with Pernod quickly ended and once again water became a mere thirst quencher.

As the Easter Term came to an end, the task of securing a teaching post from September became a priority. I recall writing a dozen applications for positions in the South and East Anglia with my interest being in the seven to sixteen age range. Within a week I was offered two interviews at quite different settings in leafy Surrey and rural South Norfolk.

The Surrey interview was first and I found myself being interviewed by a learned Headteacher in an oak panelled study. He wore a floating gown and spoke with a clipped and rather middle England accent. Every letter in every word fully pronounced and any required emphasis indicated as of importance by a slight raising of his eyebrows and voice. The Prep School was situated in splendid buildings and there was an expectation that the successful candidate would live in a flat onsite as a housemaster. The visit to the setting was brief and the teaching day had come to an end so there was no opportunity to watch teaching and chat with the staff. The boys were all terribly polite when spoken to and between each other. They looked as though they had been neatly ironed into their uniforms and had their caps glued on. There were a few flashbacks for me to my own boarding school days and my heart went out to several boys who clearly did not go home very often. The interview went well, and I was told that they would be in touch the following week.

Two days later I travelled up to South Norfolk to an independent residential school for boys from the then ILEA area deemed best educated that far away from their London home. The interview involved a tour of the school with the Headteacher who explained the varying challenging and troubled backgrounds of the boys. He sought out my views on them and the need for a twenty-four hour a day seven days a week provision. The boys all seemed pleasant enough and their courtesy in his presence was very evident. The staff were positive in their roles and the lessons I observed showed how strong the relationship was with their pupils. Periodically the language was rather ripe and some bubbling tensions between pupils showed signs of spilling over.

The school included the former Dower House, other buildings and the grounds of a once much larger family estate. During WW2 it had been a military hospital for the injured USAF airmen flying raids to Europe. It was in open countryside criss-crossed by narrow roads with a small hamlet close by. Some of the classrooms and residential blocks dating back to the war when this area was a key location of the USAF heavy bombers known as B-17 Flying Fortresses.

As the journey to the school had been so long it was necessary to stay the night with the Senior Teacher and his wife. This meant that the interview continued in a nearby village pub that evening when clearly my social personality was being teased out. I duly lost a few games of darts and bought my share of rounds to make sure that in any possible feedback to the Head I had made the right impression. During the evening I found out that the job came with a cottage in the grounds and included residential duties.

The following day I travelled back to College feeling pleased with how the interview had gone and shared my experiences and thoughts of both schools with my girlfriend. The next day I received letters from both Headteacher's offering me a position from September. It was at this point that the benefits of both made the difference between them difficult to decide upon. What it came down to was a choice between a Prep School or a Residential Special School. In reality it was more like a choice between pupils who would say, "Cut along there's a good chap!" ... and those that may say "F*** Off, you b*****d!"

It was an easy decision for me to make following the influence of Jock and the interest he had subsequently developed in me. As one of my close friends said to me, "I get it, Brian, Barrington and Joel get your vote over Rupert, Roger and Rodney!" In short, the challenges of Special Education were to be my chosen route in September.

The summer was a busy period with both personal and professional requirements necessary over the holiday break. In August I married my girlfriend Jan in Newcastle and we spent a few days in rural Northumberland on honeymoon. We stayed in Alnwick and Bamburgh and one day drove to Berwick-upon-Tweed. Having parked on the bridge we began to walk towards the town when I noticed Jan's father getting out of his car, a few behind us. My thoughts went back to the T.V. Room drama and I wondered what he was doing now ... was he checking up on me this early into the marriage? Amused, he reassured us that it was a coincidence, and he was making a delivery to a church nearby.

Not long after we collected furniture and other household items to enable us to set up our home together. At this time of year, the plant life was over eight foot high and the two-hundred-yard journey from the road was literally through a tunnel of ferns and trees before it opened out into a clearing revealing the cottage and surrounding outhouses. The cottage having been the former home of the local Sexton was made of thick clay lump walls and a red tiled roof.

As we arrived by car our new neighbours, numerous pheasants and rabbits, scattered from sight.

Part Two

Making the Grade in Teaching

Teach First are an organisation energised by the desire to 'Build a fair education for all' by developing the next generation of great teachers and brilliant leaders. In 2020 their mission statement was:

'Our challenge is to unlock the potential in all our children, not just some.'

This being based upon the view that:

'Too many kids aren't getting the education they deserve. As a society, it is time to raise our game.'

As teachers we all started with such a view of wanting to make a difference and wishing to change education from the inside.

As you read through this part of my journey in five quite different school settings you will see how my learning continued – as indeed life and not just work should be. The question of remembering to stop and think at those learning moments key to making progress in one's teaching impact.

It is important to learn at the 'chalkface' (and interactive whiteboard) about yourself … and those in your charge. It is important to question how you can change lives not least of all your own, and where your teaching craft takes you. I want for my journey to impress upon you that in being a teacher I knew I should enjoy that role, my subject and the learning I was to impart. In Part

One you will have noted that as pupil and student some great teachers moulded me, and a few crazy ones certainly influenced me. This now translates into me being the 'influential one' stood before pupils in the performance of the many roles of a teacher.

About fifteen years ago at a family and friends barbeque I over-heard a distant relative talking of her current time as a teacher. She spoke with such negativity that when she had finished it felt that those around her had 'caught her gloom' and then drifted away for a stronger drink to try and raise their own mood. At this point I asked, "Please tell me ... when were you sentenced in Crown Court ... for a seemingly dastardly crime ... to serve your penal time in teaching?"

My naughty side definitely appearing at this time as I was struck with how such a person may be having such a negative impact on so many children. I should add that she back-peddled so much on her previous cathartic dump that had she been on a bicycle then she would have slipped and severely grazed her shins.

You will see how, even when faced with the most recalcitrant of pupils in a mood of spit, blood and tears I tried to engage with the thought 'I can make it better'. It is such motivation and the need to develop a meaningful and trusting relationship with such pupils ... and indeed those with the most pleasant and co-operative demeanour ... that ensures a greater chance of success.

As a teacher my job was to see the best in my pupils ... particularly when they may have never caught sight of the best in themselves.

In managing myself throughout ... I like all that is implicit in the quote of unknown origin:

"Life is not about waiting for the storms to pass ... it is about learning to dance in the rain."

Teaching can be that way. Navigating the sunny and rainy days is what makes it so engaging.

Follow my journey ... and if it helps ... consider the words:

"If life seems jolly rotten.
There's something you've forgotten.
And that's to laugh and smile and dance and sing.
When you're feeling in the dumps.
Don't be silly chumps.
Just purse your lips and whistle.
That's the thing.
And ...
Always look on the bright side of life."

The very lyrics from Monty Python (and their film 'The Life of Brian') were an effective mood raiser ... particularly for when I felt down, and a touch lost in the role of being a teacher.

As you read through the following chapters you will see how being energised in any such way, I was able to sustain my role as a teacher with my pupils ... albeit a tad crazily too sometimes.

'So as to ... serve them all my days.'

Chapter 6

First Job in Norfolk

On arrival in the warm summer sunshine of 1978 the green of the trees, ferns and fields was a wonderful sight. Our cottage was pretty simple in its amenities with one bedroom, a bathroom with loo, kitchen, pantry and a front room with open fire. There was another room, but the cottage had suffered from lack of use and it meant this additional space was pretty damp-smelling and as such not really usable. For a first-time home it suited though and to stand at the door and gaze into the woodland, hearing the pheasants making their excited two noted crow noises emphasised our rural setting ... for there was mostly no other sound to be heard.

As we had arrived over a week before term was due to start there was time to explore the school and immediate area. So we did so on foot, walking through the gap in the ferns along a track to a field's edge and then onto the hall itself set on a slight hill looking down over the extensive grounds.

The school had two parts to it. Firstly, the old house dating back to the seventeenth century was a two-storey building with whitewashed brick and slate roof with adjoining stables converted into a cottage. This building was the residential area for the younger pupils and dining room for all meals. The converted stable block being where the owners lived. The long drive down to the entrance had wooden classrooms one side and the admin. and older residential area the other, with two staff and family flats. All these buildings being the remnants of the USAF Military hospital from the war. The grounds were extensive with playing fields and woodland. Within the woodland was our home.

To the west it was only a short walk along a quiet road to the village hamlet where there was a simple shop and post office. In the other direction there was another small hamlet and a tiny railway station connecting the area to the larger towns and cities in the county. The couple running the post office were delightful in their greeting and welcomed us to the village as indeed were the 'living in' staff members when we gradually met them over the next few days.

My classroom was big enough for fifteen pupils sat around various tables set in the middle of the rectangular room. At one end there was a roller blackboard with three sections. Two for chalk use and one as a screen. There were meagre resources for use, and this prompted a visit to the office. One side of the corridor was the Headteacher and the other side the secretary and owner. The head was pleased to see me and asked if there was anything I needed to get teaching started. My list was then quickly assembled in words and he baulked at its thoroughness, then pointed across the corridor. The school secretary smiled and agreed to order them all in time for the start of term. I sort of guessed that with her air of authority she would make sure that happened. Her friendly manner afterwards to us being new members of the staff community was very genuine and she gave many tips on what to do and where to go for shopping and leisure.

Jan had always wanted to be a teacher from early in her life. Passionate about wanting to teach P.E. she had been an accomplished athlete and hockey player. Unfortunately, she had not secured a teaching post locally but soon got a position at the Sports Centre about eleven miles away. Not the most enjoyable job but it added to our joint income and enabled her to learn more about where we were living.

In the time before term started, I planned my first week's work sat in the front room at a writing bureau I still have to this day. I had purchased a few texts from Jarrolds in Norwich as my key references for Physical and Human Geography as I was going to be teaching up to 'O' Level. They were to prove key to my teaching for the next two years. My P.E. teaching did not require such new texts as I already had some skills training materials. There was no expectation for extensive planning but nevertheless I also developed my outline scheme of work for the year to ensure that my exam groups got the right coverage, and I was not making it all up as I went along. I was sure Miss K. would have been smiling if she knew what I was doing with such conviction.

The day before term started the whole staff met for a motivational speech from the owner, laced with references to his budget. I watched fellow teachers roll their eyes and try to disguise their sighs of disapproval. As I had seen my brand new OHP (overhead projector) on my classroom desk next to boxes of pencils, crayons, pens and chalk as well as piles of brand-new text and exercise books ... I smiled inwardly. Then he made reference to specific resources of cost and glared at me. Clearly my OHP was seen as a 'luxury' and therefore an offending item. As it turned out it also became something for my peers to tease me about as I was the 'new one'.

The Headteacher then gave a briefing on duties and the calibre of the new pupils and any known troubles or misdemeanours of those returning from London. We all then retired to the staff dining room where a hearty meal was provided with table service by kitchen staff. The following day some of the staff went by train to London to 'escort' pupils back to Norfolk in reserved carriages. By all accounts the behaviour in the carriages was not totally reserved and some passengers wishing to pass through were encouraged to rethink until after the station our staff and pupils alighted.

The staff were a mixed bunch both age-wise and their route into teaching. The younger ones were not dissimilar to me with this being their first teaching post on qualification. The others had worked in schools or industry and been dissatisfied there, so found themselves better suited to this specialist setting. Nobody actually called it a Special School, but it was clear it was and that the educational issues for many of the pupils meant that mainstream had not been where their education could be provided satisfactorily. The owner prided himself in it being an 'independent' school and as such a cut above that offered by local authorities. The staff all seemed to get on well with each other but there was a note of caution about them whenever the owner was present. As the new and untested one in their midst it was better to watch and listen to their interactions and not pose too many questions of them. I wanted to let my teaching do the talking and for the start to be the best it possibly could.

The Headteacher taught maths and was forever in his gown sweeping the corridors of all, in an attempt to make it orderly. He was quietly-spoken and focussed on his teaching which he clearly enjoyed, and the pupils responded to him mostly from genuine respect. He had a peculiar way of posing a question of you and increasingly it became obvious in those first few weeks that the owner would speak through him particularly when dissatisfied. Quite solitary at times and never one for shouting it impressed on me that he saw his role to be detached from us in order to lead.

The Senior Teacher was a chain-smoking more lively character who taught History with a passion. During the war, his classroom had been the operating theatre. The glossy floor still curled about a foot up the walls evidently making it easier to wash away post-operative blood. The joke with the boys being it was best to behave in his lessons as the floor was ready should they falter. In truth, his lessons were loved as he made the subject come alive to them and they spoke admirably of his delivery. He lived on site with his wife who taught music. She often seemed in his shadow and rarely lit up unless alone and more relaxed. They were the couple who took me to the pub as phase two of my successful interview.

The Primary Teacher was a young jolly individual with a mischievous grin and manner. His pupils doted on him as he built them up in self-esteem beyond their prior imagination. He was one of the three House Masters and lived on the coast in a small holding with his partner. Full of mischief ... he was the person to bring energy and excitement to the staff room and competitiveness to any activity where his pupils could win an accolade ... for him.

The owner's young son taught Environmental Studies in a room akin to a Professor's laboratory and a wing of a greenhouse at Kew Gardens. There was no expense spared or criticised in his teaching resource requirements. He was one of the three House Masters and lived in with his wife and young family. He was pleasant and engaging ... always keen to be helpful. His manner being wearier and more measured around his father.

The English teacher was a lovely middle-aged lady who was to all around, both staff and pupils, a dreamy romantic yet captivating teacher. She was mostly one for words and books and struggled with anything technical or mechanical. Evidenced by her driving twenty miles to school one morning in her husband's car. She spoke on arrival of terrible noises and much smoke coming from the engine. It transpired that she had driven the whole journey in first gear oblivious to the fact the car was not an automatic. The A.A. took her home that evening.

The French teacher was indeed from France. An elegantly dressed man with a soft voice and marked accent. He taught French so well the pupils even mastered the non-verbal language and were keen Gallic 'shruggers'. He wore a cologne that meant everyone always knew where he was during the school day. I soon learnt that the Gents loo was best visited after him as he would refresh his fragrance there regularly thereby dulling the odour of the struggling wartime plumbing. He was quiet in the presence of others but quite the opposite when surrounded by the pupils and delivering tales of Parisian wonder. He lived in the Hall as a residential member of staff.

The R.E. teacher also lived in the Hall and was the most unlikely deliverer of any church-like curriculum. He was however a very able sportsman who played for a high performing local team at football. It was as if R.E. had been the open door to a position at the school, but not particularly his favoured role. I soon found out that when it came to any report writing it was best to let him go first. This was only discovered after I had completed my section for a year group. At this time, they were handwritten onto a single page with a section for each subject. While he was skilled with a ball at his feet, he was often completely useless with a pen in his hand and all other staff would have to rewrite their entry due to his calamitous spelling.

The Woodwork teacher was an elderly fellow who was mostly covered in wood shavings and as such not the best to sit next to at mealtimes. The pupils loved his subject and produced all manner of crafted items and assisted the caretaker in repair work around the school.

The Art Teacher was a man of immense quality both in character and artistic proficiency. To enter his room was to be overwhelmed with incredible creativity oozing from each of his pupils due to his inspirational teaching. He gave the impression he was a touch crazy, but it was a disguise to tease great things from these boys many of whom had clearly never realised such artistic skill before. He lived in with his wife and three daughters. His energy seemed boundless and it translated into whatever he did as a teacher or family man.

There was also a Special Unit for four boys with Dyslexia. The teacher was the charming wife of the owner and her pupils were there because of the attention to their need not being the same as all others. The classroom was called 'The College of Knowledge'. One such pupil being the young son of a film star who played the role of the Sergeant in the Pink Panther Films with Peter Sellers.

As the initial few weeks passed, I began to settle into a routine. The first meeting with each class group went well with me spelling out my expectations of their learning and behaviour. This was seemingly received and understood by them without question. What followed was often a surprise after the cautionary tales about them and their resultant performance in the classroom was as perfect as it could be. Relationships with them grew and my enthusiasm seemed to captivate them be it about the glacial facts of Britain, the latest football scores, or the possible solutions to the challenges of life. There were some characters keen to test me and there my own previous experiences were helpful. I had been such a well-performing tester when a pupil and this meant that in my new role as the gamekeeper that I kept such poachers of learning in check. About one in five of the pupils was of Caribbean heritage and on finding out my passion for music included reggae and ska an increased understanding and admiration was afforded me. Often it meant they would demand respect for me if someone crossed the line with their behaviour. This was an early established relationship and connection with my pupils ... one that paid dividends in so many ways thereafter.

The teaching role included residential evening duties in the 'ex-hospital' dormitories. I would seek escape at times from the relentless walking about, by going for a coffee and chat with Martin, the Art Teacher wizard. His insight and experience being extremely useful to me in my performance ensuring all were settled and safe. This duty also allowed me to get to understand the boys and their wishes, concerns and problems. I was able to relate to their separation from home and the homesickness that often swept through their lives. Any tips on getting through such trials were offered and mostly received well with an appreciative smile. Some of them had no such regular relationship with a male role model as their own father or even complete set of parents were absent from whatever and wherever their home setting was. In amongst them were some true characters who impressed me with their resilience and their honesty as a person. These attributes often rhubarb-like in that they'd been forced by the circumstances and lack of light in their home lives.

When it came to P.E. and Games, the opportunity for them to play football was indeed a welcomed release from the tighter constraints of the classroom. It was often an opportunity to conclude any differences of opinion or conflict with a timely or mistimed tackle or elbow. Never did such a moment then result in anything more protracted. The helping hand from the floor and accompanying look served to be the full stop that concluded the incident.

It was in one of the first matches we were playing in such a lesson that their code was best exemplified. One of the senior boys was running with the ball at his feet and suddenly he stopped in his tracks in an almost frozen-like upright position. The ball ran away from him a few yards, but nobody ventured towards it to continue the game. Every other player instantly stood perfectly still. Curious and wondering what was going on and whether this was a test of me I took two steps towards the statuesque pupil. One boy spoke softly and said, "Wait Sir, wait for him." The scene was one of everyone motionless and looking towards the boy in question. Moments later he then shrugged himself as he came back to life and moved towards the ball. Only at this point did everyone else similarly respond. The game continued and fun was had by all with their footballing artistry being evident and applauded.

As we walked from the pitch back to the changing rooms it was explained to me that the boy in question was an epileptic and that he had had a petit-mal in the game. The chubby and athletic Caribbean fifteen-year-old goalie detailed in a caring way that the unquestioned rule in such an occasion was to pause their own play and let him come out of his fit before continuing. His explanation was clear in stating that this was only fair in the circumstances. Such respect and consideration admirable in them and followed without a second thought. In fact, as he was such a dynamic goal scorer he was much sought after as a team player when each lesson started.

Being away from home was not easy for many of the pupils and my prior experience of boarding school meant I fully understood their emotions. With all my experience of escaping the confines of such provision I admired the planning and execution of one pupil. He had shown great ability as a cross-country runner and was coached accordingly. His skill was rewarded with the opportunity to go on runs out of the school grounds. He always returned red-faced and pleased with his latest outing. Then one day he left on a training run ... and kept running all the way towards home in Peterborough before being picked up by the Police east of Ely.

My Geography teaching became quite an art in itself with much time each Sunday morning sat at home in the cottage preparing lessons. The boys seemed mesmerised by the diagrams I produced on the roller board in various chalk colours to illustrate geomorphological features. As such the pressure was on to ensure that my research included reference to copy that I could reproduce in lessons. In addition, the added bonus of my OHP allowed for slides to be prepared and a good stock for further use. My diagrammatic skills came as a bit of a surprise as I had never really been one for art and recall my own teacher suggesting such an 'O' Level option would be best taken up by those with at least a modicum of talent. Undoubtedly the lessons I was delivering were becoming popular as there was never a latecomer to class and the engagement of all in any discussions was enjoyed.

Of course my mischievous teaching colleagues took every opportunity to launch into a tease over coffee and make reference to my bulb burning brightly (in my OHP)!

When I approached the Headteacher about adding some Fieldwork to the lessons he was surprised at what clearly he considered to be a foolish question. Once I had presented sound academic reasons with the required social safeguards he conceded. The latter being necessary in his mind as it was 'irregular to let them out'. My driver that day was the much admired Art Teacher as I had yet to take my driving test. We travelled to Kings Lynn to study the Old Town and Dockside and the work produced was just brilliant. The boys lapped up both the freedom and the implicit trust given as they collected answers to questions, drew sketches of buildings and did some surveys of passing pedestrians and shoppers. On return to school the Headteacher was invited to a presentation of their work. He was lost for words in the presence of these newly inspired Geographers detailing the depth of their learning.

Realising that the time was ripe for another foray into the wider world I put together a costed plan for a five-day Field trip to the Dorset Coastline with my final year 'O' Level Group. The need for some real-life work so abundantly clear to further their confidence for the exam at the end of the year. The Headteacher was impressed and keen to give the go-ahead but cautioned me that the Owner may struggle with the notion of something so frivolous. He then won the day for me with his description of what I'd achieved in Kings Lynn, as he put it, "Of all places!"

In the Spring Term ten eager 'O' Level pupils, the owner's son as driver (and perhaps to ensure due diligence) and myself set off on the two hundred and thirty mile trip south to Swanage where we were staying at the Youth Hostel. The trip was a roaring success with the opportunity to visit Lulworth Cove and Studland and take in the sights of places referenced in Physical Geography. The evenings spent writing up the findings of the day, eating hearty meals and playing table tennis. The weather was kind with wall to wall sunshine and no wind. One of the boys said it was like a 'Working Holiday' so I suggested he reconsidered the description on return to school when any presentation may be required. The quality of sketches was very pleasing, and another indication of the magic performed by the Art Teacher in his lessons.

On return up the coastal path from one such session at Durdle Door I noted a group of pupils coming towards us with their tweed-coated teacher. I gathered our group together to step aside. As they passed us the badges on their blazers revealed the name of their well-known public school in Oxfordshire and their conversations revealed a suggested sense of young gentry. Our cream of Londoners looked on and largely refrained from anything other than a scowl at their air of misplaced superiority. On passing we turned to walk on then heard a shriek from behind. One of our number was straggling and the public schoolboys began to throw stones at him and shouted, "Stone the Philistine!" Luckily, he was unhurt when I got to him. Their teacher then came to us and said, "Terribly sorry old chap … just high jinks … no harm done!" Then he turned and walked away. Remembering the sense of camaraderie that held fast in their ranks I ushered our boys away before rough justice was allowed to bloody the slopes of this beauty spot. Yet again these alleged troubled and difficult pupils had proven themselves to be better than the labels attached to their behaviour and academic ability.

The Head was pleased with the feedback as confirmed privately by the owner's son and the owner himself summonsed me to his office for a well done. His manner being such that on leaving slightly pleased I felt the underlying message was actually, 'Well done … but you've done it now … so no more eh!' That aside at the end of the year the Geography results for class exams and the important 'O' Level and CSE exams proved beyond doubt that we had all had a great year.

Life in our cottage was most enjoyable and from time to time we would greet a visitor of one sort or another. On most occasions it was a pheasant wandering up to the kitchen door only to run away at the sight of one of us. For the first time ever, we had a pair of nuthatches regularly coming to the bird table taking nuts and seeds with their long-pointed black bill. A small blue-grey and chestnut coloured bird and one that rarely ventures far from woodland. It soon became a favourite of mine.

When returning after dusk we would find hornets head-banging the kitchen window drawn by the light left on to guide us to the door. Rather numerous on one occasion we found out the following morning that there was a nest under the eaves by the door. The caretaker came out with a tin of poison and a spoon attached to a stick. Balanced on a ladder he tried to feed the poison under the eaves and to steady himself he held onto a strut fixed to the electric cable's earth. When I cautioned him about the danger, he replied in his broad Norfolk accent, "Don't worry about that boy … that's the least of my worries if those now hornets come out!" Sadly, this winged community was soon killed off … but we were safer.

In an attempt to develop a sense of 'The Good Life' I cleared a patch of the grass and dug it over for vegetables. A fence was put around to keep away our second most frequent visitor, the rabbits. As the lettuces and other crops flourished so did the early morning digging of the rabbits. Then, one morning the area was devastated with the numerous entrances evidencing that there had been no queue to their feast and clearly all had to dig a much larger hole under the fence so as to escape.

The most chilling encounter was a late Summer's evening when we were sat watching a horror film with our coal fire working up to a fine blaze and its flicker lighting the darkened room. All of a sudden from the chimney a bat appeared from the fireplace and flew straight towards us. The explosion of energy in us being quite dramatic as we leapt from the settee and left the room at great speed. Once in the kitchen we stood there quite bemused confirming to each other "It was, wasn't it ... It was a bat?" Shortly after our blood pressure had reduced and our bravery increased. We peeped around the living room door and put the light on. No sign of the bat at all. It had disappeared and was not there or in the adjacent bathroom or kitchen. Our bedroom was off the kitchen but this door was closed. What a relief. When we went to bed, we had the duvet pulled up to our noses and after some unhelpful comments about bats and Count Dracula, we fell asleep. Undisturbed we woke the following morning and there was no sign of the bat at all.

That evening after our meal we finished the washing up and as I gripped the bowl to empty the soapy water there it was clinging to the under rim of the plastic bowl. I leapt back dropping the bowl back into the sink. Then with a kitchen towel I stepped forward to examine our visitor. There was this bedraggled pipistrelle bat looking rather soggy from the washing-up water. I picked it up and nursing it in the tea towel took it to our woodshed outhouse and placed it in an open topped box full of straw. The following day it was gone ... hopefully gorging on the many flies and mosquitos still prevalent at that time of year.

Other creature visitors included deer bounding through the ferns, naughty squirrels on the roof throwing cobnuts at each other, a curious shrew watching me chop logs and a mole revealing itself by our parked car as if to complain a wheel was obstructing its route to a worm lunch. This was true Country File in our own little wilderness.

Human visitors were rarer, as the milkman would only come half-way from the road to leave our bottled pints in a basket. He claimed that the full walk to the cottage from his float was too far and the track impossible for him to drive along. It worked as long as he put cups over each bottle, so we got the cream before the blue tits. The postman was far more adventurous in his van or on his moped. In the late summer, the reward for delivering mail often saw the moped's saddle bags full of the largest Bramley apples he'd ever seen from our laden tree. Perhaps the most startling of human visitors were the army on manoeuvres in the woodland who suddenly appeared in front of us one afternoon. As we were returning from a local shopping trip and bumped along our drive two armoured cars crossed ahead of us crashing through the ferns. The accompanying soldiers smiling and waving as we sat in our car with our mouths agape.

Visitors in residence included ex-College friends and two of my brothers who came in varying states of health. My brother Chris was now furthering his Royal Marine training and had recently been learning woodland survival. His attempt to catch pheasants illustrating that if he didn't improve his success rate then he was likely to be a vegetarian in combat. My youngest brother Simon had come to stay with a slight sore throat. As the days passed his throat worsened and as my wife had the car the option of getting to the village to see the doctor was only to be successful if we cycled. The eight-mile round trip saw him receive treatment and a prescription for what turned out to be mumps. Periodically he recalls the event and describes it as a poor example of medical care and brotherly love. He soon got well and unsurprisingly lives to this day.

At the end of the first year the annual camp for the older pupils took place on a farm in nearby woodland. It was a tradition and quite serious. Organised by the Senior Teacher and assisted by his wife and the R.E. Teacher. About twenty pupils in various tents camped around a communal fire with a flag-pole and their own flag fluttering above. Their absence from school lightened the load of work and the school had an air of relaxation about it. Well at least I thought that … as there was plotting afoot. I received a call to go to the Primary Classroom where studious fellow teachers were crouched over a desk with a large scale drawn plan. On the board was a similar one showing the campsite and routes in via foot and track. All that was missing from this group was Winston Churchill smoking a cigar and a few senior army officers because the air was thick with military planning as if at war. A plot was schemed up to attack the camp, take the flag and kidnap the R.E. Teacher. By now I had passed my driving test and was designated the driver to take our alleged Commando Raiders to the site. The three other teachers following in a car.

Just outside the camp the teachers took all but four of the boy soldiers as infantry and I had the heavy armoured tank of a minibus. Under the direction of 'Field Marshall Owner's Son' we launched into action. The 'Infantry' emerged from the woods and set about causing havoc to the campsite chasing the shocked campers into the field. At this point I drove the 'Tank' into the site and knocked over the flag-pole whereupon my own set of spirited Commandos pinched the flag. I then reversed out and back into the woodland to await the others. Within moments they appeared excited and adrenaline still pumping. In amongst them was a blindfolded and tied up R.E. Teacher being bustled by his teaching colleagues. His photo was taken on a Polaroid camera and fixed to the collapsed flag-pole with a ransom note. Then we drove back to school in victorious spirits with our hostage.

When we got back to school it occurred to us 'Where had the Senior Teacher and his wife been?' They were completely absent from the campsite at the time of our raid. About half an hour later an irate call was received from them complaining of our action and demanding the return of the R.E. Teacher. The reason for their absence a matter of conjecture and clearly their anger being a measure of their embarrassment. A handover was organised and an agreement reached 'What happened on the campsite stays on the campsite!' The credibility of the Senior Teacher was somewhat damaged and he was unusually quiet for the remaining weeks of the term. Our insurance policy for the event being that the Owner's son was our leader ... and as such we were 'just following orders'. Never a word spoken in the staff room ... but the buzz amongst the pupils was electric.

That Summer my wife and I joined with two ex-college students for a camping holiday in Dorset, Devon and Somerset. Much hilarity had as our friends were both exceptionally tall and his feet stuck out of the tent. When in Somerset we visited the Farm on Exmoor where another ex-Otter lived. It saw us helping to round up the flock of sheep for dipping. A ram with dodgy back legs was stuck in gorse and had to be fetched out. I was nominated and due to my success required to sit on my new friend in the back of a pick-up truck as it returned to the farm. The act of dipping is an unpleasant but necessary task for the farmer to perform. To be fair the sheep were not that enamoured with the requirement even if it was to maintain their health. As we sat around a fire in the evening chatting about our first year away from University it was clear that we were all enjoying teaching. The tales told illustrating that college had prepared us well and we were indeed child-focussed in our delivery.

In the second year at the school, the academic successes continued both in the classroom and on the playing fields. Then the owner saw a programme on the T.V. about one of the country's top public schools. He noted that the staff looked 'Jolly good' in gowns and as such an edict went out that all should be so attired to raise standards in the school. Quite how a piece of black cloth was to achieve this in our woodland setting was beyond us all ... and although the Head wore one anyway the rest of us were sceptical. With hilarity the Art and Woodwork teachers announced they were exempt. This was short lived when it was decreed that they had to wear white and brown lab coats respectively. We welcomed this new look which made one look like a dentist and the other a caretaker.

Our gowns were purchased for us and the expectation was they were to be worn throughout the full teaching day. My artistic chalk diagrams were often smudged by the offending item and my right-hand side coated in white dust. I preferred not to shake it off and would be minded to chat freely at the owner's open door where he could see my chalky sheet in its full rainbow of colouring. I began to remove it when teaching and then the fact came to the notice of the Head who crept up and caught me 'naked' of my new teaching garment when he peered through the window. My rebuke was short and thereafter I had one trusted pupil at the window on 'Gown Guard' giving me a shout if the head was en route to my room.

The best staff rebuke of the gowns was had at the start of a P.E. lesson. Two lines of footballing eager pupils quietly gathered in the corridor between the offices of the Head and Owner. At the front of each line stood the Primary Teacher and myself, with our gowns over our kit. Then at a given signal all of us started to run on the spot and our studded boots made a great noise on the floor which was immediately added to by all of us singing the tune from Match of the Day. As we then burst through the doors and headed up to the pitch, we held our gowns like a bat cape and in weaving aerobatic movements lead our teams to the goal mouth in full view of the offices. Here a pupil took our gowns from us as if our respective Page or Butler and then hung them on the goal net. The ceremony complete we played out a great game of football to illustrate the improvement in P.E. teaching standards of such clothing.

Later that day we were summonsed to see the Headteacher who accused us of having not taken the issue of gowns seriously. We offered schoolboy-like excuses and faint promises of being good teachers thereafter. The respect was there but the desire to pretend was not really. The owner could see what was happening and the idea that a gown made a difference began to wane. In all honesty, he would have been better spending money on the likes of the floor in my classroom. In the wild, windy and snowy winter a wisp of snow would also blow from underneath the wooden structure. It would appear with a whistle and come up through a crack in the floorboards. This vertical white spiral mesmerising the attention of the boy closest to the draught.

My dear Gran died in the Spring and we drove down to the funeral, stopping off in the town where my brother Keith was in naval married quarters while his ship had a refit. Little was I to know that nearly twenty years later I would be headteacher of a school less than two miles from his house. It was a poorly-attended occasion with most people she had known having passed away themselves. My parents were there and another of my brothers. My father looked very lost in his thoughts. There were so many questions about his own childhood still unclear and unanswered. My mother, never a great fan of Gran, was unusually quiet which was probably for the best. My own memories were richest from the earliest years when I had been at boarding school. I reflected how easy it was for a grandchild to lose touch with aunts, uncles and grandparents and how my own brothers had limited memories if any at all of this incredible woman. Something I have tried to encourage in my own children since and indeed theirs too. Absence may well make the heart stronger ... but conversations need to be had while such as Gran are around. They can then be passed down through generations. Such was to be the basis of a regular assembly topic by me with new Year Sevens in their first term ... causing many of them to seek me out and share their own stories.

Out of school there were some interesting moments helping Martin (Art Teacher) with two projects after he moved off-site to a house in a small village about fifteen miles away. He had a Morris Traveller car and one day as he arrived at school the front suspension gave way. In his own special way, he made a quick repair to get him home later but decided that something more significant was needed. The next thing we heard from him was an invite to a 'Moving House Barbeque' for the weekend. When we arrived he had three railway sleepers, some strong rope and two spades ... no initial sight of any Barbeque at all. After an hour we had dug two holes and placed the sleepers in them at an angle. He then drove his car parallel to them and encouraged us to lift the side of the car and lash it to the two sleepers. A further hole was then dug close to the visible underneath side of the car and the third sleeper placed in that as a prop. Job done, the barbeque appeared.

A great time had by all with local micro-brewery ale to wash down delicious chops and sausages with a mighty salad. Our 'Heath Robinson of an Art Teacher' welded the car back together and fixed required new parts to make it roadworthy while we chatted on his lawn. Just before some of our number started leaving, we went through the reverse procedure of the DIY garage construction and he then drove his car out of the garden. Car fixed ... maybe under false pretences ... but nevertheless, a memorable barbeque for us all.

As if this was not enough of a barbeque for free muscle he then invited us back a few weeks later as he needed a hole digging in the garden for a new septic tank to be installed. This time we were greater in numbers and there were more spades. It took several hours, and our thirst was suitably quenched throughout. At the end of our excavation the large tank was placed in the hole, stabilised and connected. Our duties complete, the second barbeque at his new house was another hearty feast. There was no doubt that his manner and tad crazy ideas were the attraction one just could not resist. It was good to know we had been so helpful to such a brilliant colleague and his lovely family. I am sure when each of us passed a Morris Traveller or that cottage thereafter the words "Guess what I did once?" would have been the start of such as these tales being recounted.

One evening when I was on duty in the boarding house there was a frantic knock at the Art Teacher's flat where I was having a coffee and catch up. When I answered the door one of the boys stood there, arms waving and exploding with high-speed unrecognisable words. Once calmed he said, "You best come quick as one of the boys is on his top bunk with an air rifle shooting anyone that goes in the dorm!" Now this was not a sort of once heard completely understood piece of information, so he was asked to repeat it. Once realised as an incident warranting quick action, I went to the dorm door to be greeted by a boy coming in the opposite direction holding onto his buttocks where he had just been shot. As he passed by me two further pellets pursued him.

It occurred to me at this point that the offending boy had decided that he would bring his own air gun back from home to use at the gun club the Headteacher had started. The wisdom of the club a debate for another day. The immediate issue being how to disarm the 'Dorm Sniper' before someone was seriously hurt. The Art teacher appeared at my side and posed the question as to whether it may be best to sit it out until he had used up all his pellets. Then one of the other dorm members informed us that the sniper had a large tin of pellets and they would last ages. There was no way we could delay, so a plan was needed. We grabbed a mattress from another dorm and using it as a shield rushed the sniper who frantically got off a couple of shots which our 'armour' absorbed. With a squeal the sniper became a prisoner as he was pulled from the top bunk and the gun taken from him. As we lead him from the Dorm, the other boys lined the corridor clapping. "Just like Starsky and Hutch, Sir", said one of them. "We'll have that compliment!" the Art Teacher replied, with a relieved smile.

Another evening duty in my second year had gone really well, with the boys chatty and in good spirits. At lights out they settled quickly and were soon asleep. Just after ten p.m. I went for a walk around to ensure all was okay before going off duty when I noticed one of the beds was empty. It was our epileptic lad who was missing. The boy in the top bunk said that he'd received a letter from Germany where his father (in the army) and mum were living. He said that the letter had mentioned they were splitting up and he was really upset. I went to the boy's toilets and noticed one of the cubicles was engaged so called out his name. There was no reply. I could just see under the door and there were two feet visible, but he was motionless to my calls. There was blood on the floor. I went into the cubicle next to his and looked over the top. He was sat in his pyjamas slumped forward with his head against the door. He had used a knife and tried to cut his wrists and although quite successful had clearly had another petit-mal fit thereby halting his attempts. Speed being of the essence I kicked the door in to tend to his bleeding wrists. The action of breaking down the door meant he was knocked backwards allowing me access. Within minutes I was assisted by the Art Teacher in bandaging his wrists and then the Ambulance crew arrived. They set to work on him and then took him to the ambulance. As they were shutting the door one of them said, "Great work ... you saved his life ... but tell me what happened to him to result in bruising to his forehead and back of head?" The explanation caused him to smile and then they sped off to the Hospital. Bless him ... the boy was back with us two days later and his parents flew in to take him home. It was not me who had saved him ... it was his epilepsy!

Just before the end of the Easter Term I was offered an interview at the Secondary School, on the coast in North West Norfolk. The position was to teach Geography and P.E.. There were two of us up for interview. When I entered the Headteacher's Study he was slumped sideways behind his desk stroking his trusty dog. As he sat up and greeted me, I noted he was wearing a teaching gown. My heart sunk as I knew the owner of my current job had made comment of me not wearing my gown in his reference in some sort of cryptic way. The interview was going well and then the balding spectacled Head posed a question seeking clarification of the reference to me not always being suitably attired. When I explained he smiled and pushed the reference away dismissively. The result of the day being both of us as candidates were offered jobs for the September. I was thrilled as the school had a real buzz about it.

On Sunday mornings I ran a Football Training Club for the Junior Boys. It involved working on skills which were then accredited by the F.A. with a Badge Proficiency Scheme sponsored by Coca-Cola. The club proved extremely popular. At the end of one such session the boys were picking up the equipment including the wooden cones of the day. One enthusiastic boy shouted out, "Kick the ball to me Sir!" So I did. As it arrived in front of him, he chose to try and hit it with the wooden cone. The cone hit the ball and then bounced back and hit him in the face. A peach of a black eye came up the following day.

As it was coming towards the end of the term it was time for the Church Service and Speech Day, so parents were in attendance. As I stood outside the church with my fellow teachers, up strode the same boy with his eye still swollen from the bruising. Seeing me he shouted "There's Mr Johnson, Dad ... he's the one who did this!" Fortunately, his father knew the full story and contact between us was merely a shake of the hands and a courteous greeting.

After the church service we all returned to the School for Speech Day in a marquee in front of the Hall building. The Owner stood up and waxed lyrical about the achievements of the year including all the monies spent fitting hot air hand dryers in the pupil toilets. Then with a change in tone and manner he scoured the ranks of the pupils sat before him and said, "But someone has damaged them by stuffing hand towels up the nozzle!" Parents and staff reeled at his aggressive manner while the boys smirked with some obvious knowledge of the crime and perpetrators.

Then the guest of honour stood up to give his speech. It was none other than Sergeant Hercule LaJoy from the Pink Panther Films, his son (a member of the College of Knowledge) sat with the other pupils. He said with a mischievous grin, "I will not speak for too long spouting a load of hot air as I'm only too aware that one of you (pointing at the pupils) will stuff hand towels in my mouth to stop me!" The gathering of parents, pupils and staff roared with laughter as the School Owner scratched his head in disbelief then glared at the Headteacher. I don't recall much else from the ceremony other than meeting the spirited guest speaker and thanking him for his contribution to the occasion. He winked and then walked proudly away with his son.

The school term then came to an end and I was faced with my colleagues expressing disappointment at my departure as I had proved my worth and with or without my gown helped raise standards. I recall a lump in my throat as this expression of my contribution was unusual from them as it normally would be followed by relentless mickey taking … and it was not. Hugs a plenty was their expression of regret.

The boys completely undid me with their words of appreciation and admiration. My Reggae and Ska loving pupils particularly effervescent and some had tears in their eyes. Then the bandaged wristed fifth former freshly back from his parents in Germany stepped forward, shook my hand and said, "Thank you!" I was lost for words and if I had any they would not have come out anyway.

As I turned away from them, the Owner's Secretary beckoned me to the office. There the normally gruff man was quite different. Complimentary in his brief words he then gave me a small wrapped present and insisted I open it. The gift was a miniature hand-made gown in a presentation box. He burst out laughing and shaking my hand said, "Good luck and thank you for all you have done!" For the first time in two years, he had shown a part of his true character not seen by me previously.

As I walked home, I reflected on my experience and how much more I had learned of the art of teaching and how characters make it an enjoyable place for teachers and pupils to work together. Isn't that just how every school should be?

Chapter 7

By the Seaside

We drove the fifty miles up to the coastal town which was to become our new home and place of work. This coastal town described in the travel guides as 'a thriving Victorian seaside town and one of the rare places on the east coast where the sun sets over the sea'. That very sun was shining brightly as we arrived at our flat some one hundred yards from both the beach and town centre. The flat was small, but we managed to fit everything in and made it as homely as we could. The intention being to buy somewhere as soon as possible.

When term started it was a busy day with nearly as many staff as there had been pupils at my previous post. The school had a thousand pupils in the eleven to sixteen age range. The good news being that there were about fifteen of us new to the school and most of them taking up their first ever teaching position. The P.E. department was run by a very confident woman who knew exactly what she wanted from the six of us in her charge and from the start she was never short to say just that. Her enthusiasm and drive were just what I wanted to be part of. Her deputy was a male teacher who seemed to be quite laid back and it soon became clear why – he had not got the Head of Department's job when it came up. He wasn't lazy but it took something to feel he had any passion for the job at times. There was another new teacher joining, his first job too. He was from the North East ... a Sunderland fan who was passionate about his football and birth roots. As time passed, he was often mistaken by the pupils as either Welsh or Irish. Clearly the 'Mackem' in him quite amused by this. He would soon educate them and before long they dutifully responded to his "Ha'way canny lad hoy that ball owl' ere!" in lessons.

The Geography Department was run by a middle-aged man who had only ever taught at the school. He came across as very pleasant and also had high expectations of his staff team in all they did. He was one of three staff who had lived in this corner of Norfolk all their lives. They had been at school together all the way through and played football and cricket for their villages in the local leagues. During the war they went off to fight either in Europe or the Far East. One had to surrender in the conflict and had been a Prisoner of War suffering greatly at the hands of his Japanese captors. The result being he was still carrying the weight of this awful time in his outward physical appearance and I'm sure it had also scarred his mental state. All three were the undoubted rocks within the school and the core of stability such a place needed. They were the 'go to' characters and excellent mentors for the staff team no matter what their experience was. I was soon to learn that when building a team around you it is such as these 'three wise men' that you need.

It didn't take long for all of us as newcomers to realise that everybody knew everybody in the town and surrounding villages. The benefits and potential pitfalls suitably referenced in the staff room each Monday morning when a weekend could catch up with you. A number of us played for the town at football and the standard was particularly good with our Mackem colleague being quite exceptional. The Amateur Sporting reviews at morning break often celebrating great performances ... or unpicking fault when results were otherwise. Equally so when us 'Young Ones' visited a local hostelry on a Friday evening our revelry may also catch up with us. Certainly, a walk into town to do shopping almost always meant that the mother of a pupil or indeed an older pupil would end up serving us. The greeting and any further conversation always being polite and engaging such was the place of the school in the community and value placed on the staff there.

As I had spent my first two years working in the independent sector, I was deemed not to have passed my 'probationary teaching period'. As such along with others we were all timetabled monitoring visits by Local Authority staff. The intention being to decide if we were up to scratch and worthy of being qualified. It soon transpired that the year-long period was not required for me and after the first visit the LEA decided that my testimonial (including that lingering dress code reference) and a couple more visits would suffice. The downside being that the Senior Education Officer for this part of the County would be my judge and jury. It seemed it may be a tough one.

He watched me teach Geography and P.E. on the next visit and spoke well of me when feeding back to my respective Heads of Departments. Then he took a moment with me saying that when teaching about rail travel in the Geography lesson I had written 'Carriage' on the board and the correct spelling was 'Carraige'. I had a moment of doubt and was about to say something as I was confident that he was wrong ... but thought I would leave it. So I smiled and said, "Oh ... thank you!" A couple of days later I received a letter from him with two parts to it. The first part stating he wished to apologise as my spelling was right and he was embarrassed. The second part to confirm that there was no need to have a further visit and I had passed my probationary period. The question as to whether or not his spelling embarrassment was influential in my early success didn't really matter ... I was pleased and just carried on.

Working in a bigger school setting with so many other staff had numerous benefits, not least of all the opportunity to further develop my teaching performance by watching my more experienced peers at work or in team teaching such as in P.E. and Games.

The first year saw me learn so much as I worked with excellent practitioners who enjoyed the craft of their subject. The energy in the school was there to be seen. The peer supportive systems ensured even when mistakes were made the learning from them was paramount. The wise words of the Deputy Head always available and a good guide to those early in their first teaching post. I recall him saying to one female newly-qualified colleague after she had made a mistake with the management of a situation with pupils, "I will always support you one hundred percent in front of the pupils ... but mark my words if you were wrong then privately I will spare nothing in telling you just that". He was true to these words, but should have added, "... and then I promise to explain how you can ensure you don't make such a mistake again!" His bark and his bite were infamous ... his caring guidance became increasingly so.

The Head of P.E. encouraged me to go to Loughborough University and complete a residential week-long Gymnastics Course to further my teaching skills. With such a prestigious reputation for P.E. and Sport I was delighted at the opportunity. There were a dozen other teachers of P.E. from Primary and Secondary Schools, and we were fortunate to have two of the finest national coaches to put us through our paces. The emphasis being on developing both our own olympic gym competency and teaching delivery. It is fair to say that the majority of us would have baulked at the physical dimension had we known the full detail before arriving. Yet that golden thread again of skilled, confident and enthusiastic teaching by the coaches ensured we performed beyond our wildest dreams. These skills being literally caught as we were taught by them ensured our learning was secure for when we returned to our own schools. My physical elasticity was stretched to new bounds with straddles, handsprings and high-speed aerial tumbles put together in various sequences the full length of the gymnasium. The other teachers were equally amazed at this new found ability fostered by confidence that increased each day.

There were other courses taking place including athletics, badminton, tennis, hockey and rugby and we would often spot notable sportswomen and men in the refectory queue at lunchtime. There was a particularly officious dinner lady there to organise us all and ensure we followed her well drilled routine when on her territory. One such day she was getting frustrated because the line wasn't straight enough as some of the other course members had deposited kit and equipment along the wall. Tennis rackets, hockey sticks and all manner of such items were frustrating her and she ripped into anyone looking as though they were the owner of these offending pieces. Feeling left out of her rebuke and wanting to raise the level of humour we took two gym benches in the following day to raucous cheers and laughter of our fellow sporting peers. The dinner lady was open-mouthed and unsure what to say … then she smiled and tutted amusingly at us. Our silliness had won through, and the air was calmer at lunchtime. On return to school my lessons were much improved in their quality of performance and expectation. The enjoyment I had lapped up in Loughborough was now translated into pupil performance in our own gymnasium. For the first time in this setting, I realised that even in teaching I must continue to hone my skills and to do so I must remain a learner myself.

At the end of each week all the newly appointed staff and most of the P.E. Department would be joined by other younger staff members and play a variety of games in the large modern Sports Hall. By this time that included my wife who was full time on the staff teaching team. Badminton was played very competitively and boasting rights held dear for the week ahead by some. I had never really been one for racket sports of any sort and it was not my favourite part of the weekly wind-down. The greatest fun was had when playing Volleyball which by the fact it was a team sport had a more light hearted and less competitive nature to it. This had to be so as those gathered had a range of skills and some were completely new to the sport. If a team was clearly on top then at the end of each game the mix of players was changed to balance things out. This meant that competitiveness gave way to one of camaraderie and enjoyment. It worked for everyone. Laughter being heard much more than when engaged in individual sports such as Badminton.

At the end of the 'weekly wind-down' in the Sports Hall we would all shower and change into casual clothes then drive off to one of the villages inland or up around the coast. Here we would eat and drink together as well as share some funny stories about the week just ended. The sense of that professional weight of responsibility and the implicit pressure to perform being lifted from our collective shoulders was palpable as we enjoyed each other's company. The strength of the group was that we got close to each other and in that there was mutual help on offer when work or private lives got frayed.

On one such Summer Friday the topic turned to identifying a fun activity for a weekend day. After many ideas being kicked into the long grass and laughed out for their daftness, one shone through. A Car Treasure Hunt in the west of the county was the verdict. Then there was this thoughtful silence before people started volunteering roles. Of course, if it was to be a true test then there was only one role that needed confirming and that was someone to set the route and provide the clues.

When it came to the day the sun shone as much as the polished cars and the smiling faces of each pair of enthusiastic 'Treasure Hunters'. Surely even with the cryptic clues there was no way this could be anything other than enjoyable and easy to navigate. Well it was for most, but inevitably ninety minutes for some was not the experience of others. While the early birds were sat in the sun outside a very rural pub, others toiled in the country lanes. Undoubtedly some frayed discussions were had between those late to the finish and one team had to open their 'Get out of Jail' envelope with the final stop details to ensure they arrived at all. The stories told about mishaps and wrong turnings causing great laughter. The accolade for the greatest gaff of the day being admitted to by our Mackem P.E. Teacher and his Needlework partner in saying, "We got so lost at one time we tried to follow the signs to a place called 'By Road' but they pointed everywhere and nowhere!" That was certainly one for the staff room at morning break once back in school.

House-hunting finally paid dividends, and my wife and I took up residence in a small village a few miles south. With a fine pub, two shops, a primary school and church at the heart of the village … it was a relaxing place to live. Three other teachers from the school lived close by although we rarely ever saw them out and about. On one side was a young family and he worked as an electrician. We got to know more about the local area as they had always lived thereabouts. His family were originally from London and he talked a great deal of his team Charlton Athletic every Saturday afternoon. I would joke with him that he was the first fan of this club I had ever met and therefore he must be rare. He would reply, "Not that rare as I have one of their football shirts so you see they made more than the eleven needed for their players!" How life unravels, many years on I took to watching this family orientated club play regularly at the Valley.

Our first child was born in the Spring of 1983 and the joy of her arrival was immense. Not the first grandchild in the family as my brother Keith already had two sons. However, she was the first female of the family name in more than four generations so a much-celebrated addition to the extended line. Our neighbours on the other side were newly-weds and we had become great friends. He was a police officer and she was a nurse. He was asked to be one of our daughter's godparents and was pleased to agree. He was over six feet tall and quite athletic. His parents originally from Jamaica. He told the tale of working a late shift in Norwich and coming across an old tramp of Caribbean heritage. When the tramp saw him, he leapt to his feet and shouted "My son … my long-lost son!" whereupon he ran towards the startled officer who then chose to run the opposite way. In telling the tale he giggled throughout saying how this must have looked so bizarre to those coming out of pubs and clubs in the city. He added that with the county being so white that a black face was pretty rare unless you were a player on the pitch, playing for the 'Canaries' at Carrow Road.

We both went for a stroll one afternoon and spotted some small Victorian bottles in a freshly ploughed field near the road side. On picking them up and debating their former use we noted others by a track and realised we had come across a Victorian dump where such artefacts were in abundance. A little clawing away of the dirt revealed others in a full unbroken state which we took home pleased as punch with our finds. Needless to say, our schoolboy-like enthusiasm was not universally greeted by our respective wives. That story still applying to this day as mine sit unappreciated in a cardboard box in the shed ... well bar a couple that I have sneaked in as yet unnoticed.

The school First XI Football Team was an exceptionally talented group of boys. To teach them during the school day, coach them out of hours, play against some in the Saturday League and have others in the same team was a delight, and saw me enjoy a wonderful period with the sport. One year team had two centre backs who were the spitting image of Suggs the lead vocalist with Madness. In matches they would come up to attack at corners and their final footsteps were a take on the group's antics when performing the hit songs of the time 'Baggy Trousers' and 'One Step Beyond'. The following year the team had outfield players training with Arsenal, Norwich and Cambridge United and the goalkeeper at Nottingham Forest where he trained with Peter Shilton.

As the team were so successful, I arranged to take them to France to play two matches in the Loire area. The trip being in partnership with the French Department and their charismatic teacher. His spoken perfect French and his knowledge of the area was invaluable as it helped to secure splendid accommodation in Amboise. Some of the players had a further year to do at the school and ended up being picked by me to have a trial with the District Team. Picked on merit for a team that I was to manage.

The Sunday before the trial I was at home enjoying a lazy afternoon. Then there was a knock at the door and one of my players was standing there wanting to know if I could help out with a match that was due to start. The referee hadn't turned up and I was invited to be the stand-in. This was not a request I could turn down so I got changed and went to the village green. It was my village's own under sixteens versus one from the Fenland area of the county. I recognised some of the players on their side as those I'd had recommended for the forthcoming trial, by P.E. staff at their school. Of course, I knew all our own village team as I taught every one of them. As the match progressed one parent with the opposition started to make sarcastic comments about my refereeing and jeered at players on the home team. So across I went, to advise him that to be quiet would be to everyone's advantage unless he could be positive. I added that if he couldn't then I wouldn't hesitate to have him removed. The cheers from other supporters including some of his team indicating this was a request they wanted to see him abide by … or face the consequences. A moment of sense gripped him and he remained silent for the rest of a well-contested draw.

Once the players arrived at school for the District Trial with their P.E. staff the training got underway and it was clear from the thirty players present that the selection was going to be tough. A series of matches then followed when players were mixed and matched to see them in competitive roles. At this time, I was walking along the line making notes and swapping players over when I bumped into a familiar face. It was the mouthy parent from the match at the weekend. He didn't recognise me but knew I was the Team Manager. "That's my son there", he said pointing towards a midfielder. I couldn't resist the moment. "I know", I replied, then adding, "I remember him and ... you from the weekend!" He did a double take and then went a rich ruby red with embarrassment. I winked and walked away. Whatever he thought at that moment about his son's prospects must have had him agonising for a week. By which time the selection letters arrived ... and he must have been incredibly relieved his son had been picked. This man attended many matches thereafter and was reserved in manner at every one of them. At the time the painful experiences of such parents 'playing football badly through their child' was just starting to wear thin with referees and coaches. It was some time before the F.A. gripped hold of it and set a code of conduct in place.

When playing local league football myself, there were players who abused the referees with all manner of comments. Our team took such behaviour seriously and would drop a player cited during a game and ban them longer if sent off. On one occasion I was playing on a cold Saturday afternoon and the sunny blue sky turned to cloud, it snowed, it hailed and the sun reappeared. That afternoon the language was as blue as the sky at the start and end of the match. Nothing to do with decisions or foul play but most certainly the fact it was so very cold. In the sleet storm the referee took us all off to the changing rooms but the heating had broken down during the game so the room was freezing. This meant that the language then was directed at the ref. to encourage him to get the match going again so that we could at least warm up. I didn't score many goals that particular season but I got one in that match. One of their defenders tried to cross the ball to another player just outside their penalty area. I slid in and volleyed it into the goal ... and kept on sliding in the snow, just missing putting their advancing goalkeeper in the back of the net with the ball already there. As I stood up and was being congratulated by my team mates all I wanted to do was to remove the large volume of frozen snow from inside my shorts and pants. We won the game four-three and it took the whole journey home before my full personal parts were approaching the stage after numbness on the return to normal body temperature.

The weather at school that winter was quite exceptionally cold. The joke being that when the wind blew it often made the rain falling in Lincolnshire blow horizontally across the sixteen miles of The Wash and not actually land until it got to the Norfolk side. One member of staff claiming that a crisp packet dropped over there would hit you in the face minutes later at school because the wind was so strong. Certainly, when it snowed that same wind caused ten-foot drifts and school was closed as the main road was impassable. It was of course proper snow in those times.

In our village area someone organised a snowball fight and pupils of all ages took on the teachers and other parents living locally. It was a great fight with no quarter given by either side and undoubtedly some old scores were settled in the chaotic scenes. At the end of this skirmish the teachers and parents held fast and were likened by one ice covered parent as brave kinsmen to those who served at Rorkes Drift. Such an imagination indeed and in weather so very different. The tales of the Battle of Shelduck Drive living on for some time afterwards in the village folklore.

Injury free through three seasons of football I managed to break a bone in my right foot when I stumbled at a barbeque and even before I'd had a beer and eaten a sausage! A visit to the hospital saw me in a full leg plaster and after two days at home I decided to turn up to teach. Now teaching Geography on crutches was easy and it may be that they felt a touch sorry for me so were additionally well behaved. Teaching P.E. was more of a challenge but my credibility with the pupils was added to for they had never had hockey taught by someone on crutches before. Added to that, by a teacher who then played an active twenty-minute game with two crutches and a hockey stick used so menacingly and efficiently. Crazy seemed to be a descriptive label attached to me and to make matters worse I cracked the plaster so had to go back to get another fitted.

The Summer Term was one when the weather was always good and an early tan ensured for all in the P.E. Department. On one such day I was teaching Geography the whole afternoon while Ian Botham was destroying the Australians at Edgbaston in an Ashes cricket match. On a regular basis I hung out of the classroom window to seek updates on the score from a pupil pitchside and off games who had the teacher's radio tuned into the match. From my classroom runners were sent to other rooms to pass on the unravelling score and the cheers could be heard across the school as each Aussie wicket was taken.

This energised the staff and First XI Cricket Team to play out a match of their own to be watched by all the school and non-playing staff. The pupils had an impressive batting and bowling team and decided to put us into bat first. We scored well at first then collapsed for less than eighty runs. The pupils padded up in confident mood. Then our Head of English, a rather quiet and gentle teacher, was given the ball and asked to bowl. To that point their runs had been creeping along towards our total … but no more. His fast bowling ripped through their batting order with ease and we won the day. As he left the field his GCSE English set stars in the cricket team asked if he'd ever played much before. He replied modestly, "Yes, just a bit in the Lancashire League!" They had been undone by a semi-professional cricketer who had swapped his passion for the sport, and taken up Poetry and Classic Literature and they now liked him even more for both.

Enjoying my teaching at this school as much as I did, I felt restless for a new challenge and an opportunity came up at another town nearby in Special Education. It was as the Deputy in what was called a Senior Tutorial Centre and would now be known as a Pupil Referral Unit. I attended interview which comprised of the Headteacher, Educational Psychologist and the Education Officer who could now spell 'carriage'. My two years' experience in the Independent Special School and never-give-up-on-anyone mantra saw me through and after five years in teaching I was appointed Deputy Head.

My colleagues at school questioned my sanity for making the jump from well-disciplined and self-motivated pupils in a forward-thinking school for this setting with the best of the worst from West Norfolk. 'You need the bumps feeling on your head!' being their take on my supposed loss in sanity.

However right they thought they were ... and indeed a few times I wondered after handing in my resignation ... I knew it was right. It felt like destiny.

Chapter 8

Down the Coast

Set in the grounds of one of the three large secondary schools in this coastal town and seaport was the Tutorial Centre. It took boys and girls of secondary age from the west of Norfolk. Most had been excluded from mainstream schools because of their disruptive behaviour or they had been placed because of their vulnerability in such settings. Of the twelve on roll only two were girls.

The boys were all from ages in the eleven to sixteen range with only four of them in the same year group. Their presenting behaviours varied and included such as violently aggressive, mentally disturbed and passively non-cooperative. The girls had either been teenage pregnancy or suffered some form of abuse. Each was a character with a story to tell and some ability needing to be rediscovered. Despite their expressed hatred for school, they had a sense of comfort and security in being present. The Headteacher had worked at the school for several years and created a learning environment where the challenges could be extreme but the results could be so rewarding.

I was responsible for teaching Maths, Environmental Studies and P.E.. There was no formal lesson teaching of any of these subjects. It was basically an introduction and then individually tailored work for each pupil. The planning required for each day being quite extensive. That prepared not always necessarily used as events may overtake learning requiring interventions for which I had no preparation at all … but soon became conversant with, to prevent injuries to other pupils and myself.

One pupil was from a beautiful and tranquil village with a large pond at its heart full of small golden crucial carp and rudd. His manner was unlike the calmness of his village and I likened it to a volcanic explosion if he made an error in any work or felt someone was teasing him. His strength when angry was quite devastating with items being broken. His strength when working calmly quite brilliant at Maths. To deflect his anger with humour and then refocus him quickly was an art in itself. When it worked he was a mouse. He loved being in the Centre but would literally swear blind he hated everything about it. He could use the phrase F★★★ Off in so many ways it became clear it was really his 'and', 'if' and 'but'. It was important to remember that if he didn't behave that way then he couldn't attend. It was part of the entrance exam and a prerequisite for maintaining his place on role. There it was, the key to coming to terms with them and their challenges. That very behaviour was abnormal and unacceptable in mainstream … it was normal and challenging to accept in this setting. The key being work with it and try and fashion a desire to change.

Another boy would prefer to spend most of his day laid on top of a desk simulating a sexual act and referring to how his parents bred dogs with each thrust of his body on the wooden desk surface. The reference to animals in any work was his hook point and could often secure on task behaviour for at most fifteen minutes duration when a new strategy was required. Sometimes the threats of violence from others if he didn't stop being 'weird' was more successful and his hyperactivity would decrease. His presenting learning difficulties and lack of any sustained education weighing heavy on his self-esteem.

The youngest boy was from a children's home and had been passed around like a parcel at a children's birthday party game. With real issues of trust that he would constantly play out to test relationships and then choose deliberately to fail at in any tasks. This was his way of showing a rare moment of actually feeling he was in control of something in his life. His approach to the Centre was to arrive so he could run away and only come back so he could be taken back to the Home by his Social Worker. He loved Environmental Science and was the keeper of the indoor plants and tender of the germination trays. His red mist often being subdued by his green fingers.

Another younger boy had the same name as an older boy but went by the nickname 'Einstein' which he loved and was because he had been caught cheating in a Science Test. He had psoriasis and was for ever scratching his hands and face because of the discomfort and also from habit. He had Tourette's Syndrome and inter-dispersed his involuntary swearing with real insight and interest in to anything presented in class. For his gruff nature always mellowing when his granddad came to collect him. A man he loved and unashamedly admitting to feeling so.

One older boy lived near to the Centre and would burst into the building as if he was a bank robber. He would then search the place to find anything new and try and pocket it before slumping in a chair and going silent. His big brother would often collect him after a half day with us and on one occasion I spotted a shotgun in the boot of his car. The advice from the Head being not to say anything for fear of a rather scary reaction.

Other boys were a mixture of the behaviours already mentioned and would blow hot and cold about anything presented or asked of them. But they turned up every day. The girls were quiet and withdrawn preferring always to be close to the Head.

At the end of my first week when the 'F★★★ometer' had registered a high three figure total in my direction, I met up with the Friday 'Wind Down' Team from my previous school. They were dumbfounded to hear of my wonderful pupils and the fact I was referred to by my Christian Name or a swear word. They questioned as to how the education being provided was going to make any difference and result in better outcomes for the pupils and all others in their lives. After only one week I certainly didn't have a winning answer, but I talked of wanting to make a difference and being resilient in my efforts for and with them. That got me an extra pint in the pub and a shake of the head in disbelief that this was a good career move for me. In their eyes I was now one of the 'quirky' teachers.

In the weeks that followed some green shoots started to show. It seemed that what I was doing was having an impact. Alternatives to certain behaviours particularly swearing started to occur. The notion of three steps forward one sideways and two backwards sometimes just about summed it up … but there's progress there if you read it again! The fact they were beginning to acknowledge their behaviours and hear alternatives that they may then choose to try, was real progress.

The behaviours were sometimes vicious and to physically disarm one of them wielding a knife was dangerous but necessary. Although the Educational Psychologist was present at interview there was little sight of them during the day when the feeling of being a lion tamer without a chair, let alone a whip to crack seemed very real. Some classes she provided added to the Psychology of Behaviour I had learned at University but strategies and case files were short and incomplete.

It wasn't all gloom and doom though for the ripple of giggling, the bursts of laughter and the expressions of fun were there too. Achievement made was noted and celebrated with the resultant work snatched and stored safely. This being done to prevent it being destroyed as it sometimes would be if the achieving pupil wanted to maintain the historic credibility of maladjustment. When I suggested we visit the town swimming baths for recreational swimming and to teach some how to swim the Head gave me the same look as my 'Friday Friends' and former colleagues. So we gave it a try.

They were nervous and timid in this public space. Staying close to me and seeking reassurance they would be okay. Their swearing not out loud but almost in library voices. The fact they were vulnerable may have been due to them being in swimming trunks ... but it was a moment to build on. Once in the water and less self-conscious they wanted to swim and took on board the teaching of it with greater attention than in the classroom. These sessions would not include everyone for that would truly have been a formidable challenge for more than a core of six of them. In time all the boys longed for their trips to the pool. On one occasion to remind me of why they were at the Centre they threw a beach ball at one of the Lifeguards. It hit him on the back of the head and he spun around demanding who had thrown it. My loyal pupils all instantly pointed at me and I was thrown out of the pool that day. All very funny until my six swimmers had to come ashore with me. It was the first time the mischief had been in humour and without malice. A point we debated on our return to the Centre.

In the Summer Term we agreed to take some of them to the Royal Norfolk Show as a treat. Their work and behaviour warranting the trust that would be afforded at such a high-profile venue. My wife and daughter accompanied us and 'Einstein' took a shine to both and stuttered and stammered in his vocal resistance to prevent swearing. On winning a Koala Bear at one stall he came bouncing back to my daughter in her push chair and offered the Koala to my wife. He struggled to get the words out, "I w-w-w-won this a-a-and it's f-f-for your d-d-daughter",with each word he screwed up his scarred face as he resisted the swearing punctuating his words. Then with a smile he handed it over and pleased with himself he turned proudly to walk away. At this point he remembered something and spun around to exclaim, "But mind the f★★★ing claws they are sharp!" Then slapped his forehead in disappointment and said "Sorry Miss, Sorry Sir!" There was nothing we could say other than to thank him. The truth be told ... those claws were very sharp!

One afternoon when teaching Maths with three of the younger pupils, the one from the children's home suddenly became angry and launched at Einstein. I stepped in and pulled them apart. At this moment the angry boy pulled a knife from his pocket and stabbed me in the left arm. The knife was only small but nevertheless it was stuck in my arm. I took the boy down to the floor and held him with my injured arm while pulling the knife out with the other. He was angry and wriggling. I shouted at the other two and told them to go and get the Headteacher. To my astonishment they chose to start to barricade the door and when asked what they were doing, one replied, "Look Sir ... what he did to you was wrong ... so you can do whatever you like to him and we will stop anyone coming in while you do!" Einstein stood scratching himself frantically upset by the whole incident.

The Children's Home kept the boy off for several weeks and when he returned he was sheepish in my presence. During this time, I had decided to seek an appointment back in mainstream to work with children with special educational needs and had secured a position in Warwickshire as Head of SEN in a large comprehensive. My year at the Tutorial Centre had taught me a lot about such children and indeed about myself. I was sorry to be leaving but excited about my new job.

On my last day at the Centre the staff and students said some nice things about me and the difference I had made. But it was Einstein who captured it in his own inimitable way as he thrust a wrapped present into my hand and said, "There you are, that's for you ... thank you! Now f*** off ... cos you obviously don't care anymore!"

He turned away with tears in his eyes and did not look back. His thank you and good bye was filled with honesty and regret.

His words still resonate with me to this day. My year in his company highlighted how caring, and showing such care, is the key to unlocking such as him. Now ... where had I learned that?

Chapter 9

Along the Canal

Moving to the Midlands was an attempt to further my career in special educational needs by stepping back into mainstream and working with a broad spectrum of pupils of secondary age. My previous three posts had prepared me for leadership so to take on a Head of Department role and Support for Learning co-ordination across the whole school curriculum was the right move.

My new school was in a North Warwickshire town. A secondary school for about a thousand pupils in the eleven to eighteen age range. It served a semi-rural area and had several coal mining villages within its catchment. The town was of Roman and Medieval origin and gained importance for its leather-working, tanning and hatting industries. As such it was semi-industrial and a market town for the north of the county and nearby Leicestershire and Staffordshire. The Coventry Canal ran through the town and proved to be of great importance to many of the pupils I ended up teaching.

As one long-serving teacher shared with me early on at my new school, "Education does not always rank highly with some of the youths you will come across. The most important thing will be fishing on the cut (canal), then going to the pub underage, then a girlfriend, then god knows and after that going to school!" As time passed some was proved to be right but much was proven wrong as we worked hard to make school far more interesting. This spark on our behalf in time lit their imagination and engagement.

My first week was quite straight forward in respect of establishing a routine and organising my team. One evening I decided to visit the local area to gain my bearings and get a better insight into what the outlying villages were like. As I tried to enter one village where I knew there was a working mine, I was stopped at a police road-block. After the officers had established who I was and where I was from, they politely denied me access to the village. The Miner's Strike was in full swing and 'strangers' were not welcome by the Police. This happened again at another village so I gave up on my reconnaissance and drove to my parents where I was staying.

Each weekend I would drive back to Norfolk to be with my wife and daughter. The two hundred and thirty mile round trip a bit of a chore each Friday night and Sunday evening. This lasted for several months and then we bought a brand-new house in a village ten miles from school. We actually sold our Norfolk house to a couple who were both teachers at the same school I had previously worked at. We had a lovely view from our new house down to the canal where reeds, grass banks and blackberry bushes flanked the water-side opposite the towpath. The twenty houses around us were newer than two years old with a young married couple in each and some had children. That community afforded us the chance to mix with engineers, store managers, hairdressers, builders, a pit deputy and a welder. No teachers and therefore when out with any of them education issues rarely came up in conversation. It was easy to switch off from the day job.

The staff at the school had mostly been there some time and the routines were well established. The Headteacher was a balding man with boundless energy and a traffic light system at his office door. You only entered on Green and you'd best be ready to on amber. When it was on red you got the impression that he was either busy or had got wind of your impending arrival and his eagle-eyed secretary had pre-warned him. His deputy was a Welsh former rugby playing man, now Chairman of a Staffordshire

Club. Each lunchtime he would bring his healthy packed lunch to a sun-drenched corner of the staff room to tell the funniest of tales and the odd risqué joke. His favoured sport in school being to wind up his own Head of Department for Maths. He was a brilliant mathematician who the pupils enjoyed being taught by because of his style and manner. He was the man who made sure the school worked like a well-oiled machine. The Head was often put out when staff would defer to the Deputy rather than run the lights at his office.

During one lunch hour while a group of us were enjoying the Deputy's wit as we finished our homemade packed lunches the head appeared. He summonsed his Deputy to accompany him to the senior boy's toilets. On arrival there the Head pointed out the sketch of the pair of them in graphic nude detail on the toilet wall with anger in his voice. The Deputy tried to calm him explaining he would have no difficulty finding out who the artist was. The Head cut him short saying, "Oh never mind that for now ... why have you been given a bigger willie?" The Deputy shrugged his shoulders and smiled. I don't believe he ever sought out the artist or indeed questioned whether he really had the wall sketch varnished to preserve it for posterity. Such thoughts were pointless to pursue and their answers may only serve to spoil the wonder of his much-appreciated mischief. Here was another 'go-to man' on the staff. Note to self at the time ... the likes of them make schools work ... so gather them around you.

My Department's area was on two levels with a classroom on the ground floor and a small office and library suite on the second. The upstairs part always helpful when the Educational Psychologist or Hearing-Impaired Teacher came to do follow up assessments or any training with me and my staff team. The classroom was just about big enough for the English bottom set of fifteen- to sixteen-year-olds I had on Friday afternoon and smaller groups from the middle years.

One of my teachers had been in teaching for over twenty years and was very old school with her approaches and philosophy. She wasn't averse to describing the pupils as being retarded and bringing her up to date on the impact of the Warnock Report and the concept of a special educational need was sometimes a task in itself. One of the younger girls had a hearing loss and often took her aids out so that any usual high-pitched screech by this teacher was just not heard. Many of us envious of such a positive impact of a disability.

To break into other lessons and support the teachers in modifying their curriculum content and delivery to ensure it was accessible to all was a joy and quite revolutionary. One English teacher captured the rationale for it when he exclaimed, "I spent ages preparing my lesson and lots of the pupils just didn't get it ... I don't know why I bothered!" Taking him to a deeper understanding of how you can create a learning need if the work isn't matched to the pupil's learning ability was a journey worth making. To his credit, not only did he get it he also became a disciple for my innovative approach at the time. It reminded me of the lecture at University when a lecturer had mischievously provoked debate with the following:

"Why is it that some Maths teachers are satisfied with some pupils only getting four out of ten? Do you wonder if they do not understand that the other six out of ten may not have been taught very well or indeed the stage of learning for such a pupil was not at that point?"

This too was a light bulb moment for staff colleagues and it was very much captured by the Deputy Head who soon became my lead disciple. However, that very old school Head of Maths (or was it Math?) saw this as educational terrorism.

It wasn't long before the Senior Teacher looked for opportunities to celebrate the success of my team and further its influence. We soon found that we were working with staff members rewriting learning materials for them to use. What a huge leap forward for them from their previous role of being sat next to a pupil confused at the explanation given by a teacher ... and then translating it into a far more accessible language. This work then leapt forward further after some training was done with History and Geography staff on the readability of their texts and they were able to see the mismatch with pupil reading ability and comprehension test scores. Within these first two years our influence and credibility improved vastly and the previous term of Remedial Department was no longer to be heard of.

Providing 'Home Learning Packs' on Spelling and Reading was soon taken up by many of the parents and carers of the lower ability classes. My greatest coup with such at this time being with a fourteen-year-old lad and his Dad. The farm they ran was a huge responsibility and massive test on balancing commitments to school. To get his father in and trained in the use of such materials saw him blossom. The father's pride equally so. This boy could drive a tractor and plough a huge field with great skill ... something he glowed about. To have him come bounding into class enthusiastic in his description of a book he had finished or new words he now recognised and could also spell showed the impact of the Home-School initiative. From this small acorn moment it was a joy to watch him become a maturing oak reader.

At this time in 1984 our second child Allan was born in Nuneaton. At first, he was not that keen to come into this world with a long and draining labour for my wife. Each day thereafter the loving attention from his adoring sister ensured he was showered with kisses. Her broad smile at now being a 'big sister' a sight in itself. For as much as I was really enjoying my job the drive home was eagerly awaited so as to be all together. He became well-known in our small community for his great desire to try any challenge once he could walk. The announcement, "Here comes 'Big Al'!" being a statement of his developing personality and 'give it a go' nature. The Teaching Salary on Scale Three with a crippling mortgage was difficult and our only credit card was reserved for fuel ... to get to work. Such were the days for all of us in the profession at this time.

As the miner's strike continued, the stress visibly impacted on many of the pupils who had fathers, brothers and other family members working in the pits. A sense of hopelessness was most evident in those in their last year at school who had aspirations to work in the coal industry. For generations that is how it had been in their families and now the future was looking evermore bleak when two of the pits were then faced with closure. The sadness in the eyes of their parents was there at each point of contact with them. Their voices often breaking too as they described how times were hard either being on strike or being deemed a 'scab' for breaking the strike picket so as to feed their family.

In school the mood permeated into the daily operation of many. Hard as it was to avoid pessimism it often became a worrying norm. Then to cap it all we were told the school was to be inspected. It left many wondering just how much further could morale dip?

When Her Majesty's Inspectors [HMI] arrived everything that didn't move in school had been polished and everything that did, oiled ... including a few older staff members. This was my first such experience of an inspection and in my naivety or otherwise I wasn't quivering as were some of my colleagues. My view was that a normal day in our school was at least good and if we could do any better, then it would be interesting to see what they thought. Such a philosophical view causing the Senior Teacher to send me away with a 'leadership flea' in my ear. For the first two days I had only seen a HMI from a distance when coming out of my Tutorial room with my sixteen-year-olds. Then I was informed that an English lesson with a low set of thirteen-year-olds had been chosen for a visit.

The class in question were a fine group of twelve pupils who enjoyed our lessons together and had been fired up in enthusiasm by the projects we had pursued. The current one was about writing accounts for different audiences. Our focus was the different expectations of writing as a newspaper journalist and writing as a police officer taking a statement. The pupils understood that the journalist would add a touch of embellishment to their story to please the readers. They understood the notion of sensationalism. In comparison they also understood that the police statement would need to be a factual account and more precise. To prepare for the next lesson I had spoken with one of the newly appointed P.E. Teachers and he had agreed to help me out in creating a scenario for us to take our work onto its next stage.

As I stood at the classroom door welcoming my class to the lesson, the HMI appeared and walked into the room and sat at the front. As the last few pupils entered the room, a balaclava-wearing person in a heavy long black coat burst into the room shouting and pushed by a few pupils. On getting to my desk, he took a small bag from it then turned to the HMI and gave him the 'slap on the cheeks' much associated with Eric Morecambe and Ernie Wise before turning and rushing from the room. The pupils were in total shock and amazement at what had just unfolded in front of them. The HMI was sat bolt upright in his chair and confounded by what he'd just seen, and his face cheeks still tingled.

I turned to the class, settled them and then asked them to think for a moment about what they had just seen. After a few minutes one half of the class were reporters and the other police officers. Their task was to write down what they had just seen, be it for their newspaper readership or the courts. Without a peep from them off they set to writing their words. The HMI having gathered his wits walked the room to see what they were up to. The lesson finished with them sharing with each other so they could go to either final print copy for their readership ... or get the final evidence needed to present in court. They were literally on fire with enthusiasm and were disappointed as the lesson end drew nearer. I told them we would carry on the following day and how impressed I was with what they had done. The HMI hung back as they left and admitted he was speechless at how I had created such learning from a seemingly chaotic act. As he spoke, I wondered what state the P.E. Teacher was in after he got back to the staff room and took off his disguise. His reflective thoughts were something I was desperate to hear.

The following day as the same class started to finalise what they wanted to say in their newspaper and court the door opened and in came the HMI to sit at the back. From this class of low-ability pupils great words were spoken about both tasks. The newspaper account and headline was full of drama and sensationalism with excellent descriptions of the 'theft', the criminal and the impact on those gathered. As one girl said, "We have made it sound much better than it really was to excite our readers!" This allowed us to unpick the line 'Why let the truth get in the way of a good story?' The police account for the court was precise to every timing and action. It included references to witnesses in different parts of the room. As their lead 'Investigator' said, "We've done a job on this ... as good as The Bill would Sir!"

I then presented them with a coat and balaclava saying it had been found in the car park. They perused over it hypothesising about the criminal's sex, size and weight. On examining the pockets, they found a bill from a Volkswagen garage, Rizla papers and tobacco, a bus ticket for Wolverhampton and keys with the school logo on. After some discussion they worked out that if this was a member of staff acting the drama out then it must be the new P.E. Teacher who had been seen smoking as he left school getting into his VW Beetle who they knew was a Wolves football fan. With the lesson drawing to an end, we agreed that the Newspaper would be printed next lesson and the alleged criminal would face the Police to be charged based on the evidence to hand.

I couldn't have dreamed that this topic could have been so successful. The HMI had by now found his words and spoke of how much he had enjoyed both lessons and the work produced. Whatever he said to the Headteacher, I never found out for there was no green light offered to me. It was enough for me to be proud of all my pupils. Afterwards I felt sure that they would have captivated their families each night at the tea table as this learning adventure unfolded.

Our inspection report was a good one. With my lesson being cited. Was this same confidence what I carried with me through into later school leadership? Was this where it all started, and I would later have the confidence to manage OFSTED ... and not be spooked by visitors in suits?

My line manager during my time at the school was the Senior Teacher. We got on very well despite the fact he had asked me an absolute 'googly' of a question at my interview, "How would you change behaviours in schools where the psychology of the individuals concerned was quite complex?" He kept a straight face when saying it. Next to him the Headteacher turned and looked in a puzzled way at him and the Educational Psychologist on the panel just screwed up his face closing his eyes. The focus was definitely on me to say something very profound that clearly would make the Times Educational Supplement (TES) and desk of the Secretary of State.

My first reply was, "Well to be perfectly honest, that is a huge ask for someone to answer when only being interviewed for this position ... and if I really had the full answer then I would not be here now as the book I'd have written would have been a best seller and I'd have retired on the sales income!" The head smirked ... the Educational Psychologist smiled broadly with his eyes alight ... and the Senior Teacher rocked back in his chair. I then added an answer with two examples of pupil behaviour illustrated with start point, strategies and reviews. It seemed unwise to resolve the problem faced by generations of worldwide teachers with a Doctoral Thesis style answer ... and I was right. The nodding from the Headteacher and Psychologist said it all and the Headteacher quickly asked the next question.

As an individual, the Senior Teacher had a long term plan for how the Curriculum should expand both in content and meeting the needs of all students of all abilities. My work in making the curriculum more accessible to the lower ability pupils was just what he needed and he lapped it up. I often wondered when sat with him if I should ask why he had posed that damn fool question in the interview and what his reflection was afterwards on my initial answer.

When compared with the Deputy Head, the Senior Teacher was quite a contrast. I am sure they brought balance to the senior management team in as much as they were so different in their start point. One quite serious, considered and cautionary ... mostly a 'half empty person' while the other was more light-hearted, reflective and solution-focussed ... more 'a half full person'. The fact remained that it worked and it was a point worth remembering for the future.

Soon after the Inspection my endeavours were rewarded with the opportunity to do a two-year Advanced Diploma in Special Educational Needs [SEN] at West Hill College. It involved attending lectures each Monday afternoon with ten others from across the West Midlands tutored by the impressive John Visser. This provided a great update on the law and practice for SEN in schools and empowered me further in pushing for a greater observance of a more inclusive curriculum at school. It also reinforced in my mind that although mainstream education was my current role, I would look for a way back into Special Education at some time in the future.

The issue of our salaries in teaching came to a head with industrial action looming. It puzzled me greatly that the respective teaching unions seemed to get on less well with each other than they did with the Education Authority and Secretary of State who was resisting teacher salary increases. What developed next in our school at times seemed farcical with one Union out for three days, another only citing part day walk outs if the largest union were out and another being very clear they would just sit in the staff room on site when the school was subsequently closed anyway. This caused some upset between staff and the tensions came close to boiling over more than once. With several local councillors and the MP having children at the school we were targeted for increased action. As such, three sets of three days saw me have additional time at home but a reduced wage packet at the end of the month. Although my Union paid some of the money, the impact on our already sorely tested finances was hard to sustain.

When we were in school the removal of a supervision requirement of pupils at breaks, lunch-time and end of school were included in our strike action. At lunch-time this meant we walked off-site and into a local pub for lunch. Perhaps not our finest hour as in time some staff would have a couple of beers before returning to school to resume the afternoon teaching role. This meant that unless peppermints were available to them to part mask the alcohol, the pupils had to be fairly tactful in any comment made. I recall being asked to go to one of the Craft rooms to collect a pupil and on arrival had to do a double take of the situation. As I entered the room all the boys were at the benches with a saw in their hands. The nearest to me put a finger to his lips and said, "Shhh, Sir don't make a loud sound!" He pointed at the teacher who was sat in his chair with his feet on the desk. He was fast asleep. When I asked them what they were doing the reply was, "Silent sawing ... so we don't wake him up ... and really upset him!" It seemed to be quite true.

Eventually the strike action came to an end after the Secretary of State had made quite a few 'This is my last and final offer' statements and a salary increase was granted to us. After all the anguish and disruption to our school it had been worth it from a salary perspective but the after effects remained. End of day school clubs ceased as did many lunchtime activities both of which had enriched our school day for the pupils. The sense of camaraderie in the staff room was still tainted with an element of distrust towards those who had done nothing but gained as much as those who had been out of pocket. It took for the Deputy Head to make a comparison with parents of our pupils down the pits to ensure the real world outside school wasn't forgotten. At this point our relative sense of being well off was no longer overlooked.

When walking across the field to the Sixth Form building late after school one day, I saw two teenagers with a crisp packet which they were sniffing glue from. It reminded me of that real world that some of our pupils lived in locally. Their behaviour was reported, but the subsequent action and support unclear ... that is if there was any. This was indicative of the troubled world of some pupils ... one we knew little of.

A tremendous shock to me a week later when one of my Tutor Group a tall and intelligent Sikh boy with a wonderful personality and a great deal to live for, committed suicide in his bathroom at home. The day before he had been joking with me at the end of the day registration. The following morning, I was called to the Head's Office to find his grieving father sobbing his heart out. His son having taken his own life that morning. The father at school was trying to retrace his son's thoughts and previous day to make sense of what had happened. All I was able to do was say he was a happy and popular boy with a great sense of humour ... no help at all to the grief-stricken father. This devastating news had to be shared with the rest of the Tutor Group. It took many deep breaths and nervous clearing of my throat to get the words out. It really was a tough one for me and the first of its kind in my teaching career to that day.

My passion for fishing was furthered at this school as one of the Art Teachers lived in a village about fifteen miles away where the canal was famous for its head of tench. This fish also known as the 'Doctor Fish' with the Latin name tinca tinca is strong, stocky and a beautiful colour of green. We fished for it on many an evening with great success. Our friendship developed from this and we ran the school's fishing team for the following two years. Matches against other schools were on Wednesday afternoons and the preparation of boiling hempseed was done with the help of Food Technology colleagues. This was a new school sport for me after football, cricket and so on. To be sat on the riverbank offering advice on bait was hardly taxing at all, particularly on sunny afternoons. The fishing skills and depth of piscatorial knowledge of the pupils was indeed a revelation. Now the teacher's words on arrival started to make sense. This was more than a sport, this was a passion and a way of life for them. It was one of those keys that you can use to unlock pupils and get them to engage in learning. I'm sure as you read you can cite others you have found and used.

The School Fishing Team had come third in the Nationals years before and one of the boys had placed second in the individual competition. The Art Teacher and I agreed to organise a trip to Eire for them as reward for this prior achievement and the season, just finishing. We travelled by minibus to Holyhead, made the night crossing to Dun Laoghaire and then drove onto Athlone where we were staying for the week. Our host was the famous Irish Angler Sean Egan so there was much to learn from him to make our week a success. Indeed, his coaching advice ensured we had a tremendous week fishing and enjoyed the hospitality of the town itself. After one tough afternoon on a small river we sought Sean out for advice for the following day, which would be our last. He was quite brief and just said, "Don't use the maggot …

just use the worm!" So the following day that is what we did and after minimal bites and a few fish ... we all thought let's try maggots. From the first cast with this change of bait we couldn't stop catching large roach and bream all afternoon.

At the end of the day, we packed up and drove back for supper. After showering and presenting ourselves for food, in came Sean to ask how we had got on. We had agreed that the team captain would respond. He explained how we had followed Sean's advice and fished with worm and had little success and then once we changed to maggot it had been a roaring success. Sean looked at us and with a dead pan face just replied, "Ah well, you would!" With these four words we were disarmed and fell about laughing.

The school was broken into during one warm holiday period and although there was some damage nothing else could be noted about the intruder's motives. A couple of weeks later the smell in one of the Art Rooms became unbearable and on searching the large drawers where work was stored, the culprit was found. It became clear that when the break in occurred the perpetrator had left a calling card in the drawer. He had defecated in the drawer and the warm weather that followed had made the smell increase daily. The Head of Art claimed to know who had done it and eventually took the opportunity to make a statement accordingly. In the School reporting session, he wrote in one boy's report 'What can I say about an artist that shits in the drawers in my room?' In the checking system that followed the Head of Year and the Deputy Head conspired to let it through and it ended up on the Headteacher's desk for his read through and final comment. Shocked, he demanded an alternative teacher comment. The report change was made and the pupil's behaviour picked up on with humour mixed with a touch of rebuke. The phrase 'don't dump your problems with me' being used several times when he finished off his exam year.

Although my salary position had been somewhat improved by the pay settlement, the package afforded teachers working abroad for the Service Children's Education Authority (SCEA) came to my attention when I was flicking through the TES one Friday lunchtime in the staff room. After a discussion at home, it was agreed I could do no worse than apply. Two weeks later I was invited to Eltham Palace for interview and the feedback from it was there with two job offers for either Hong Kong or Germany. As my wife's parents thought both were too far away, I declined the Hong Kong post and accepted the one in Germany. The opportunity was too good to pass up for my career and more importantly us as a family.

On return to school, I gave notice of my resignation. Once again colleagues and pupils were disappointed at my decision. The Senior Teacher took time to say that teachers found it exceptionally difficult to return from such schools and that the quality of education just didn't compare. I heard his words but had more of an insight than he was aware of, for where I was to go to was where I had started school and completed my reunion of a gap year.

The year finished with a trip for our entire year group of staff and pupils to the Drayton Manor Theme Park. Up until this point such a place had not interested me and never been visited. The pupils were given their briefing by our very competent and confident Head of Year then off they went for their fun day. Returning at lunchtime they devoured their homemade and school version of a packed lunch alongside the staff with their picnic hampers and a few bottles of chilled wine. Such were those days, nobody batted an eyelid.

After lunch I ventured to join the pupils on rides encouraged by some of my tutor group. My first trip ... flight ... on a rollercoaster ride was quite enjoyable and I screamed less than I expected. The second go was more fun and then the following ten or more were absolutely hilarious with me beating some of my tutor group back to the start of the queue for another ride. I even had them holding their arms outstretched and skywards when twisting, turning and rotating upside down on the ride with accompanying yells. On the journey home my credibility with my Tutor Group suitably enhanced by this juvenile behaviour ... with other pupils just saying, "Your Tutor is really crazy!" It was true and I had enjoyed myself beyond all expectation. The point being though that they wanted to be with me ... the connection was real.

As the three coaches neared school, the excitement of the day on various rides proved too much for only one of the hundred and twenty plus of us. The Head of Year was sick all over the front of the bus as we arrived back at the school gates. The rebuke from pupils lasting until the day they left to enter the world of work or college. Certainly not the way such a charismatic leader would want to be remembered ... but he had broad shoulders and to be fair the year group had the deepest respect and admiration for him.

At the end of term fine words from great friends, colleagues and dear pupils. My fourth teaching post completed. Once again, I had learned a great deal from everyone and was ready for travel abroad.

Next stop ... back to Germany.

Chapter 10

Back in Germany

I flew out to Germany midway through the 1987 Easter Holidays. My family not able to join me for a couple of weeks as accommodation was still being prepared. Once together we were temporarily housed in a large flat which was part of the residential provision for the secondary school on Joint Headquarters (JHQ). Soon after moving off-base to the village of Waldniel and a large three-bedroomed flat.

My school was a few miles away and within walking or cycling distance. Prior to arriving I was unaware of the history of the place and WW2. It was on a site originally established as a monastery by monks in the fourteenth century where in 1909 the Order of Franciscans started their ministry. These monks looked after six hundred patients mostly with learning and physical disabilities and varying mental health difficulties. Then after financial problems and with the rise of National Socialism, the site was taken over in 1937. As part of their 'New Order' the Nazis questioned the right of such people to live. At least thirty children were murdered and buried within the grounds and all others either died at the hands of the Specialist SS Division at the site or were transported elsewhere to be killed. This was at the time when their terrible 'Child Euthanasia Programme' was in place to rid their society of those with such a disability.

In 1952 the buildings became a Military Hospital and then in 1963 a school to ease the pressure on the secondary school at JHQ. When I arrived, the two schools were about to be amalgamated and renamed. My role was Head of Support for Learning with a department of five full-time staff. I was to be working with pupils aged eleven to eighteen with learning disabilities being met in a mainstream setting. How poignant this role being in such a place. One of the first things I did on arrival was to visit the gardens where the murdered children were buried. I stood by the cushion stone on the grassed area between small trees and noted the inscription 'Den Unschuldigen Opferrn' ('To The Innocent Victims'). I don't recall a single sound from birds in this haunting place.

The cautionary words from the Senior Teacher at my previous school started to ring untrue as I was introduced into a school where the resources and staffing levels were far superior to anything I had previously experienced. I had been aware in my own childhood and gap year that there was an angst for the Military that those of school age received an education at least on a par with the best in the UK when accompanying their father on a posting abroad. The school was all that and more for teachers and pupils alike.

Historically the place of children with special educational needs in such Service Children Education Authority (SCEA) settings had always been seen as a challenge and often meant one of two options. The first being the child would be placed in a UK Boarding School so the soldier or airman could have the rest of the family with him on an accompanied tour. The second being the soldier or airman was on an unaccompanied tour for the two to three year duration. No sooner in post, I began to ally myself with the Educational Psychologist and Education Officer with a view to try and break down this harsh ruling of separation. As such the Department committed itself to the integration of such pupils into our school setting. There were a few challenges and hiccups along the way but we prevailed. Our emphasis on initially supporting new pupil cases in class, then changed to the redesign of teaching materials to ensure full access. All the tried and tested methodology from North Warwickshire implemented with the support of staff who embraced the challenges some new arrivals posed.

Those with learning difficulties found the language both in new oral presentations and pre-prepared texts took account of their lower ability without dumbing down the learning experience. Additional support packages were also put in place replicating the Home Learning previously used in England with my star tractor driver and his father. Regular assessment of their progress allowed for re-evaluation of such schemes with subject teachers and pastoral staff. The impact on the children being remarkable and gaining our work praise and increased credibility amongst staff, parents and the military education team.

Two particular cases were a test for some staff because they presented the need for a completely new teaching approach.

An eighteen-year-old girl was referred to us with Cerebral Palsy. Her father commanding the RAF Police at a nearby fighter airbase by the Dutch border. He was keen to keep the family together and came to visit me at school to talk things through. The facts around her poor co-ordination, stiff and weak muscles, tremors, speech and learning difficulties were discussed with the Educational Psychologist also present. I was honest with him as to the breadth of what we could offer and stunned him by saying, "So there isn't a problem ... when will she be arriving?" He sat there with a tear glistening in the corner of one eye. So much relief felt ... I was expecting an emotional hug from this Squadron Leader with a chest of medals ... he regained his composure and nearly shook my arm from its joint. The Ed Psych said he would sort the detail out when he returned to the office.

A month later the girl arrived and took her place in a small support class of fifteen year-olds. Training was provided to staff on both her condition and strategies to employ with her learning and any medical responses should she have a seizure. As each week passed her delightful smile broadened and her confidence grew. There were, of course, moments when things went wrong but they were quickly fixed. More often than not she started to show the classic symptoms of a teenager and that was well within the skills of staff to respond to and nurture her through. After the first Parent's Evening I was faced with one of my brilliant staff team in floods of tears. A complete mess with smudged eye makeup and quivering lips. This being the result of ten minutes emotional and heartfelt feedback from her parents. Evidently my staff member hadn't been alone in crying with joy … and a great deal of relief.

I'd never felt under pressure with this dear girl as the important thing for us was to make school fit her … for that way it was going to work. Then when my youngest brother came to visit me at home a link was discovered. He was now in his early years in the RAF Police and the girl's father was his Commanding Officer. The connection had been made by the Squadron Leader and now the success of her placement at school was linked to his view of my brother and me.

Her condition continued to show signs of deterioration as the next two years passed. It didn't stop her from achieving exam grades and more importantly growing in confidence. The best example of that being when she enjoyed a work experience placement. When she finally left school, it was to go to a residential Further Education Specialist College. Her self-confidence at interview and charming manner winning the hearts of the staff team. She had truly shown she was not to be held back by her condition and that she was a 'do-er'. We were sad to say good-bye to her but immensely proud of how we had impacted on her … and grateful to her for all she had shown us about her resilience. The letter from her father expressing gratitude for all we had done was touching. The line in there about keeping the family together being the key message.

A twelve-year-old boy of mixed race background was to present a quite different and difficult challenge. His father was a junior rank in the army and his wife was from Belize. Both charming people but very concerned parents. Their son had experienced significant behavioural difficulties in the Primary School and on secondary transfer the reports indicated that he may best be returned to the UK to continue his education. The parents naturally anxious about their son also recognised that if the father was to return with his family then it would mean impending army promotion would not occur. If he was to stay in Germany on an unaccompanied tour then his wife would not cope and they were fearful neither would their marriage. The challenge therefore and associated pressures were considerable.

The boy had a wild look in his eyes at times and was presenting as restless to tasks that required him to concentrate. He often required clear unambiguous statements to be made in all the requests, directions or challenges to his actions. He also needed time to assimilate his response without being asked another question. Patience with him ... clarity of spoken word ... and shorter tasks ... started to pay dividends. To further our own understanding of him it was agreed that a full reassessment of him would be in order, so a review with the Ed Psych was organised.

The boy was a bit nervous prior to going in and then forty minutes later came out with a smile on his face and a bounce in his step. When I asked him how he was and how it went he replied, "Oh it was fine ... but honestly sir if you think I have got problems you need to listen to him!" as he pointed back to the room where the Ed Psych was writing up his findings. With that he went back to his class and I went to find out what had happened in this two-way assessment that seemed to have just concluded. The Ed Psych was a dear friend as well as colleague and amused by the boy's remark. The assessment identified real anxiety at home and worries the boy had for family continuity. It also noted that our strategies were working and the boy was feeling calmer and more able to engage productively. As a result, his place with us was sustained and some counselling offered to the family.

He remained with us for the rest of his father's tour in Germany and as a result the soldier was duly promoted. The boy was seen as the lovable rogue by many and the teaching of him while never simple was achieved with greater thought and a sprinkling of tolerance. He would periodically do something to remind us all of his other side. The best and probably most amusing being in an Art lesson. He had kept moving around the room and was becoming a distraction to other pupils. The teacher then told him to stand by her desk as if glued to the spot. At the end of the lesson he was still there and she said she'd be back shortly. On her return the challenges of his behaviour were revisited with his Head of Year present. He accepted his mistakes and punishment and was told to go back to our suite of rooms and prepare for going home. But he didn't … or to be more correct he couldn't! For at a moment when the Art teacher had gone to help another pupil during the lesson, he had poured strong glue on the floor and stood in it. This glue some thirty minutes later was set and he was literally glued to the spot as had been requested. He smiled and shrugged his shoulders. That night he went home without his footwear which was chiselled from the floor that evening and returned the next day.

The example of his literal behavioural response warranting great humour in the staff room thereafter. There was certainly a greater thought given by everyone when issuing instructions to ensure it didn't result in embarrassment to anyone on the staff. When he left there was certainly a big gap in the conversations over coffee each day. He was missed and mention of him always ensured a smile. He had helped staff better understand the challenges of such pupils. They were increasingly seen as having additional needs rather than problems. It's important to learn from such children and I have always felt his short story has prompted many to think just so.

There were other minor 'behavioural problems' that came to my attention during each day and Heads of Year would often ask for advice. This presented us with the opportunity to work together to ensure clarity of expectation and a code of conduct with equitable restitution for anything below expectation and recognition for that expected or better than. It also led to the senior team conducting a full review of rules with an emphasis on things being clear and unambiguous. For the first time I engineered the notion of 'rubber boundaries' rather than set consequences irrespective of the pupil's needs.

I wonder how often schools actually do such a thing. How often do 'problems' presented by a pupil cause the school system to ask the question of themselves as much as the seemingly wayward pupil? I have always tried to influence colleagues into believing this is something they should do … and not shy away from?

An interesting dimension to any behaviours requiring parental meetings was that if such a meeting didn't go too well and the parents took a controversial stance with the school then the respective Commanding Officer would be referred to. The implication being help us sort it or the family could be sent back to the UK! It made me wonder if such a relocation package would have been a way forward in managing the lad who 'dumped' in the art drawers at my last school?

As a tutor of a group of sixteen-year-olds I was given the opportunity to visit my pupils on their various work experience placements. Being on a camp there were a great deal of opportunities for them to enjoy both in military and civilian settings. One of my boys was with the armoury and learning how to take guns apart and service them before they were reissued for use. On one visit to him I passed through the various iron gated cells of security to see him working on a pistol used by one of the Close Protection Officers for the Commander in Chief of RAF Germany. It became clear that the trigger mechanism was 'altered' by the officer to make it almost touch sensitive to seemingly get a shot off first in an emergency scenario. Such being the challenge of a close protection role that each time the gun was in for a service the armourers were duty bound to fit a new trigger mechanism.

One of my girls was working at the NAAFI in the camera shop selling duty-free high-tech equipment. It had been noted that several times just before lunch and mid-afternoon she went a bit 'dreamy' and staff were perplexed. It transpired that the bright fluorescent lights were causing minor seizures. Until then her medical condition hadn't been noticed as such. She was subsequently moved to a different part of the shop without further issues. Her photosensitive epilepsy was pursued at the Army Medical Centre and tests carried out. A chance finding brought on by the extreme bright conditions in that sales department. Our knowledge of epilepsy and seizures resulting in a new understanding of 'elevated neurological activity' being added to our skill set as a department team.

After about a year of being in a flat, we moved into a house in the village. It was nice to be fully immersed in the German community and be able to cycle to the shops in the local Stadt. With plastic small child chairs fixed to each bike, my wife and I were able to cycle afar on the great network of cycle paths running parallel to the roads. Quite often the children would fall asleep very quickly and sleep for the duration of the ride being oblivious to the countryside around us. They enjoyed visiting the small supermarket in the square where the fruit display always looked like someone was employed to polish it to a sparkling standard. Once they had started pre-school, they were picked up each morning by a military bus with an escort on board and taken to JHQ where their school was actually in the same building my youngest brother had started school many years earlier.

One evening a three hundred pound bomb exploded on camp and thirty-one people were injured by the flying debris and shards of glass. The bomb had been situated near to one of the boarding houses for my school and rocked the building. Naturally it caused some panic and distress to the younger pupils in residence. Thereafter there were checkpoints at the entrances and armed soldiers constantly patrolling the whole site and perimeter. When the children were picked up for school there was now an additional person on their bus. It was a young soldier with a machine gun which caused intrigue to the children, but a significant concern to parents waving goodbye.

The IRA had resumed activity in Germany against British servicemen and their families with several bombs and shootings taking place. Nearby a young Asian RAF corporal and his baby child were shot dead by a terrorist standing at the roadside. His wife escaping injury in the attack. This very tragic event completely spooked families and many chose to stay on camp to be safer. Our car had British plates on it so we bought another locally and had it registered with German plates so as to blend in when out and about. All military and civilian personnel received an extendable mirror with accompanying torch to check under their cars for a bomb before driving off. The first requirement being to know what the underneath of your car looked like so if there was something looking suspicious then you could avoid using it and notify the Army Bomb Squad. Having a local German registration removed that need and we would often travel into nearby Holland to do shopping and go for a meal in Roermond. Sadly, two non-military tourists were mistaken for soldiers and shot there one weekend so we reduced our visits and made sure that we were cautious about speaking English loudly when walking around.

We continued to live in the German community and felt relatively safe even though there was no level of apparent security. At the time friends and family visiting from the UK or being visited on short breaks to home found it a touch stressful and this made us wonder whether staying in Germany was a good idea. I often reflected that the same campaign by the IRA was being conducted in London with some awful bombings resulting in numerous deaths. As such it was about trying to stay safe and thinking carefully about what we did and where we went.

Living in Nordrhein-Westfalen meant we were in a pretty central position to access routes via the autobahn for day trips and longer breaks. To be able to drive through the Eiffel Mountains to Cochem on the Mosel and tour the vineyard slopes, or into Belgium or Holland to some picturesque architectural cities was easily done for a day out. Longer forays into Denmark, Bavaria, Brittany and Austria for holidays became the norm. Such a change from a week in Whitby which had been our highlight holiday before leaving the UK. That was the point really about moving to Germany ... to open up our horizons and have the where for all to enjoy life much more. The salary I received from SCEA came with additional allowances and free housing as well as duty free access to many goods and petrol coupons ... all being additional incentives and rewards. The improvement in our lifestyle was incredible and much enjoyed. No longer worrying if the crippling mortgage could be paid and whether one of the children could have new shoes. The change for us was simply brilliant. The two youngest children were skiing before they were five years old on the slopes of Alpbach in Austria where we travelled each Spring half-term – something we never thought we would ever be doing when we were walking the tow path of the Coventry Canal. At times like this the IRA threat just melted from our thoughts.

When parents or the in-laws came out to visit, they too marvelled at the lifestyle we were living and how relaxed life was for us. Work was work and it was taken seriously and committed to, but it had opened up this huge change in our circumstances. One significant change being the arrival of our third child, a son Tony, born at the RAF Hospital in Wegberg in 1988. The very place where my brother Chris was born twenty-eight years earlier.

When my parents came to visit, we took them to Berlin for a few days. The route was through East Germany via the Military train from Hannover. As my teaching status gave me an equivalent military rank of Squadron Leader or Major the travel was in First Class. The white linen tables with Military Train embossed china plates and silver cutlery with BAOR (British Army of the Rhine) labelled wine in crystal glass was an eye opener for us. The closest thing at the time to a journey on the Orient Express in the late 1980s. Travelling through areas where photography was banned due to Russian tank marshalling yards and other Soviet bloc military installations being track side was very James Bond-like for the children. Berlin was an incredible place to visit and the real-life situation of the Cold War so very apparent.

My brother Simon was now at RAF Gatow so he took us to various sites such as the Olympic Stadium. To stand where Hitler had been very disgruntled at Jesse Owens winning numerous medals was a stark reminder of terrible times. As indeed were the ruins by each City Bahnhof to allow for returning Jewish Berliner's to orientate themselves for any potential land claims. We all got to travel through into East Berlin by Checkpoint Charlie. The puffed-out chests of various soldiers bristling with guns and eyeballing each other seeming quite surreal. I recall standing on the East side of Brandenburg Gate looking back towards the West wondering how life was for those separated since the end of WW2. The white crosses on the western side of the River Spree fences were marked 'Unbekannt' showing where 'Unknown' East Berliners had been shot and died trying to escape. Another reminder of the 'here and now' and testimony to the risks they were prepared to take. Two years after our visit it was an emotional time in Germany when the wall came down and the two nations were reunified. German colleagues in our school repeating the cries of Berliners "Die Mauer ist weg!" ("The wall is gone!") and talking of their family and country being together once again.

My father-in-law had a spirit of adventure when he was staying with us. On one occasion he went off for a bike ride to investigate the options for a family meal in the village. When he returned, he was enthusiastic in saying that he had found a restaurant that looked good and that he had the prices of food. He then said, "The food all seems to be around the same price except one meal." When asked what was on the menu he replied, "There is Montag, Dienstag and Donnerstag which is between seventeen and twenty-three Deutschmarks ... Freitag and Samstag seems more expensive ... and Sonntag by far the cheapest!" Bless him he was so pleased with himself and was quite crestfallen when told he had just informed us of the restaurant's opening times. Nevertheless, he enjoyed the subsequent meal and thereafter always requested a Schnitzel with a glass of Pils.

When we took him and his wife down to the Mosel for a day-trip we visited several vineyards and wineries to the west of Cochem. To walk in between the vines laden with grapes was a joy for him. As we left one such small winery in the village of Ediger Eller one of the female staff heard him talking about the wine he made and engaged him in conversation. She then fetched her father who asked about the wine he made in Newcastle-upon-Tyne. It seemed to the rest of us that this was not going to end well and indeed when he replied "Oh I make Elderflower and Carrot wines" the look of disbelief was easy to be seen. The German wine growers tossed their arms in the air turned and walked away laughing. I'm sure that I heard one say, "Dumme Engländer!" We advised him to be a bit reflective about his wine comments after that as we moved along the valley. My memory of his wines being that while the Elderflower was quite palatable, some of the others made Newcastle Brown seem like Bollinger.

Having been deflated on leaving the Royal Navy Careers Office in Brighton many years earlier to now have gained the status of an officer rather amused me. My grandfather, two uncles, father, mother and three brothers all had served 'Queen and Country' and none had reached such dizzy military heights. Here was I, a mere teacher, now responsible for a squadron of I know not what, due to working in a Service School. My only lifetime uniform memories previously being a member of the 49th RAF Nicosia Scout Group and as a Spitfire Pilot in the Primary School Christmas Panto. This newly acquired status of an equivalent military rank gave me access to both the Army and RAF Officer's Messes … places they had never accessed.

Early in my time in Germany I was to find out how being dressed correctly for functions was of paramount importance. I recall being reprimanded by one of our Deputy Heads for wearing a short-sleeved shirt which was revealed once the announcement was made 'Gentlemen may remove their jackets' one warm summer's evening. Some months later at the Oktoberfest celebrations in the RAF Officer's Mess I was amazed to see Phantom and Harrier pilots stripping to the waist and lining up at one end of five cleared tables. Beer was splashed across the table-tops and one after the other of these fast-jet pilots ran at the tables and launched themselves on top of them. Their speed and the beer causing them to slide quite a distance along the tables. This evidently being the 'aircraft carrier landing' and a regular performance at such an event. On completion they redressed and continued with what may be considered more officer-like behaviours. When I enquired about what I had just seen, of a high-ranking RAF friend he replied "Oh now you need to understand these chaps have to let their hair down from time to time … and the rule is it doesn't matter how badly behaved you are as long as you are dressed properly!" Now with a smile I better understood the shock and horror of my short-sleeved shirt faux pas.

Tenure in this military world was decided by a review every three years to determine whether your performance as a teaching practitioner, your contribution to the wider community and your general conduct warranted you being offered a re-tour. I passed the 'grade' and began my second tour with many plans for both developing the Support for Learning team in school and us as a family. At such a contract renewal point each teacher is rewarded with a week of professional development back in the UK.

I organised a session with my College Lecturer from West Hill in Selly Oak and several school visits to update my practice and see specialist provisions for Hearing Impaired pupils. It was a great week with much to think about developing once back at school. At the weekend before returning, I also got to go fishing with my father. As I approached the checkpoint at Elmpt to cross from Holland back into Germany I was stopped and pulled over for the car to be searched. A Military Policeman let his sniffer dog go to my car and straight away it became quite animated at its suggested find. The Policeman's attitude suddenly changed from being quite chatty to one of serious authority. When asked to open a flat bag I revealed my fishing keep net which clearly still held the strong odour of bream. Disappointed dog and owner then let me continue with my journey home.

As the saying goes "Old fisherman never die ... they only smell that way!" Or is it that their nets do?

On being back at school all fired up with new projects and the prospects of taking in more pupils with complex needs, I was looking forward to at least another three years. Unfortunately, further acts of terrorism by the IRA saw an increase in bombings and shootings. This spooked my wife much more and the topic of return to the UK reared its head again.

Soon after, I applied for the Deputy Head post in an EBD Residential Special School in Yorkshire and was invited for interview. We travelled by car via the overnight ferry from Hoek van Holland to Harwich then drove to York where we had breakfast in Betty's Tea Rooms before continuing on to Newcastle. Here we stayed with the in-laws the night before the interview. On that day we travelled down as a family, me for the interview and them for the opportunity to explore the village and area around. The interview went well and they loved what they saw of the tranquil setting on the edge of the Moors and Forest areas.

A week later the job offer was received and accepted. Once again, I was to be faced with a staff team who were disappointed and pleaded for me to stay. My heart strings were severely pulled and tested by them. It was followed by several weeks of me wobbling about my decision and for a week or so I walked about with the ever returning question in my head of 'Should I stay ... or should I go?'

Just over four years after our arrival in Germany we were to be moving on again. The challenge of a Senior Management non-teaching role awaited in Yorkshire and the decision was made ... mostly for the safety of the whole family ... that we should return to the UK.

Part Three

From Toil to Success in Leadership

"A Leader is one who knows the way ... goes the way ... and shows the way."

John Maxwell

"A genuine Leader is not a searcher for consensus but a holder of consensus."

Dr. Martin Luther King

As a teacher aspiring towards school leadership, it was strong in my mind that the essence of great leadership was the opportunity I would have to influence ... not the authority the position may hold.

On becoming a member of the Senior Management Team and, in due course, a Headteacher it was a case of:

'Dear Future, I'm ready ... and ... Dear Past, thanks for all the lessons.'

When you make that leap from teacher to Deputy and Head you do so with aspirations and a strong sense of self-belief. Rightly so. You know there will be challenges but are you prepared? Ironically not necessarily so, and at the time it was definitely the case that the better a teacher you were, the greater the chances you may well be promoted away from just such a role. Part Three will take you through that continued learning and the realisation that sometimes the easiest part of school leadership is actually the pupils. Certainly, worrying won't stop the bad things from happening ... it will just stop you from enjoying the good.

Once in that position the important thing was for me to look back so as to see how far I had come. The stories that follow in Part Three will show how it can be a bumpy ride and that it can hurt too. The key to getting through such times being that you should never be a prisoner of your past ... for it was just a lesson, not a life sentence.

In time it was when I took on the great unknown of a totally broken and failing school that I realised the necessity of reigniting the incredible depth of hidden strengths of my very new staff team ... and those in myself ... that I had perhaps lost sight of.

The team we created there had stopped trying to just educate the heads of each damaged pupil ... they had begun to try and educate their hearts. They literally had moved on from teaching these pupils just to count ... which was fine ... and begun to teach them 'what counts is best'.

As a result, the school thrived, and it truly was because every pupil was one caring adult away from being a success story. The adults around them were believers again ... and our school was reborn as a very happy and highly performing setting.

There's a lot here about adversity and the huge challenges faced in leadership. The drive required is implicit in:

'When someone tells you, you can't ... just stop and think for a moment ... they are likely to be showing you their limitations not yours.'

The enthusiasm and drive needed to be a headteacher is unquestionable ... and if you can't see where you are going it is always beneficial to have someone, perhaps a peer, who has been there before. The role of school leader can be a lonely one and therefore having such a critical friend and mentor is important. In this stage of my career, I hadn't such a person. It took for my next leadership position for this to become practice in the profession.

On looking back now there was so much we could have learned from those where professional supervision, when provided, helped reduce the risk of serious oversight and helped with reflection on ones feelings, thoughts, behaviour, well-being and general approach to work.

Fundamental to me making it through this ten-year period in my career being a line from a canny Scottish Head of Year when I taught in Germany. He would often say, "God gave you two ears and one mouth as he or she wanted you to do twice as much listening as talking!"

Try as I may ... you will find I mostly got that right in these three schools. It is what I have always believed referenced the difference between being a confident but humble leader ... rather than one who was arrogant.

Chapter 11

Now then Lad!

A small village on the edge of the Moors and some eight miles from the coast was to be our new home. The school was for forty-eight boys aged seven to sixteen placed there by the LEA because of their emotional and behavioural difficulties having resulted in them acquiring a statement of SEN. All were residential and six staff lived in flats or houses within the wider grounds of the Hall dating back to earlier than the eighteenth century. Having once been the seat of a Member of the House of Lords it had been sold to the Education Department when the family male lineage came to an end. The pupils were deemed to be best educated away from their family setting as termly boarders. It had a good reputation albeit the local population were weary of the pupils and preferred the school to be a quiet and fairly remote part of the village.

The head was as classic an example of a Yorkshireman as one could find. The line "You can always tell a Yorkshireman ... but you can't tell him much" just about summing him up to a tee. He had been at the school since Noah was a lad ... or so he would say. He smoked a pipe wherever he went within the school buildings at all times of the day, thereby giving notice of where he had been or was about to arrive. The LEA constantly requested that he should embrace technology and get a fax machine. His rebuff being, "Now listen here, I've got caretaker on t' roof shooting at any pigeons that look as though they've got messages to be responded to!"

Despite all this he knew EBD inside out and how to get the boys to respond to the challenge of change. It was based upon the line he often used, "We can do this the hard way or the easy way ... I'm good at both ... so which one do you want to choose? Mind though ... think carefully before answering me!"

The previous three Deputy Heads had all lasted two to three years and then gone on to Headships of their own. The story touted by staff being that they'd done their own job and that of the Head ... so after a couple of years they left on promotion to get paid for it.

The Senior Teacher had been at the school a number of years. It was quite unclear as to why he had never put his name forward for the Deputy Head position. He was rather cynical in his outlook and believed in his own ideas and his own way. Sometimes contrary to the whole school approach but seemingly he was unmoved by this. He was respected by the boys and in particular the older ones whom he mostly taught.

Other staff were a mixture of individuals with varying agendas either revealing career hiccups, dissatisfaction or boredom. They were great within their own classrooms but had spare energy capacity in the staff room for being a touch awkward and ill-tempered. The delivery of their subjects done with a fair degree of academic skill and more often than not a genuine interest to inspire the minds of the disaffected pupils. The Woodwork teacher (as he would only be known) had resisted any attempt to update the title of his role despite it being accepted in all schools up and down the country over the last four decades. He had actually started teaching at the school the day I started school in Infants. This was something that seemed to impress him more than it worried me.

The Primary Class teacher being a real mother hen figure for her six seven- to eleven-year-olds. All her pupils so young looking ...

so innocent and fresh-faced ... and everyone with a twinkle in their eye signifying trouble available. She had been teaching for many years and was very much of the old school approach.

All teaching staff did an evening duty and periodic weekend day. All Senior Staff had a full twenty-four-hour duty each week and did one in four full weekend days on call.

The domestic staff loved their roles as cleaners, as did the catering staff and were the backbone and barometer of happiness in the school. The Domestic Bursar, Doreen, their leader was a dynamic individual whose raison d'être was to ensure the pupils had the best in food and homely comfort while with us at school. In truth it was probably much better than most experienced when they returned home.

Each of the five residential areas had two Care Staff members who worked a weekly split shift and lived in on their duty nights. These staff were mostly unqualified in this role and for many it was their first such position. Three of the women were mums and brought that experience to their work, one of the men had worked at a Children's Home and another with Youth Groups and the Scouts. Their Team Leader was a Professional Social Worker and a comparative ray of sunlight in the whole school staff team. He was on the Senior Leadership Team with the Head, Senior Teacher and newly appointed me.

So much to learn so quickly of staff and pupils. A veritable rainbow of behavioural issues to unpick, redirect and hopefully long term, to change. Early on the threat of the IRA seemed to be a rather insignificant challenge and one that may have been easier to overcome. My first twenty-four-hour duty appeared to be going well when news broke that three boys had run away. They were brothers from York and the word was they were heading home. Two staff went out in a minibus to see if they had crossed the valley to a village where the bus to York passed through. There was no sight of them so I informed the local Police Officer who came along to get their details and photos. He was a jolly individual and by all accounts a frequent visitor to the school for such an event. Although this news made me feel better, I remained anxious for the safety of our three escapees.

An hour later the Police Officer returned with news that if they were going to York their sense of direction was completely adrift as they had been spotted heading south and not west. He announced that a patrol was out looking for them as night fell. Two hours later news arrived that they were in the Police Station of a coastal town fifty miles away. We then had to get to the Police Station before it closed at which point, they would be transferred to Hull. Luckily the Head of Care was available to drive me there and we collected them from Police Officers who were extremely pleased to hand them over. Their reason for running away was quite simple and unrehearsed ... they just wanted to be at home with their Dad. Two days later this urge struck them again and they were off by foot. Nobody offered them a lift and they were spotted across the valley with an improved sense of direction indicating they were after catching the bus. Once again retrieved and returned to school they settled down and slept. At this point the notion of three brothers being on roll was severely questioned by staff not least of all the Senior Teacher.

He was clearly more unhappy that they were from the older group and his responsibility. His upset being that his standing in the staff room would be damaged by this. This was short-lived for him when they ran away for the third time at the weekend. Once again found with the help of the Police and returned. The weekend was my first such forty-eight-hour on call duty and the Senior Teacher was very pleased that it had happened again on my watch. His comments in staff briefing reflecting there was no shame on him and his school section. An indictment of the relationship in the staff room and the way in which such competitiveness was more about saving staff face than determining what could be done to change pupil attitude about the school and the need to run away with such frequency.

Staff briefings in my first year were often bear traps prepared beforehand by some staff members. It was at this point that my patience started to falter with them and I just about managed to bite my tongue and not give them as good back as they were seemingly enjoying directing at me. An early lesson for me on crossing the line from member of staff to Leadership Team.

I chose to find another way of establishing my authority, responsibility and primary role in trying to refocus their own recalcitrant behaviours. Over a couple of weeks, I sat in each of their classrooms to observe what they were teaching and how. I then discussed with them what I had seen and sought from them a rationale for the content and employed delivery strategies. This was a first for so many of them but it worked. Initial hesitation and even a touch of indignation soon passed and saw most mellow and then open up in a professional conversation. It became blindingly obvious that when I complimented them in any way and offered some ideas on possible changes that they were shocked that a friendly supportive colleague was actually the Deputy Head. From then on those in the Primary and Middle school sections were more relaxed about my presence and solution-focussed approach to their daily practice. They were keen to collaborate and enjoyed the working relationship. This 'Hallelujah Moment' not being earth shattering in education at all … just an earthquake in this establishment allowing current methodology an opportunity to break in. The Senior Section Staff withdrew into a shell and although as individuals they similarly enjoyed their interactions with me, the Senior Teacher seemed to enact a collective mindset with them.

This challenge had to be picked up in a different setting. I chose the moment to be in a Senior Leadership Meeting on a Friday afternoon. After much debate about presenting behavioural rewards, sanctions and lessons learned I introduced a new weekly agenda item related to the Curriculum. My report about Primary and Middle School identifying the various positives and where there were shortfalls, how they were being addressed as next steps in a partnership approach. On completing this report, I turned to the Senior Teacher and praised the individuals in his team for productive initial conversations and said how I looked forward to a similar full presentation of the Senior School at the end of the month. The Head puffed on his pipe and from within the resultant cloud of smoke I noted his smile and nod. Game, set and match to the new Deputy Head. I took a moment to reflect ... had I expected I would have to do this in my new role? As that thought was held ... the truth was had I managed to find a route to success and change? No time to dwell ... just get on with things.

Staff Briefings became more positive. Negativity was banished unless such a voice could then add ideas in a solution-focussed manner. The Senior Teacher became unusually withdrawn and rarely spoke as he puzzled at his loss in this morning setting. This then saw the whole school academic curriculum being reviewed with a view to such achievement being a goal all our pupils could reach and therefore should reach. Within the year meetings addressing planning; testing and assessment; new and accessible resources; and styles of teaching and learning all became the norm. I was beginning to break down the underachievement of pupil outcomes which the Governors and Local Authority had also let slip and never questioned.

As a family we lived in a three-bedroomed house in the wider school grounds. The village had a pub, school, church, butchers, newsagents and post office doubling as a general store. Our two youngest were at the Primary School where they were two of twenty-one children there. With six in the Infants and the rest in the Juniors our arrival in the village had bolstered the roll and we were made very welcome. In the first month my wife and I went for a meal and realised on finishing that they only did cash.

The owners said we didn't need to worry as they knew who we were and could pop back anytime to pay. That same week I took our eldest son along the valley to the Cubs three villages away. On arrival I did brief introductions but was stopped mid-sentence and told, "It's alright, we know you're the new Deputy at the Hall!" This certainly was an introduction to the village way of life and the fact everyone knew everyone ... and probably all about them too! When our third child started at the school, we were certainly big players in the village. The publican had three there and a farmer and farmhand also had two each. Between four families we had the best part of half the school population.

When our eldest son was in the infants we were called to the school as the teacher claimed she wished to discuss his 'disruptive' behaviour. Sat there on seats fit for five-year-olds we heard the teacher explain that at story time he tended to giggle and nudge the boy next to him and smile. Clearly showing almost genuine astonishment and outrage at this we agreed that such disruption required nipping in the bud and we said that we would speak with him when we got home. The excitement of a six-year-old to such gripping story telling clearly drawing out in him behaviours that unsettled the experienced teacher. On getting home a loving hug sufficed as a punitive measure and nothing was mentioned at all. Interesting that two years later, when I was a Parent Governor and Vice Chair, the Head revealed that the children had an unfortunate phrase about the same teacher indicating a link between her name and her nature. The suggestion being she was an 'idiot'. I offered no remark. The look on the head's face suggested I didn't need to.

In the Summer, the school was the venue for the Village Show with the Manor House respected residents being key to the judging. As a family, all five of us made entries to various competitions in baking, house plants, decorative floral and craft arrangements, largest weed and vegetables. We came away with numerous first, second and third places and a modest cash value of nearly five pounds. Our credibility in the village and place as accepted villagers dramatically increased. It then became common place for us to be greeted with the words 'Now then' accompanied by a nod and a smile.

The Summer also saw me take up sport again by turning out for the village Cricket Team. It started with a chance conversation with the newsagent who clearly could sell coal to the Welsh and sand to the Arabs. When I popped in after school to order a newspaper delivery a couple of times a week he asked if I could play cricket. Having replied I could he said he would be in touch. When the next newspaper arrived, written on the top of the first page was 'Game tonight please be at village green for six p.m.'. I duly turned up and enjoyed a match we easily won. I then started to receive newspapers more often than arranged with similar messages, so I popped in to see the newsagent and suggest he just phone me. He reluctantly agreed and then charged me for all the additional newspapers he used for messaging. When I described this event to the School Secretary, she told of paper boys who on finishing their last weekly round would go to him for payment and come out with no cash as he had encouraged them to spend in his shop and they went home with sweets and magazines.

I played each year for the next five years and enjoyed the camaraderie of the team and the competitiveness that is bred in Yorkshiremen for their cricket. In the Summer that would mean matches every Saturday afternoon and at least one midweek. The midweek games being eight ball overs to save changing over so often and getting through the game before light faded. We played at some interesting rural grounds and regularly won our games. The strength in our batting mostly due to one of the village farmers and two brothers in the butchers. When they hit the ball, it was done sweetly, and many runs would follow. Our bowling was by two very differing characters. One quite thin and balding. The other a fair chubby character with a mop of hair. Neither looking as though they would amount to much but when the ball left their hand it terrorised opposition batsmen and would skittle through many of their wickets. I batted a bit and bowled some too but never set the world alight with either. That was apart from the match between the Village and the team put together by the Manor House. Here bankers and other city folk joined a few local ringers from the bigger teams. In one such match I took three wickets in an over with one being the Head who was playing for the opposition. My celebration at taking his wicket rather muted as I would have to face him behind his desk on Monday ... without a Cricket ball.

Towards the end of my time playing for the team one of the good fielders had become a less frequent player. We knew he hadn't been well and that this reduced his appearances. His nickname all the way from school days in the village was 'Spit'. This may seem a not particularly nice or positive name but it had great meaning to all that had grown up with him. In the village where the road bridge crossed the beck the children would play 'Pooh Sticks' on the way home. He would not offer up a stick but would spit down into the water. The flow under the bridge then taking sticks and spit to the other side where all children would be waiting to see who had won. His spittle was always the winner and so he took the nickname.

I recall seeing him in the village pub one Friday evening and then on the Tuesday his death from cancer was announced. As a team and a village, we were shocked and saddened. The funeral was immediate family only and indeed they had known of his fight against the illness. His view had been to tell nobody outside the family and keep it secret. He didn't want any difficult conversations or quiet moments because of what he was going through. He just wanted to live on as long as he could having fun and laughing with his mates. His son had a wreath made, shaped as a cricket bat and 'Spit' was buried across the road from the cricket pitch so he could watch us play thereafter. I said my goodbye to him sat at his grave-side and pulled the ring on a tin of beer and poured it by his headstone. A drink for a dear family man of his favourite brew. Bless his heart he was a good cricketing friend and may he Rest In Peace.

In school the changes in the Education Curriculum had started to show impact but there were no examinations allowing the pupils to be matched in any comparative way with their peers in mainstream. The thought of exams for the latter two-year groups causing panic among those teaching in the Senior School. The time was right for a change in their approach or a change in their presence. Brave times were called for.

When I remarked that 'Our programme of Life Skills meant that the pupils could shoot a good game of Pool and when they ran away, they could do it relatively safely because they had been taught to read a bus timetable', the staff gasped. I added that testing and assessments carried out in the Middle school predicted examinations were not beyond them and therefore needed to be pursued. Within three years of starting at the school we had a change in six of the teaching posts with experienced and resilient mainstream teachers joining our team. Examination results started to show ability previously untapped, and pupil confidence and self-esteem also began to impact on their behaviour too.

The loss of some teaching staff to the idea of educating our pupils was tough for a few of the Care Team. They had seen those leaving as friends before colleagues and thus had seen their departure as a personal matter rather than a professional one. In turn the changes in a more professional Care Curriculum with targeted behaviour plans for each in their charge became the next challenge. Aided by the Head of Care and then his replacement this took root and their subsequent performances were more successful for the pupils and satisfying for them. Throughout the Head took a back seat and allowed me a free hand to make changes. This being in keeping with his early words which were 'If you want to become a Head, I will give you every opportunity to learn and practice.' The reality being I was learning by doing ... there wasn't much coaching. At best it was 'caught not taught'.

Soon after these changes were also in place, I realised that the chance to become a Head wasn't going to be too far away. I applied for half a dozen and got interviews at all. Some I wasn't successful at but I learned the 'game' ... others were revealed to be a nightmare of a school and I withdrew from. It became clear that perhaps another challenge be sought. Then with the arrival of the OFSTED model a chance conversation with the SEN Inspector alerted me to the fact training was available and that could result in a position with them. The Head encouraged me and off I went for a week in the Arundel area going through training and a selection process. On completing it I had a good feel about the whole experience and the possibility of further prospects. As I drove the long journey North I practiced my resignation speech to the Head. I knew I wanted to pursue this new line of work and take my family away from the intensive residential setting where all too often my work pulled me away from them.

When I got back to school, I discussed it all with my family and they agreed it may be a good way forward. Then my wife said that the Head had been taken ill and I had best go over to school and be brought up to date. On doing so I found out that he had suffered a series of heart attacks and was quite poorly. This meant he was signed off indefinitely and I was now the Acting Head. It came as no surprise that his lifestyle had sadly caught up on him. When I visited him in hospital, he looked pale and grumbled that his drinking, smoking and eating habits would be scrutinised the following day. I took this to be his shorthand version of an impending 'medical telling off' and that the cardiologist would be expecting a huge lifestyle change.

The Head was quite poorly and much in need of being away from the daily challenges of a normal day let alone anything remotely difficult. Having him around smoking his pipe more often than not had dampened the desire for a pupil to kick off with his behaviour. The Head had referred to such behaviour as a pupil 'turning his hog out'. Two incidents we had worked on together had taught me a lot about not overreacting when such a tremor resonated through the building.

The first was when one of the fourteen-year-olds in care had been let down by his social worker regarding transportation to a home visit. Naturally his disappointment was understandable but the sound of chairs and other furniture being thrown around and then the telephone call box being violently kicked drew us from the Head's office. The angry boy threw himself at the Head knocking him to the floor and as he lay on top of the Head, who still had his pipe in his mouth, he began shouting, "It's not f★★★ing fair … it's not f★★★ing right!" The Head rolled him over to the floor and held him so I joined in. As the anger rippled through his body and he tried to kick out we alternated between firm and relaxed holds trying to talk with him. No impact on his anger was evident and the insults were increasingly directed to us.

At this point the Head started just to talk with me as if the boy wasn't there at all. A conversation followed about my car and children then his dog and forthcoming holiday. The boy was bewildered and said, "Oi … I'm still f★★★ing here you know!" Then his kick attempts and threats of death to us subsided somewhat as he listened. In this temporary lull the Head's wife popped her head around the corner of the door and said "Hello, I'm going to the shop would you like some tobacco while I'm there?" Immediately the explosive energy and A–Z of profanities just stopped. The boy went completely passive and just lay there listening to the conversation that followed. Another five minutes saw the three of us still on the floor having a conversation about what had just happened and what could happen next. The 'contain … control … deflect … rebuild' process had worked. Nobody was injured. Insults issued were forgotten. When we stood up, the boy apologised and said "Should I get ready for tea now?" It was over.

The second was a boy of sixteen who had got into a fight and been brought to me. He stood in front of me with his head down and when asked what the fight was all about said "Oh it's alright for you, cos you've not been made to have sex with a pig!" My brain froze and my jaw dropped as I tried to comprehend what was unfolding in front of me. As he tried to talk more, I asked him to pause so we could go to see the Head a few yards away. Here the complete tale about his weekend visit to home and a job in a small farm was told in infinite detail and he claimed that he had been encouraged to have sex with a pig. The Police were quick in attending, took a statement and said they would be back in touch. The 'Do not Panic' approach no matter what is said or done … and listen carefully to all that is being said was very important. Over the next few days, the farm site was visited and the owner interviewed. The explanation given was that our pupil had entered into such an act with the pig and been caught. When asked where the pig was, a carcass hanging in the refrigerator unit was pointed out and the police officer was offered some pork chops from it. She declined. No further action was taken by the Police other than advice given to the teenager and his family relating to future home visits. I recall meeting the Police Officer shortly afterwards and her remark was, "You know whatever you might think about the lads at your school … when you meet some of their parents you realise all things considered that the lads haven't turned out that bad after all!"

This was the case of some such as the father of one at Christmas who unfurled a roll of twenty- and fifty- pound notes to buy raffle tickets. "My Dad is a drug dealer sir!" explained his sheepish son. Then there were the adoptive parents of an eight-year-old who asked Social Services if 'this child' could be returned as they hadn't realised his behaviour was an issue. In my mind that likened him to a shop purchase on 'sale or return'. No wonder the Social Worker stepped out the window after a meeting with them to avoid losing her professional decorum. There were many though who were the salt of the earth and good honest people perplexed by the brain-wiring issues of their sons resulting in mixed behaviours and unimaginable grief in the family home. Such as these never giving up and truly showing a love and devotion to their troubled child. Whatever we did at school, no matter what we achieved, these parents and carers were often unable to sustain it so working with them became of paramount importance.

We would prepare the boys for weekends at home and then follow up with their parents the outcomes, lessons learned and next steps. The LEA officers didn't like this on the basis that they had funded us for seven-day boarding and it wasn't always so. Lost to them that such work was about transferring behavioural progress out into the community and home settings … otherwise the behaviours were only institutionalised to time at school and untested elsewhere. One broken toothed mother with the letters F. U. C. K. O. F. F. tattooed on her knuckles captured it in a review when she launched towards the LEA rep at a review meeting and shouted, "Oh F★★★ Off … this school is turning my son's behaviour around and I'm F★★★ing chuffed with the results you Tw★t!" I enjoyed the challenge of including her energetically expressed remark as indicative of the words needed for a new annual target for her son.

When pupils did stay for the weekend it became clear that many of them had not enjoyed the opportunity to be a child engrossed in play. Some of the care staff often too eager to get them outside with a ball to kick around or coat to wear as they went for a ramble in the hills. We had received a huge box of LEGO and one Saturday as the snow fell outside it was emptied out onto the carpet floor of the main hall in front of the fireplace. To see eight-year-olds playing with those of fifteen and jointly build intricate networks of roads and buildings as they lay sprawled on the floor making noises or having conversations between the various toy figures was truly wonderful. It was indeed just a very natural family moment where siblings were just children exploring through play and having fun. The staff had to be held back from getting involved as they thought they should be engaged in the activity unfolding before them. When lunch came the boys asked if they had to put the plastic wonderland of a townscape away. To be asked if they had finished playing or wanted to continue was received with, "Oh great ... we can carry on then ..." revealing their desire. On this occasion as the hall settled to the lights out time for all those that had stayed ... the LEGO game remained on the hall floor. Those that were playing, pleased it would be there for a further day. All others respectfully admiring their building skills as they carefully stepped through it on the way to their beds that night. A lesson learned for the Care Team on duty about 'Play and Children'.

In the Head's absence all manner of behaviours continued. The staff ability to manage it and then try and unpick 'the why' so as to help the pupils develop self-control was a new dynamic to their working practice. Periodically, without rhyme or reason, somebody would explode and chaotic behaviours would require intervention. The difference now being the need to skill up the pupils and look beyond punishment to potential solutions. I enlisted the Psychiatrist who had worked with several of our pupils to assist in the work with the Care Team. On one occasion he was covering body language with them and how it could calm or escalate behaviours when I entered the room. I sat down to listen and he spoke to me. I had my arms folded as he asked me a question and he turned to my staff to explain how I had taken up a defensive stance. Somewhat surprised I felt it only right to add another explanation with it being my own childhood had involved adults saying, "Sit up straight and fold your arms". I explained to him and my staff that such a response from me and other children at the time being 'I am now listening ... you have my full attention'. It was a conditioning I had responded to. The Psychiatrist smiled, paused ... then continued with his presentation. He laughed with me afterwards about it and said that he was pleased to report that the staff team were improving in their engagement in the training. He cited examples of their practice having changed and how the feedback from pupils was that school was improving. It was a tipping point for me for as it was becoming clear we were starting to make real inroads. The outcome of the staff changing their behaviour being that so much more was working in our school. Definitely a case of 'when the adults change the children change' ... a great book there to be written ... as indeed it was by a wise colleague, Paul Dix, in the future.

Around this time our school inspector from the LEA arrived to look at aspects of our provision and talk things through with me. I recall saying to him that I was 'acting up' which he found very amusing in the context of our school being for children with behavioural problems. He said he would find a place for that as a quote in one of his speeches or books. This was the first time I was to meet Gervase Phinn. In future years his success as an acclaimed author and speaker made me think of telling my story and how I really did 'act up' in my life as a way of both coping and finding success.

When the news broke that the Head would be retiring on ill-health grounds it wasn't really a surprise. The Governors set about arranging for a replacement and I was faced with a dilemma. I had heard back from OFSTED and been offered a position with HMI status working in Special Education with the EBD team. Then following an interview resulting in me being offered the position of headteacher, two jobs were on the table and a decision required. My previous thoughts of taking us as a family away from the high pressure of the school setting still very real in my mind. Yet, the chance to be the Head of something I had nurtured as Deputy was too much of a draw. So there it was, my first headship and we moved into the large flat within the hall itself.

The majority of the Governors were genuinely pleased to see me being successful. This came as no surprise, as for them all to agree would require those from the three political parties to step aside from their rigid political differences and think school before their doctrines. The Chair, who was a Tory Councillor, City Banker and President of the Village Cricket Club [the latter being of credible status in Yorkshire], grinned as he shook my hand and congratulated me. He then questioned whether I would shave properly and remove what was then described as a designer stubble beard. Such important questions often his chosen specialism. This was the man who as Chair of Governors of the Village Primary thought the children should wear blazers and caps. As his confident Vice Chair, I leant across the table and told him to "Behave!" Needless to say, that for better or worse, the beard continued to live on my face as I took up my formal position as Headteacher.

A few staff decided this was a good time to leave and the calibre of open-minded replacements ensured that the progress continued at an even faster rate. The changes included a new Deputy, Senior Teacher and Head of Care. As a new team of four we were enthusiastic in our desire to make the school a happier place and one that was far more professional in every way. What we wanted was success in the academic curriculum to further build a sense of self-worth, self-belief and enquiry in the pupils. We also wanted for this to translate into a Care Curriculum and them then being guided towards managing their own behaviour. It sounded grand and the staff and governors bought into it. That first year saw the pupils do likewise and for a setting once described as for 'naughty boys' the change was so evident and the village no longer twitched when any of them were allowed to go out to a shop.

Until this time the idea of pupils being reintegrated back into mainstream was seen as pie in the sky … described by my predecessor as 'an opportunity to embarrass us all'. Now we had two boys worthy of trying to see what could be done. Both had shown that should they be referred to us as new pupils then they would fail the entrance exam criteria. No behavioural challenges, no swearing, good academic progress and very influential in their peer and staff relationships. Following formal reviews with parents, LEA and nearby school settings everything was set.

The first case was of an eleven-year-old who started school in the nearby coastal town attending with two of my own children and others from the village. The secondary school had a very good reputation and I had previously done staff training with their SEN Team. Our boy, now their pupil was nervous but eager. The resultant success enjoyed being testament to their staff team during the day and our support on his return. He was literally buzzing with excitement and pride. This translated into a heart-warming review at the end of the first month. Then headaches started to blight his day and he became withdrawn. We had known that at Primary School such headaches had frustrated him and in turn lead to the tantrums that caused him to be placed with us when his behaviour became unmanageable. His previous year with us had not seen any such problems and now it seemed they had returned. Subsequent medical tests revealed this dear child had a brain tumour and we feared the worse. The operation successfully removed the tumour but the side effects impacted on his speech, cognitive ability and mobility. Months after coming out of hospital his trial at mainstream and his place with us both came to an end. The upset was openly displayed by staff in both settings for he had captured all our hearts.

About a year later I had a story recounted to me from a colleague who ran a Special School in the boy's home town of York. Now in a wheelchair he was described as a feisty and confident pupil keen to speak up and look for change if he felt things were not right. As I was being told this, my friend indicated that he believed the boy had learnt all those attributes when in my charge. The story was of him being summoned to the Head's office because of challenging an action by a teacher as being unfair and unwarranted. When the head demanded of him to put the situation right and leave his office the boy had evidently let down the wheels on his wheelchair and refused to budge demanding to be heard. As my friend shook his head saying this had been a first for him, I enquired how it had been resolved. He explained that the boy was actually correct and subsequently he had to get the member of staff to put the whole situation right. I was so pleased to learn that my work was impacting beyond my school. I know that this boy went on to enjoy great success and respect within his new school. He had made the best job of what fate had presented him with and his story was certainly one to be told over and over again.

The second case was of a fifteen-year-old placed in a secondary school in a market town again with good pastoral and SEN support staff. The Head was keen to show how inclusive his school was, particularly to some of his doubting staff who wanted some pupils to 'leave' not for a supposedly reformed EBD pupil to arrive. This boy could charm the devil into behaving and get him to trade his horns for a trendy baseball cap. It wasn't long before the staff greeted every monitoring visit by me with further examples of how well he was doing. It seemed nothing could go wrong. Then one day as I arrived, I was ushered to the Head's office as an incident had just occurred in the Technology Room. The description of the event seemed to suggest all was undone. The teacher reported looking up and seeing two boys in discussion, one with a chisel he seemed to be waving in a threatening manner at the other. In fear of what might happen the teacher rushed forward knocking the chisel from the boy's hand and took him to the floor. This pupil was our star fifteen-year-old.

The boy was brought into the room to be faced by the head, teacher and myself. It was intimidating for him and he looked anxiously towards me and said, "Sorry Sir, I think I have let you down!" When asked to recount his version, he described how he had been talking with the other boy about a TV programme they had both seen and enjoyed. He said as he was talking, he had the chisel in his hand and was waving it as he nodded at the amusement of the TV programme. Then to his amazement he suddenly found himself on the floor with the teacher on top of him. The Head looked embarrassed at this recount by the boy and the teacher's head dropped. The other boy then was brought in and completely concurred with every single word told.

The moral here being that not everything you see is really what is actually happening. In addition, the teacher's view that he had made his mind up about the incident because of the prior history of this pupil was seen as being the biggest error in the whole event. My response to the Head was, "Oh well it seems that there's been a lot of learning that's gone on here today. I'm sure you'll be able to fashion it to further your ambition with such as my pupil who I really think should now be yours full time". The deal was done there and then and the pupil became a shining light for the Head in furthering his quest for an Inclusive School.

Returning to school I found out that notice had been given of an impending OFSTED visit. The notice period allowing me to take my staff through what that meant for us as a school community and how the inspection team would arrive at their judgement. This was a new experience for us all as there had not been the like in any of our previous school settings. However, my training in Arundel paid dividends in developing staff understanding and allaying any fears. As the day grew closer the quality of what we did just seemed to be even better in every respect to the point we just wanted them to come quickly in case our show bubble popped.

When they arrived their manner and engagement with pupils and staff indicated that they really understood Special Education and in particular boys with emotional and behavioural difficulties. The lead inspector being a calm and thoughtful character was likened by the boys as a detective 'looking for the good'. As it turned out he found even better than that in all facets of our provision and related exceptionally well to all in our team. The discussions we had reinforced my belief from my own OFSTED training that the inspection process should be done with and not to the school. This man made sure that everything was seen, recorded and judged fairly. When it came to the final feedback the relationship between the two of us was highlighted by something that surely would only happen in an EBD School. Under his chair was an old defused WW2 hand grenade with the words 'For use in Inspection Feedback, remove pin and retire if wrong judgement' written on the lever mechanism.

As he went to sit down, he noticed it and chuckled. I explained that I had placed it there to help him focus on how good we were. He said he wanted it as a memento and I insisted that he presented his findings first. In hearing him describe our school I could neither have wished for words any better nor felt any greater pride. My Leadership Team were present with our Chair of Governors and our Link LEA Inspector. I was not alone in feeling emotional and some showed it brushing away tears of joy … and relief. We knew what we had created for the boys was very special but to hear it captured so by the inspection was a great feeling for us all. When the Lead left the room, I kept the grenade knowing it may come in useful at some time later in my career.

The LEA struggled to find any words to match the recognition by OFSTED, or indeed say even a hearty well-done. The first real contact from them suggesting that if it was correct then why weren't more being reintegrated back into mainstream? That was hard to take as the staff deserved the recognition, but alas it was symptomatic of a hierarchy that was overly robust and at times bullying with schools and their leaders. A College of Education had captured the impact of the report and our educational approach to behaviour. As such, I became a Visiting Lecturer on the Master's Course there and recall the amusement of teaching peers with one of my introductory lines, "You will know when you have got their respect, because when they tell you to F★★★ Off, they will say F★★★ Off Sir!" Sharing theory and practice with them was an enjoyable experience. It was also a personal historic moment to be a lecturer at the very University where the once Principal of my training place now presided.

The LEA were coming under a deal of criticism for their bullish approach and I had already witnessed a Secondary Head openly rip into the Director for her insensitive remarks. The resultant gasp and awkward silence ended by the various assembled school settings splitting up and heading off to their own meetings. When alongside my Special Head peers waiting for the start of our sector meeting with the LEA, our brilliant OFSTED report was discussed and the congratulatory comments I received very welcome. The meeting was to discuss working practices and a new way forward for us all. It was laden with innuendo and veiled threats about performance and the shortcomings of leadership. There was no quarter given in the finger-wagging and clearly each speaker had been banished from referencing anything slightly motivational. Mutterings nearby alluding to a desire for shallow graves being required for those scolding us. One usually quiet member of our ranks, turning his head and adding "Great idea, do you think anybody would miss them?"

To my surprise when talking about documentation requests sent out to schools the LEA admitted only receiving around a fifty per cent. return which seemed to satisfy them. I turned to a long-standing Head and voiced my surprise at this figure. His reply was, "I don't send them anything back ... never have!" When I asked how he got away with that he laughed as he replied, saying "Because I know the likes of you send one hundred per cent. back!" This was a big lesson for me and as the discussion continued my peers berated LEA officers for asking for details which they held centrally and a clerk should collate anyway. I began to realise that I was guilty of trying to do too much and that this often included some things that were of no benefit to my school. As I drove home afterwards, I thought long and hard about this and how it was draining for me and impacting on my family contact. The aggressive delivery by LEA Officers of a total demotivating content continued to puzzle me. Surely this was no way to run an education system.

Adding to my portfolio of roles I was asked to both apply to become a Magistrate and also consider doing likewise to join the Police Authority with its governance responsibility for North Yorkshire. The latter was offered to me and I became an Independent Member on a team of others from Political and Magistrate backgrounds. I soon took on responsibility for Youth Liaison and had oversight for aspects of Rural Policing and the Firearms Section. To already have an insight into Police matters through two of my brothers now having come out of the Forces and joined the ranks of the West Midlands and Derbyshire forces was helpful. The structures, financial challenges and shortage of staff were real issues in meetings with the popular and very dynamic Chief Constable leading discussions. They were interesting and similar in so many ways to the education system. My position confirmed by the then Home Secretary who I met at a conference hosted at Blackburn Rovers FC where he was keener to talk of the merits of his team and point out where his season ticket seat was, rather than the national challenges of policing. Our meetings were chaired by a formidable and cool customer of a Councillor who was rewarded for her work regionally and nationally by becoming Lady Angela Harris of Richmond. Some seventeen years would pass before we caught up again in the House of Lords over afternoon tea. As an experience this role added to my understanding of the bigger stage in running organisations and the need for scrutiny to be with a view towards excellence in the delivery of services.

The week after the demoralising meeting with the LEA, I found engagement with the Police Authority business quite refreshing albeit quite time-consuming. If presented with such an opportunity, I had been advised I would be wise to take it on. A different perspective of leading, managing and accountability can be very worthwhile ... and indeed it was. Then my focus was swiftly returned to school with several pupils in crisis needing a great deal of attention.

One fourteen-year-old was struggling with his behaviour and had requested I attend a meeting with him and the Psychiatrist. As a result, it was decided he would be put on the medication Ritalin because of his attention deficit and hyperactivity. The explanation given to him was done so carefully reducing his sense of fear at needing such an intervention. As we left the clinic he turned and held my hand and said, 'Thanks for coming with me ... thanks for helping me get my life back together'. Words from his heart and indicative of school being seen as a way forward for him.

The following day one of the twelve-year-olds who had associated mental health challenges but didn't meet the criteria for intervention was in a severe distressed state and had been found shaking and sobbing in the school grounds. After eating his evening meal and seeming calm, he entered a period of crisis again and kept threatening to take his own life. We took it in shifts to sit outside a room set up for him to sleep in to make sure he was safe. He kept waking and calling out for me. So, I sat up through the night with other staff and responded to him each time he came out of a brief period of sleep. The following morning my wife and I took him home to where medics were waiting from the Mental Health Team. This boy had withered in the previous twenty-four hours and was but a shell in this emotional self-anxious state and now without the will to live.

As if not enough, at the weekend I received a call to say the hospital required me to attend. One of the sixteen-year-olds had been at home and hunting for presents in his parent's bedroom. Seemingly not having found anything with his name on it, he prepared a ligature and tried to hang himself. The first his father knew was a banging noise coming from upstairs. On entering the room, he found his son twitching as he hung from the ceiling. Now in Critical Care he was on a ventilator and wired up to all sorts of equipment – my presence had been requested by the family. As I arrived the Consultant described what had happened and the probable outcome for the boy. It was not good.

I entered the room to see his parents stood beside him looking exhausted and broken. They beckoned me forward and asked me to say something to him. The equipment was beeping and there were few independent life signs from him. I leant over him and from God knows where the whispered words that fell from my mouth were "If you think pulling this stunt will get you out of doing your studies then you are mistaken!" At that split second, he twitched, and the machines bleeped a different sort of noise. We were all ushered from the room and ten minutes later the Consultant came out and to our relief pronounced he was conscious again. He then turned to me and said, "Whatever it was that you said ... my goodness it worked!" When I left to go home, they took him off the ventilator as his recovery progressed.

I was drained when I got home and slept long into the following morning. On Monday there were some questions that had arisen about one of our young teachers who lived in the next village. After taking advice I was advised to suspend him and the LEA said they would look into the matter. The teacher was stunned but offered up no comments at all. Concerned for his mental health and well-being I contacted his local Union Rep and explained the situation. I also asked for him to be visited to check and to make sure he was safe.

That period of seven days had really tested my resolve and without me realising at the time had started to cause cracks in my own well-being and inner strength. In the days that followed I was pleased to note that the Ritalin was being taken by the boy and he was feeling good about himself. Likewise, the broken boy was now in the hospital receiving care and psychiatric attention for his condition. Finally, the boy who had attempted suicide was out of Intensive Care and in the Children's Ward back to his 'prior normal self' causing havoc, so they wanted him discharged. The member of staff was signed off sick now as well as being suspended so the investigation was halted.

One afternoon I found myself lost and confused just before the end of the day. I felt my mind was spiralling and I just couldn't collect my thoughts in any rational way. Two hours later sat in front of a friend, my GP, I just broke down in tears. I was not well at all. Overthinking and overworking I had tried to make so much right and care for so many others but I had lost sight of me. The doctor told me I was more than stressed I was close to depression and breaking point. In a very direct way he told me I had to stop everything and rest. I was signed off work. The relief at that moment was indescribable and quite bizarre.

The next few weeks living in the flat in the centre of the Main Hall building of school were just endless cloudy times of confused thoughts. I knew I had crashed mentally and that in the nick of time I had got out before I completely burned. My family tried to understand and help me through, but it was as new to them as it was hard for me. The support of colleagues was challenging for they knew not what to do and the LEA weren't there for them either. The burden of responsibility for my new Leadership Team was such that they had a focus and it was to run the school and wait to see what happened with me. I had seen them grow in their own confidence ... with some concerns about how they might do on their own ... and it was time for them to try and step up to the mark and hopefully thrive in the opportunity presented.

This episode in my life had not been a result of just a few weeks or incidents. I had passed through the motivated and focussed stages of what I now know to be referred to in the 'Stress Curve'. I reached my peak and OFSTED had shared the moment more widely. Then rather than sit back and take stock of what we had achieved together I had ploughed on relentlessly and without realising I had started to physically tire. In turn that became exhaustion and the point at which it all became crystal clear to me was when I was sat in front of my GP. The anxiety caused by my confusion and lack of direction was the sign that burn-out was critically close, if not passed. At this time a mentor and close working supportive headteacher would have been my guide perhaps even noting the trajectory of my health. But these were not such times. The likes of author and speaker James Hilton had yet to arrive and open up the topic of how to cope as a leader in the ever-increasingly complex and ever-changing education landscape of school leadership. When James did, he explained with unbridled honest words reliving his dramatic personal crash as a Headteacher, then unpicking it all and writing how to be more resilient. He would in the years to follow help take away the shame often felt, and then introduce an honesty that allowed for such as I was feeling to open up and go on to reinvent ourselves as stronger souls.

Unfortunately, I had already witnessed the mental dissolving of a much valued and respected Senior Educational Psychologist within the LEA where many of us thought the support available had come up short and sadly his life ended. This learned fellow man had been part of my interview panel and an advocate of the methods put in place and outcomes achieved. His voice all too often overlooked and ignored. He had once promoted the need for a review of residential provision on the basis of 'Where is the Care for the Carers?' He recognised that this work was at the frontier of teaching and we often joked it was the 'Wild West of Special Education' and one where the staff had to be looked after. Needless to say, despite his best efforts and those voices of others in residential schools nothing transpired. So, when the likes of me broke down at their workplace there was nothing on offer from them or indeed elsewhere professionally. It was definitely the case that such an event was seen as a weakness. Indeed, this was still a time when such feelings and difficulties were mostly ignored by many such employers and particularly hidden by men, because of a feeling of shame and failure.

I thought back to my colleague who was the 'nil per cent. returner' and wondered if he had survived that long by sometimes just saying 'No' and focusing otherwise. Did he have a mentor or close confidant? How did he switch off so he literally didn't breathe his job twenty-four / seven? These and many other questions were rattling around inside my head supported by a medication that I was not sure was making me feel that brilliant anyway.

Then one day I found myself in Pickering admiring the historic Steam Train pull into the station full of joyful tourist passengers. As they got off the train some walked towards the engine to thank the driver and fireman. They responded with gleaming white teeth smiles and from behind their oily and coal smudged faces their eyes glistened appreciatively of all that was said. Then they prepared the engine for the return journey across the Moors before sitting and chatting on the footplate. Their work done for an hour and now downtime, relaxation and reflection. These two men chatted away within earshot. No moans, no worries, no battles in their day to be taken home. When had I created such times for thoughts other than work? The answer was simple ... not enough and too often, not at all!

As time passed it became clear that the waiting for self-repair couldn't continue and it was best to resign and take some purposeful time to really get better. A key requirement being to get away from the school, so we bought a house in the nearby seaside town of Scarborough. Relief absolute when we drove away. No real goodbye to my great pupils and so many staff stars. Moving forward it was for them now to make their own future. I had one memorable afternoon when invited to a splendid afternoon tea with the Domestic Team. My hard working and constantly smiling barometers the very last to see me. Their leader Doreen, a giant of a person full of kindness and honest endeavour. I could see that they hurt at my departure and their concern was expressed in more than words.

Life was now about coming to terms with myself and the multitude of troubled thoughts. It was not long before I happened across the book 'Counselling for Toads – A Psychological Adventure' by Robert de Board. I do believe it helped save my life from even darker actions as it explained counselling as a method of dealing with psychological distress with an admirable clarity. Set in the context of Kenneth Grahame's 'Wind in the Willows' I was able to understand Toad's breakdown and the challenges for Rat, Mole and Badger. I had no Heron as my counsellor but the story helped me to analyse my own feelings and develop improved and revitalised emotional intelligence. At the end of the book Toad is ready through transactional analysis to set out on a new adventure. After a period of several months, I was too.

In time I broke out of my silence and lack of contact with the outside educational world and found friends and ex-colleagues full of aspirations for me. After discussions my energy was refreshed so I applied for a number of positions just to see what may come back. My confidence for the future was boosted when I received numerous job offers. The choice of working in a Scottish University teaching on their Special Education Course, or in a Special School in York to assist an old colleague the Head in turning it around were the start. Then came interest from further OFSTED Inspection Teams for contract work following on from that I had already enjoyed in the Midlands. Finally, an International School in the Middle East asked me to fly out to offer them some advice. So much to be considered particularly as three of the four would mean time away from my family.

As this chapter in my educational journey came to an end, I realised that:

'There is no shame in being a broken man … you just have to pick up the pieces and start rebuilding'.

That was what I now needed to do.

Chapter 12

A Gulf Apart

In the Spring, feeling refreshed and much better about myself I attended a meeting in the Randolph Hotel in Oxford with the joint owner of an International School in the Middle East. A European woman openly enthusiastic about her school and totally committed to the need for its status to be recognised with an International Accreditation at any cost. She greeted me like some sort of long-lost friend. We discussed ideas and as a result I was flown out to the Gulf to meet with her again and her husband, a very professional man who fully understood the importance of the staff team and its leadership in making their school successful. Judging by some of her sharp remarks, her approach seemed more in keeping with some of the questionable motivational strategies employed in my previous LEA. After two days of talks an offer of work was made to me and arrangements agreed for a return visit as a Consultant to advise them further. An envelope full of fifty pound notes given to me as renumeration for my services.

My next visit gave me the opportunity to spend a great deal of time with the Headteachers of the Secondary, Primary and Special sections of the school. I gained a quick insight into both their take on performance and areas for improvement. Then I had time to wander freely into any area to cross reference all I had heard. The thousand pupils in the four to eighteen age range and over one hundred and fifty staff welcomed me wherever I went. On the second evening I was asked to present my thoughts at a sumptuous meal at the owner's huge villa in a suburb of the city. The Gallic impatience of his wife being moderated simply by a small lifting of his hand enabling the owner to hear all before reflecting and responding. His legal background revealing his systematic approach to what was the issue and then what was to be the best way forward. He liked what I had to say and how his school could be transformed. It was at this point that her position as Director of the School then came into question. They begged a private moment and withdrew for about half an hour. On return I was offered the position formerly occupied by her. She sat quietly, her half smile revealing a discomfort but general acceptance. In the following discussion, celebrated with champagne, it was clear that her acceptance was made all the easier by talk of an extended holiday break in Europe. Once again, an envelope full of fifty pound notes was handed to me, clearly a customary act.

Two months later I flew back via an overnight stay in Dubai. The temperature in August being in the high forty degrees centigrade and everywhere looked parched. The heat, very dry, caused perspiration to be my wish, but sweating profusely was the actual reality. Any opportunity to stay indoors and enjoy air conditioning taken with real enthusiasm. The next few days spent visiting various Government Offices to gain the correct paperwork for employment and right to stay. On completion I was now able to open a bank account, gain a driving licence and hire a car. That level of independence being key in getting to work and around the city for shopping and meeting colleagues. I moved into a two bedroomed flat which came with maid service and a pool in the adjoining complex. Now I was all set for term to start.

I met my three Headteacher's each week as a group and again separately to be updated on their plan for the term ahead, staffing compliment, student numbers and any exam or test results of significance. The expectation being one I would have considered as normal, seemingly not quite so for them. As such a coaching session on future working practice and our collective vision was needed quickly. They were keen to engage with me and it seemed from regular aside comments made that it was an easier format than any with the owner's wife.

The Secondary Head was a Science Teacher from England and when in the UK only having been a Head of Department. His friendship with the wife of the owner key to his status. Clearly a very competent Scientist but he had limited leadership experience and influence in a developmental sense. The Head of Primary had been in such a post in Scotland and his operational experience seemingly far more competent. The Head of Special a Canadian with limited leadership experience prior to his appointment. The whole school had no Development Plan and the notion of anybody monitoring quality of teaching and learning, and implementing any continuing professional development was seen as quite alien. In fact, what came across pretty quickly was that for many of the staff from the UK their motivation for being abroad was to escape such accountability. The challenge ahead in achieving an International Accreditation became a task requiring some serious actions that could over time be painful to such individuals.

It came as no real surprise to the owner who would come to school at the end of each week to be briefed by me. His knew his wife had run the school in a very autocratic way and, with her Secretary, they had often spread a degree of fear throughout the staff team. He openly acknowledged that her absence meant that I had a free hand to put in place important changes. He understood they needed enough time to take root before she returned. His enthusiasm for my approach emphasised when the Head of Secondary was quickly replaced and returned to England.

Within two months monitoring and evaluation was in place, with the emphasis on any deficits in standards being remedied through staff training and coaching. Key skilled middle managers were appointed to lead on such tasks and they soon became the leaders of change and improvement. The Heads now had teams to refer to and share their management role with. The school began to take on a more professional feel which most were enjoying. The quantum leap being when I established a staff room in the centre of the campus. This was richly appreciated and became a hive of activity as seen in any normal school setting. Previously it had been banned by the owner's wife as she saw it as a place where teachers would be idle, leaving me to wonder what sort of example had she based this school on in the first place.

My daughter had accompanied me out to the Middle East with the expectation of being a Teaching Assistant. It was to be a 'gap year' for her before going to University to study Speech and Language. Her promotion to class teacher for children with learning and communication difficulties being a popular appointment and one that allowed her to flourish as a practitioner. Her reference for such a responsibility being that of her successful mother, now the Deputy in a SLD School. It wasn't long before the referrals to her class increased and the complexity of SEN met with consummate ease.

I provided further training to the staff team in the Special School on current UK practice each morning of a weekend day for a twelve-week period. It was received with enthusiasm by both teachers and teaching assistants. The impact being that word spread in the city and numbers in the school increased by thirty per cent. as places were sought by parents seeking this newer quality provision for their children. My daughter became well-known and very popular. On one occasion she had to explain to an Arab parent that his son couldn't have a place in her class because he was twelve and mainstream ... and her class was for four- and five-year-olds with SEN. It seemed quite simple and obvious but took some time for him to realise no matter what the offer of inducements were ... it was just not going to happen.

The curriculum throughout the school was based on that in England in all sections. The examinations in Secondary being

IGSCE and sat in Years eleven, twelve and thirteen. Everything was taught in English with the exception of Arabic and Islamic Studies. The staff were mostly English, but also included those from Ireland, Wales, Scotland, Poland, Ukraine, India, Philippines, Lebanon, Egypt, Canada and Palestine. As the term passed, they were gelling as a team and enjoying being engaged in a professional manner about moving the three schools forward. Then the owner's wife returned, and their morale and sense of having a voice evaporated overnight. She was livid with the idea of a staff room and the loss of the Secondary Head. For the next few days, she patrolled the school seeking out all manner of other changes with a view to having a showdown with me.

It happened on the afternoon of the owner's regular briefing and as the three of us sat down she launched into a tirade. The elasticity of her recent cosmetic surgery was severely tested as she contorted her face with anger and dismay at my work in making 'her school' now 'a den of idleness'. Having heard enough the owner did his hand lift to encourage her to stop and breathe deeply. We then outlined the content of our weekly meetings and decisions made. His weight of argument well practiced in court proved to stem her rage and then came the killer question, "We appointed him to do this job, so we either let him or we lose him. Is that what you want?" Before she could answer 'Yes', he added, "It is not what I want and it should not be what you want!" So ended the first test of her patience and my role.

Just afterwards I became aware from the newly appointed School Manager, the curious thing about the country's education system was that each September both students and staff swapped between the various international schools. Students did so more often than not because the school and parents came to a better deal over school fees whereas staff often bartered their skills for better wages and contract benefits. Our discussion then focussed on how neither would contribute to great stability in our school. It was as clear as daylight that the owner's wife could disaffect the staff and reduce the chances of us keeping them with us. Undoubtedly, continuing success in our outcomes meant that teachers could be poached by schools looking for such quality. If the staff felt insecure and unhappy then the other schools could snap them up with a better salary and any offer of additional inducements.

This conversation was had with the owner and his eyes rolled, and I'm sure his heart sank. Dealing with an opposing lawyer or a difficult member of staff was well within his range of interpersonal skills. He knew this challenge was considerably more difficult … it was his wife. I'm sure the outcome was helped by me receiving an offer of an interview back in Yorkshire to turn around an EBD School where the leadership team had found themselves in great difficulty and no longer in post. My name put forward by the Regional HMI and the call made to me by the Director of Education in that Riding. I returned to the UK for a short period and met to discuss possibilities. It was clear that my prior health difficulties were not seen as a professional flaw, just merely an indication of how I had neither been appreciated nor looked after. This was so refreshing to hear and put me another 'mental mile' away from that difficult time. They wanted me to sort the school out and take it to where my previous place had been … excellent for all.

When I returned to the Gulf the owner was waiting to see me. I outlined what had happened and the offer made. He cut to the quick and made promises about my role, responsibility and independence from interference. The visit to the UK had furthered my sense of achievement in picking up the pieces but it was a step backwards so I committed myself to the owner and his school. No mention was made of any potential difficulty with his wife. We actually agreed that every opportunity be given to her to take front and centre stage position on any celebratory events, which she loved and performed with regal efficiency. It seemed all were happy and the progress could continue.

Each day I would walk the school three times and make my presence well-known throughout. The opportunity to watch improved levels of teaching and feedback positively to the teacher, then seal the words of congratulation with a handshake were soon valued and much sought after. Walking down the corridor it was common to find classroom doors open and teachers hovering as they waited to invite me in. The students similarly looking for opportunities to show and glow their work to 'Mr Kim' as I was known. Parents and carers at the start and end of the day were keen to talk and express gratitude for proactivity with any problems raised and the air of 'happy study' they felt that had become more prevalent. These parents included members of the extended Royal Family who would reward any act lavishly and be keen to say they were in debt to me for what, in my mind, was just the performance of my role.

During the year that followed the riches of the Arabic families and the matter-of-fact attitude this instilled in their children became very apparent. At the start of the day, it was not uncommon for a child in Kindergarten or Early Years to arrive in a limousine with three household staff. One to drive, the second to carry the child into school and the third to carry the child's bag and lunchbox. All three being from the Indian Sub-continent and performing their role with care and precision. Their faces would drop when I would tell them to put the child on their own feet and hand them their lunchbox and bag. I would then welcome the child and tell them to walk into school before I turned to wish the three staff a good day. At first shock and worry on their faces. In time a wry smile as they realised that we were all working towards this over-indulged child having some daily tasks requiring his or her own level of independence.

When there was a knock at my door, just before the end of school one day, I was confronted by an anxious sixth former who had been placed in detention for a misdemeanour. He pleaded with me to excuse him from the punishment saying he would give me the keys to his brand-new Lamborghini for the weekend if I would sort it for him. Similar offers of yachts, speed boats and so on being the norm for such rule bending. Tempting as it may be for some, it was clear that the balance of power would shift if such an offer was accepted ... never mind it being totally wrong! There would be a play on words by some students saying that if their parents found out that they had performed any wrong act they would suffer a loss of face at home and with their peers. This was completely turned around by challenging any wayward acts with the question, "If you don't start doing your work (or perhaps ... behaving) then you will bring shame on yourself and your family!" This worked as it was very much their 'Achilles heel' in all matters.

If that posed a brief question in my mind as to how that would go down in the UK it paled into insignificance when incidents occurred of bad behaviour and the use of swearing. To have the Head of Islamic Studies stood nearby and announce to a student that we had decided that their unworthy actions warranted 'extra Islamic Studies' was serious in its design and impact. The thought of saying that to a recalcitrant teenager in England with the consequence of extra R.E. conjuring up all sorts of subsequent scenarios.

The key piece of learning regarding influence and power of such students was captured one day in the playground. There was a great deal of noise and many older students gathered in one corner of the school by the Mosque. When entering the scene, the crowd of baying teenagers fell silent and two were stood yards apart resembling a scene from a Spaghetti Western. I recognised one as a Palestinian boy and the other a local Arabic boy. He was not just any boy, he was from the Royal Family. I turned to him and asked him what was going on and his reply was that the other boy had used bad words about his family. When I said, "But, you bring shame on your family by fighting in this way!" He quickly replied, "Do not worry Mr Kim, for I will arrange for two Bedouin to come from the desert and take this boy to meet God!" At that precise moment by brain was on speed dial calling for a connection to my EBD Memory Vault for a suitable response. The problem being there had never been such an incident so calmly explained as being so easily fixed by a killing. Part of me wanted to put my arm around the member of the Royal Household and say, "Now listen here son, I'm on your side!" But then, sense kicked in and I lead both away to my office for restorative justice and preservation of life to be the winning solution. It worked and both played football for the school team as good friends. I'm sure the Palestinian was a good deal more cautious thereafter and so it was as he lived to graduate at the end of the school year.

The vast majority of students were very polite and keen to work hard at their studies. Incidents of difficulty were in fact very rare. Smiles and energetic greetings increasingly heard in the corridors, playground and classrooms. The Arabic staff noting a new air of happiness that permeated through the school. "Inshallah Mr Kim this will stay here thanks to you!" being the remark made by the Head of Arabic Studies. He was a wonderful character from Gaza who tried to explain the difficulty of his Palestinian national status and inability to travel home to see his grown-up son. When in any doubt of local customs and ways of addressing issues related to parents, he was always at hand along with the Head of Islamic Studies to offer me support. She had a smile on her face irrespective of all else going on in the world and announced that as good a man as I was, I would be improved by becoming a Muslim. Serious words spoken with a smile waiting to burst into laughter. I thanked her for trying to save me and said that the Church of England had been chasing me for many years without success.

The morale within the staff continued to grow and this was evidenced in them sharing professional dialogue in that den of alleged iniquity, the staff room. It also transferred to Parent's Evenings when honest and forthright feedback was given on student progress and exam predictions. The emphasis being on what could be done in partnership to improve the situation rather than a moan and blame. An indication of this change in staff culture being highlighted at the end of a term when a plane full of staff flew out of the city airport. Being a dry country, access to alcohol was usually the preserve of those invited to the British Embassy. As the plane took off the P.E. staff were up and out of their seats to get a few beers. One being passed to me and then they toasted me to cheers from all others. A moving act and one they felt safest doing in airspace rather than on the ground in school. There were several such moments like this throughout the rest of the year and it was very evident that they had bought into the changes and felt the school was theirs … as indeed it should have been. I would add that after this flight with an overnight stop in Dubai the celebrations continued and three staff missed their connecting flights the following morning.

The new year started with the arrival of half a dozen staff fresh from schools in the UK to replace those that had left for schools elsewhere in the city. A disappointment to lose them not least of all from Primary and Special where they had contributed to such improvements in every aspect of the provision. Amongst those being my daughter who was off to York to start her degree course and her close working partner a teacher from Poland who in time rose to the position of Head of Special in a competitor school. Her departure evidence of how the loss had the potential to damage sustained development and impact positively on another school and indeed her own career. Another departure was of our young and inspirational Art Teacher who had set alight his students. He had also been a much-liked and energetic member of the staff room. His love of Manchester City puzzling the students as at the time they were not a team on their horizon of fame. He had previously dazzled the First XI team in a staff versus students match. He wore his club shirt with the letters EIDOS for the kit sponsors. The P.E. staff pleased he was on their team because of his quick feet only matched by their quick wit. One of them informing him that the letters on his shirt stood for 'Eleven Idiots Dreaming of Success'!

With prior knowledge of departures, I had managed to recruit a new Headteacher to both Secondary and Primary. A married couple absolutely oozing with confidence and keen for a new challenge. They both recognised the opportunity of coming to join us. The first two months of their tenure enabled greater change in practice than their predecessors had achieved in the whole previous year. They had been in posts elsewhere in the country and been interested in the speed of our developments. On arrival they literally hit the ground running. Their predecessors had been steady practitioners but the difference the new pair brought was a total professional drive and the ability to communicate it with outstanding practice of their own. The staff responded by finding yet another gear in their own commitment to raising standards further.

The owner's wife was still in Europe and this undoubtedly ensured that the pursuit of excellence was easier to achieve without her scrutiny. Without a doubt during this period the school was at its very best. Staff were upping their game and, at the same time, they gathered evidence sources for the validation process of the forthcoming International Accreditation. The respective Headteachers, School Business Manager and myself forming the key committee with sub groups within each school sector then working with Middle Leaders at the helm. Weekly visits by the owner then allowed for updates to be given to him and confirmation of next steps. All was better than good in our school.

Then the owner's wife returned and the mood swing in school was of tsunami proportions. One teacher fled the country devastated by an outburst directed at her. She slipped away by plane one night and the pleasure of her success was evident in staff briefing the following day. Further staff similarly threatened to do so and sought reassurance from me that this injection of vitriol was just a blip. But her timing was calculated, as her husband was busy with work and he had stepped back from school for a period. The impact of her return was like watching a sunflower wilt before our eyes ... but at speed.

Staff briefings became laden with moans and fault finding about anything and everything conceivable. Often the staff sat before me shell shocked as she vented her spleen with alarming rapidity. The Arabic staff confused as their English, although good, could not keep up. This meant I then had to summarise the content removing as many barbs as I could to make it easier for them to digest. Then one day we came closest to revolution when the owner's wife ripped into the cleaning team. Unhappy with their work she fined them all a week's pay on the spot. A dozen of them shattered by this as their wages were already low and their conditions poor. The staff team were outraged and lead by the Brits had a collection for the cleaners. The amount raised exceeding their wages which just added to the sense of anger. When she found out what the staff had done, she exploded. No matter what was said she could not grasp the implications of her actions. As if to capitalise on the moment she fired the Business Manager. This seemed to be more a statement of her status than his performance.

As the Ministry for Education were keen to authenticate the SEN provision within the school, we were tasked with a mound of requests for paperwork for them to consider. This provided an opportunity to work with the Head of Special and we created a big evidence base to keep the civil servants busy for a month. True to that design they came back in five weeks and announced they would not be returning the materials provided. This did come as a surprise and then we found out that the accreditation of SEN across the country was to be based upon the standard we had provided as a statement of our provision. As was the curious way of their system, we were not accredited with their newly imposed standards and had to repeatedly ask if we had actually passed ourselves. Frustrating as this could be it was always worth remembering that LEAs were often just so back in England. In time the call came one day and was more of a 'Oh by the way you are accredited now for SEN!' This success then inspiring the owner's wife to have a few days lauding the staff and students ... and bathing in the glow herself. This positivity welcome yet confusing for the staff. Soon all went back to normal and staff would scurry away should she be seen heading towards them.

My escape from this unpleasant working environment continued to be weekend visits to the Beach Club where a friend had a catamaran which I would often help crew. These days were a delight after the fury of school. On one such rest day we sailed in a series of competition races. With no prior experience I skippered in a race which we actually won. On heading back with my nautical friend, he was bubbling with praise for my skill, all of which was the result of his modest tutoring. Later sat ashore in the shade with a cold lemonade to celebrate, we looked back over the week just ended. We shared the highs enjoyed and lows endured. His job as a Loss Adjuster for a multinational oil company giving me a different perspective. "There are times when you cut your losses and move on!" he said. In the bright sunshine the depth in those words struck home.

In school the following week I secured a meeting with the owner and shared my concerns for the stall in our work and the damage being done. His mood changed from his normal calm and respectful manner, to one of anger. The challenge of change was something he sorely desired and the obstacle to it was the woman he loved. He left the meeting saying we would talk again.

The following week two things occurred that would dictate a solution to the situation. Firstly, I attended a high brow function at the British Embassy and after a humorous chat over many glasses of wine with a member of this Arab country's Royal Family I was introduced to two RAF Officers. We compared notes on all manner of things including similar experiences at RAF Camps in Lincolnshire and Germany. Then they offered a bit of advice as jet fighter pilots freshly based in the country. They first asked what I was doing in the New Year and when I answered I expected to still be in the country they replied, "You might want to rethink that!" and winked. In previous weeks we had all noticed the increased number of thick necked American personnel in their fatigues in the shopping malls so this 'tip' was fully understood. Saddam Hussein was still in power in nearby Iraq and tensions were rising daily. Reports on BBC World Service and CNN making many twitch and worry.

Then I received a call at my flat from the UK. An old friend from Yorkshire who worked as an OFSTED Team Leader had recently inspected three schools and failed each. Two of them were EBD Special Schools, one in London. Both him and the HMI who was an advocate of my leadership had put my name forward to the Director of Education of the London LEA. In our phone conversation he encouraged me to attend an interview for the school adding, "The school is in a mess and failed in every category. There's only one direction it can go ... so come back and take it there!" I really didn't need any further encouragement. Faced with the possibility of my work being undone by an International tyrant, as well as one more local, what had I to lose?

I found myself in the Council Offices of a London LEA meeting with the Director, SEN Inspector and Chair of Governors. They recounted the sad demise of the school and the subsequent loss of the Headteacher. It was not a pretty story at all. I was asked for my thoughts and they were greeted with energetic nods of the head. Then asked to sit in the adjacent room while they considered things, I picked up the local paper and noticed the high prices for renting property. When they returned to sit with me the Director offered me the job there and then. They announced that nobody else had been or was going to be interviewed. In replying I added that the salary would have to include free accommodation, which he agreed without blinking. Their enthusiasm at unloading their huge headache and embarrassment was such that I was convinced I should have also held out for a chauffeur and magnum of champagne each Friday at four p.m.. We shook hands, then the Director said that this meeting remained Confidential as the school were unaware of what was happening, and this also meant that I could not visit. As strange as the scenario was, it paled into insignificance with the prospect of a war looming in the corridors of my school and the Gulf as a region.

I flew back to the Gulf and went to see the owner. He was unhappy that I was to leave but honest in saying that it removed a fight from his agenda with his own wife. Our discussion was frank and I shared with him a list of issues that would need fixing before his school haemorrhaged staff and students. He took notes and apologised for my efforts not being fully realised. We agreed that I would meet his wife and explain to her what was happening.

The following day as I waited to enter her room her Secretary peered at me over her glasses sympathetically as if I was the condemned man. On entering the room, I was greeted with much the same level of enthusiasm as at our first ever meeting by the owner's wife. Then she started to speak with the words, "Mr Kim I am sorry ..." but I interrupted and said, "Me too, and as your husband knows I will be leaving in two weeks to take up a position in the UK". Her jaw dropped, indicating she had not been told anything by her husband. I added, "In the light of your desire to be the School Director again, perhaps I should relinquish the role now and just enjoy my time otherwise until I leave?" And so it ended. She was clearly happy albeit I sensed she was frustrated at not being able to deliver some sort of 'coup de gras'.

219

I spent the next few weeks organising my departure. Saying good bye to my key staff off-site and enjoying my last visits to the fascinating old Souk with Arab friends.

One such evening, it was one of them that said to me as we wandered through the market with our nostrils full of the smell of sheesha, "Mr Kim, have you noticed that God must like crazy people?" When I enquired why he thought that was the case he replied, "Well look around you, it must be so, for he has put many of them on this earth!"

How true his words were and how good it was to fly away from one of them.

Chapter 13

From the Ashes

I arrived at Bromley South railway station on my first day and was picked up by one of the two Deputies. We had spoken briefly on the phone a week earlier. This being my first ever contact with any of the staff. As we drove towards school, he gave me a first-hand explanation of what had happened to the school. He emphasised it was a good place and that the staff were good people. He added that the school was just 'in bad times'. His deep sigh speaking volumes as to how it had impacted on him and was still hurting.

To walk into a school that had failed its OFSTED Inspection on all counts and just seen its headteacher sacked was definitely my biggest challenge to date. To be appointed without seeing the school or meeting the staff may have seemed foolhardy, but it was my new reality. On arrival my first impression was of many sets of suspicious eyes looking me up and down trying to work out who this person was parachuted in to fix things. As one member of staff soon put it, "How is it that we need somebody so special they have to be brought from a Gulf war zone to lead us ... was there nobody in the UK?"

My introduction was a balance between my experience with EBD pupils and the quest for the highest standards possible with the caveat that any journey taken was one in partnership with them all and that we had to have fun in the process. It was clear that the idea of having fun in teaching in that school was a distant memory and the haunted looks on many, showed that finding their smiles may be one of the most difficult tasks ahead of me.

The school was for around eighty boys aged seven to sixteen years old with severe emotional and behavioural difficulties. A title which was to change several times over the next few years at the behest of the Education Department with EBD, BESD, SEBD and SEMH being played around with … but the client group staying the same. I often added the acronym WTFK when colleagues started playing the 'acronym game' when talking of their provision and forgetting to mention 'children'.

Explanations were sought as to where WTFK originated from when I was at an early meeting with Special Head colleagues from across the borough. I had slipped it in when the acronyms were flying around with regularity. In an attempt to bring us back to talking about children and needs I had thrown in this new one. After several uses of it there was a pause and some had 'confused faces' (not meant to be a collective noun for LEA Officers). The question came up, "Kim, what are the WTFKs?" My reply ended the latest game of Top Trumps in my career when I said with a straight face, "Who The F★★★ Knows!" Thereafter sense prevailed and we spoke of real children. Additionally, my credibility with my new peers was acknowledged with a chuckle … for labels were not enough!

The staff were all seasoned at the school and the previous head had been a very effective Deputy by all accounts but seemingly lost his way in respect of leading the school as a Headteacher. He had been well respected, however they recognised that his primary role had been unfulfilled and then the difficulties followed. There were two Deputies. One a well-versed and competent practitioner with both theory and practice on her side. The other, much longer serving, a most likeable man who seemed to be a touch shell shocked and needing to be propped.

At this point I knew that many others in my position would say that the best way forward would be to affect a big staff turnover in order to move a school on from such a dire position.

This judgement call needing to be made as soon as possible as it would have profound and immediate consequences. I had to think carefully and know who my staff were and what they were capable of before I acted. That first day I quickly gauged the quality and potential of the senior and long-serving staff … and made a decision.

The Leadership Team was extended by me beyond the two Deputies to include the three Key Stage Team Leaders and the Senior Social Worker who ran the social work and therapy team. This was a good move as they were the link to the staff and respected. Through them ideas and strategies would be translated into practice to reap potential success.

The Governors were a group of well-meaning and supportive individuals who needed to develop their role and responsibility in holding me to account. The quality of teaching was overall fairly poor and the behaviour of the pupils without a doubt challenging beyond belief. So much to do and now I truly understood my friend's remarks about there was only one way the school could go after he inspected it. This school, the pupils, curriculum, behaviour, staff, governance and leadership and management were definitely rock bottom.

Two days were spent as a staff team going through establishing a behaviour code, rewards and sanctions, curriculum expectations of teaching and learning, and how end of day meetings would review practice and identify next steps for the following day. The start point was that the behaviour of pupils was the reason for them being with us. If it was extreme resulting in injury or significant disruption and damage, then a pupil would be excluded for a short-fixed term. They would then be returned to the fold to 'try again'. The idea being each time a line was to be drawn in the sand saying 'You need to end this behaviour and move on'. In the first term about four in five pupils were excluded and returned. For the first time this was the school saying 'We accept this is how you do behave, but you must understand it is not acceptable. We will work with you to make you better prepared and more able to improve your own behaviour.'

In that time, I was head-butted, punched, kicked, spat at, had a finger broken and sworn at using every profanity available. Throughout it was important to be unmoved and resilient. I had to be seen to have strength in affecting change, as by doing so the staff would see me stand strong and they too could begin stepping up to the mark.

One rather disturbing moment being with a sixteen-year-old who was keen to leave the premises and yet doing everything he could to trash everywhere and abuse everyone ... but nowhere near the exit route. As two of us tried to calm him and his repeated spitting was both splattering my clothing and dripping down the outside of my face, it crossed my mind that twenty-five years earlier perhaps working in a Prep School might have been a better choice. My thoughts also returned to the Gulf and despite the outbreak of war there, I was now trying to calm the significant conflict here ... and it seemed that this setting was riskier.

The boy, as strong as an ox and now becoming extreme in his physical assault on a member of staff, was being held to prevent further escalation and more importantly hurt. At this point his enriched Anglo-Saxon expletives were rattling from his mouth in all directions. "You are a f★★★ing bast★★d, I'm going to f★★★ing kill you you c★★★!" being directed towards me.

Recalling the 'engage to deflect strategy' tried and tested with North Yorkshire's fine young men I thought I'd try it with one of London's equals. I replied, "I'm sure you are wrong as I met two elderly people at the weekend, and they remain convinced I'm their lawful son ... so you see I can't be the 'F★★★ing Bast★★d' you claim I am ... or they are completely off their trolley!" He looked perplexed at my explanation and certainly upset with my ability to use to such expletives, replying, "You are crazy, you are … and you shouldn't use those words!"

He had a point, which I acknowledged with a knowing smile, the spit now dripping past one of my ears. "So what's this about killing me?" I enquired. "I'm here to help you and the staff turn this place around so the world doesn't label us all as losers and failures." At this point his anger subsided and it was safe for him and us to let go of him. "I'm tired now and need to go home to rest" he said. Then he sat on the floor where he remained for twenty minutes while the Deputy and myself tidied ourselves up and got a cup of tea each. We sat on the floor with him and his anxieties about home and worries about the future beyond the summer and leaving school poured out. At this point, one of the psychodynamic therapists appeared and took him to the section of the school where that invaluable work was delivered so skilfully. Later in an end of the day debrief he reported back and included the apology the boy said he would deliver the following day. Which he did … and I accepted with a shake of his hand. This being my signature with the boys that 'a deal was done … and now we move on.'

Such inner torment and sense of trouble racked many of the boys and they would swing between complete academic engagement and on task behaviour to a most dramatic explosion of anger, tirade of abuse and hurling of chairs in a flash of a second. These souls were deeply troubled and the therapists work helped somewhat in calming and refocusing their inner storm. There were others though for whom it was a well-learned and played out game to deflect from any attempt to enhance their schooling. The curriculum often not engaging their imagination or curiosity. Sometimes the expectation that the next hour will be an academic single task was clearly beyond their ability and interest level. Here the Deputies and Team Leaders started to challenge thinking of the staff, as to what could work and why. Staff

Briefings saw sharing of 'What Worked Well' and 'Even Better If' moments from lessons related to pupil progress in their studies and behaviour.

When HMI came back for the first visit, they saw the green shoots of this starting to work and noted the school was calmer. The relationship with the HMI was proving to be key in the process. We challenged each other as to the What, Why, How and When in everything. This was not a process of being judged, this was a partnership in making something work better. I knew it was important to 'listen and consider ... then engage and work together'. This being a quite straight-forward strategy and one where I needed to be a confident equal ... so it could really work.

After some very long days, which often included being in my office over the full weekend ... there was now a School Development Plan and it detailed responsibilities, costings, success criteria and timelines. This pleased the HMI greatly. I shared with her the comments of the LEA SEN Inspector where the admission "I knew the school was failing!" had been said to me without a flicker of emotion ... but there was no explanation given as to what had been done with the former Head to stop the slide into chaos and failure. HMI and I agreed that the LEA had been culpable in the sorry state of affairs and as such it would pay to be guarded in taking any of their advice as time progressed. This was borne out by a poorly chaired review meeting with the LEA when two of their members seemed more keen to attribute the success to their personal engagement with the school. They did so without reference to all the hard work of a team of staff who had started to believe in themselves and find a collective energy to improve. Interestingly, after this meeting neither came anywhere near the school for the rest of the year.

As for the SEN Inspector, it became evident that being cautious was her way forward. When I outlined a plan to introduce an off-site educational base for some of the Year elevens she said it would be frowned upon by OFSTED and criticised by the LEA. My response was to ignore these words and go ahead with the project. An immediate return being that attendance for this group jumped from forty to eighty per cent. in a term. When the HMI came in for her second visit she asked if she could get a Case Study done on it as it was a great example worth sharing more widely. By the time that was written the attendance was just below ninety per cent. The fact that education both academic and work-related had enticed these pupils in and they had displayed minimal behavioural problems was of little interest to the LEA. It seemed after having disagreed with it they could not swallow their misplaced pride and admit they had been wrong. Naturally this didn't bother the staff leading the work ... but it did add to their contempt for the LEA's SEN section.

It is easy ... perhaps too easy sometimes ... to bow to the established words of the LEA and other learned organisations. However, experience had taught me to be resilient and have the strength of conviction in my ability to move things forward. I was not afraid to be a maverick. After all ... nothing ventured ... nothing gained!

Before leaving, the HMI fed back to me in my office and cited numerous areas where the progress had been better than she expected. Warm examples of relationships between staff and pupils were mentioned by her as evidence of a significant change in the school. We joked that the only omission in her report seemed to be in not referencing the headed goal by me in the lunchtime playground football match. I felt it was important to note all improvement detail and it was duly added.

A hearty breakfast club delivered a welcome but probably unhealthy cooked breakfast each morning. Staff and pupils sat side by side eating and talking in the closest thing many would probably experience to a family setting. This ensured a good start to most days. Subsequent behaviour and engagement in class work was excellent as the soporific effect of bacon, eggs, sausages and beans with a cup of tea ensured no drama disturbing the calm air of our changing school. Should anybody then struggle and need support the teacher leading learning could call for one of the senior team or Behaviour Support Assistants.

One morning I was called to an English lesson where the teacher, after many attempts, could not deflect a pupil's attention from ridiculing one of his peers. The reading of the text constantly being stalled ... so my presence requested. On arrival, the disrupter went silent ... the lesson progressed ... the disrupter became a distinguished contributor to learning ... and before half an hour was up, I was immersed in a Shakespearean production of immense calibre. At the end the pupils left buzzing with enjoyment and the teacher stood at the door speechless. I got up from behind a desk at the back of the class and said, "That was bloody brilliant ... well done!" I left the room and as I walked back to my office, reflected I was hard pushed to recall a better lesson with such pupils. This type of school had a charm about it ... no two minutes the same, let alone two days and that's what made it such a draw.

As for the teacher ... he grew even more in confidence from this moment forward. Another example of how important it was to never underestimate the powerful impact of support and congratulation of one of the team.

When required the two Behaviour Support Assistants were available to collect, refocus and return a pupil to a classroom and enable learning to continue. Both women, they were excellent at their job, but with different skills and approaches.

One was Afro-Caribbean with a huge personality and wonderful broad smile. When called upon she could undo the knots any pupil had tied themselves up in, and convince them that being back in class was the best thing for everyone. Often achieved by explaining to the pupil that they would help her by getting back quickly as the required paperwork was a great chore and made her grumpy. Even the most hardened and obstreperous of boys would succumb to her skilful ploy.

The other assistant was a small white Londoner likened to a Jack Russell dog by the pupils. Just to see her coming down the corridor was enough to convince them that the conversation to follow would be a greater challenge to their eardrums than the lesson would be to their brain cells. On seeing her they would put their hand up and shout "Oh it's you … okay Miss, I'm going back in and I promise I will stay and behave!" She had an answer to everything and could turn anyone inside out with her questioning. She would capture a look on her face of 'Why are you making this so difficult for yourself?' and provide half solutions like an easy crossword for the pupils to finish and follow. To stay out and spend time with her still meant they'd have to commit to change so it was a case of choose the easiest route at that specific moment. Both these staff had been to the University of Life and should have been pursuing a Doctorate in Behavioural Science.

These two stars taught me the importance of getting to know my staff well … very well. When looking for improvements one can often find such artful change-makers already within your team.

The Care Support Team comprised of three part-time therapists specialising in Art and Drama Psychodynamic approaches and two full time social workers. The lead being a fully-qualified Social Worker originally from Canada. Their work in unlocking pupil issues and supporting them then to access school more fully was of paramount importance to our provision's success. Attempts by the LEA to close it for financial reasons were resisted by me and fully supported by staff and Governors. The added dimension of working with the teaching staff and their assistants ensured school programmes addressed issues being picked up in their one to one sessions. The social workers worked with the family and added quality to the continuity of expectation in pupil behaviour. A bonus of all of this work being it happened on-site and did not require absence for attendance.

Psychiatrists from a London Teaching Hospital hot-desked on-site at our invitation to add further competencies to our provision. This was vital to ensure the most complex behaviours including deteriorating mental health conditions of some pupils could be met. The rapport between teachers, therapists, social workers and mental health workers absolutely outstanding and valued by all. This was a first-time experience for me with a wealth of skills being available for the most needy, and often mostly forgotten SEN pupil population. Across the road from the school the largest Mental Health hospital facility in London housed a specialist school for high-needs pupils. The link with their brilliant head-teacher furthering the continuing professional development of both myself and my ever-growing competent team.

This was a key moment in my career and was to have a significant impact on my thinking going forward. In a future headship this type of model would be replicated as an in-house specialism to support the wider sense of rebuilding pupil confidence and engagement. It had been right here to fight for this provision to be maintained as a quality enhancement to what was offered to these needy boys ... my pupils. This 'wrap around care' was set to be implicit in all my current and future plans to help improve sustainable pupil outcomes.

By the time the third visit came from our HMI we had a new Deputy Head. His witty and often mischievous Irish humour, wealth of Primary expertise and brilliant teaching ability further transformed the quality of teaching and learning across all three key stages. This was noted by the HMI when observing lessons and discussing with him our academic progress tracker and the link with a behavioural targeting scheme and tracker. The two-day visit was going well and all reports coming back from review meetings, lesson observations and pupil interactions indicated that we were definitely 'in the zone' and able to showcase our best practice.

On her second day she had observed the Key Stage Three Assembly and witnessed pupils showcasing their work with pride. Commenting on this, she revealed an in-depth memory of certain pupils and how in the last eleven months their whole demeanour to school had been transformed. Keen at morning break to speak with me, we were interrupted in the main hall by the pupil who had previously questioned my parentage. He was not a happy soul and swore as he impatiently tried to interrupt us. I paused and spoke with him … it was enough to convince him to come and see me later so the HMI and I could complete our conversation. At this point the HMI smiled and said, "Kim, this school doesn't need me anymore or the former poor label from its OFSTED. You and the staff have done a brilliant job and the school is excellent. Well done!"

There it was … within a year we had turned the school around and grown in the process. My excitement was bubbling as she finished talking about what she had seen and admired us for. She added that I should keep it to myself for now. She had worked out my Deputies and suggested that I hide them so they didn't leak the news before I had the staff together at the end of the day.

In respect of my longer standing Deputy, he was a real character and a handful when it came to the HMI visits. At the first one he was likened to a dog worrying sheep so was banned to his office, where he relaxed and came out later smiling and saying it had worked for him and the staff. His anxiety expended in that brief isolation. At the second visit he decided to bombard the Inspector with 'what we can do' evidence. He took it so literally he actually stopped her from doing a lesson observation by drowning her in information about pupil work and progress. She commended him for his enthusiasm and the richness of evidence provided. Then finally at the time of the third, he had the news shared with him nearly two hours before the staff. Immediately he burst into tears of relief and hugged me. I then sent him to his office again to keep the news confidential from the staff until the end of the school day.

Once all the pupils had left site, having been collected by their taxis, the full staff team were all gathered in the staff room. They were sat there waiting very nervously, keen to hear how we had done in this, the third visit. When I broke the news, my voice faltered with emotion. It was greeted by an enormous cheer and then several of them just burst into tears and hugged each other. The joy of achievement and the relief after all that work was immense. That same team bar two changes in personnel had risen from the ashes of abject failure to be a beacon of light and centre of excellence. The year had been about putting structure in place, challenging mediocrity, aspiring for excellence, supporting each other, believing in the sense of being a team, valuing all and ... yes, having fun together. It had worked!

Even though it was a week-day, it was agreed that we should all reconvene in a nearby pub as the celebrations warranted a few strong drinks. The emotion there still so powerful, that tears replaced laughter, and laughter in turn reverted to tears. My Leadership Team gathered around me requesting a silent moment to allow the teacher who asked about 'why has someone been brought from the Arabian War Zone' to add his postscript. The thank you for taking the job comment being a great moment for me. The rebuild of Kim complete now, as well as this great community.

Meanwhile, outside the pub it started to snow and a bit of fun in the car park saw our Social Worker inadvertently cut the head of a P.E. teacher with a snowball (containing a piece of loose stone!). The trickle of blood down the P.E. teacher's face being of no consequence to her as the celebratory drinks had anaesthetised her senses completely. Hours later the staff drifted away through the falling snow to their homes, exhausted by the news and drained of energy in their celebratory evening. The realisation of their success ensuring that when they fell to sleep their smile surely remained.

I closed the school the following day. The snowfall doing likewise across the rest of the borough.

The pupils were pleased at the news, and questioned what that meant for them in the days going forward. They wanted to know if it meant that I would be leaving to go and fix somewhere else. I had no such plans and told them so. In time some said "It's a shame you didn't f★★★ off!" It was important for them to remind me why they were at the school and that the job with them was not yet completely finished.

Some pupil behaviours posed challenges over the following months. The collection of police evidence bags regularly being filled with knives and other offensive weapons brought in to school but thankfully never brandished in anger at all. One day news broke that a fourteen-year-old had stolen some percussion explosives from a railway building, and brought them into school. These explosives were used as a method of warning those trackside that a train was approaching. One had already been detonated and caused a small tree to topple. The news was that the boy was being pursued in our small woodland area by others trying to hit him with stones, as other explosives were in his pockets. This was a new dimension to my experience with these pupils and now I could claim that active Bomb Disposal work was only a footstep away. The boy was found intact and his pocket contents handed over with him to British Transport Police.

Some weeks later he was in the thick of it again, having upset two older boys who pursued him at lunchtime towards the basketball court. Here he climbed up the stand and sat in the hoop. When the duty staff arrived from nearby, he threatened to kill himself because of the threats issued by the other boys. When I arrived, he embarked on that attempt and only by sitting on the Deputy head's shoulders was I able to hold him with one arm while cutting the hoop nets away from his neck. Safely to the ground he was taken away by his Therapist.

Lots of further work with him resulted in real breakthroughs in his behaviours which unhappily were not being sustained out of school. Sadly, this resulted in his death in circumstances that never became clear to us as a staff. His funeral widely attended by many in the local Afro-Caribbean community and staff from the school. His coffin open throughout the service reminding us that he had an angelic face ... even in death.

He was not the only pupil we lost that year. Another had stepped in to try and stop a fight and was pushed away. He stumbled backwards and fell to the ground striking his head on the kerb-stone. He died within days from the resultant brain haemorrhaging. His well-meaning actions had resulted in this tragic accident. The impact on Key Stage Four Staff was significant as he had truly turned the corner with his behaviour and become as close to a good role model as they had to show off to those coming up through the school. He had also been one of those that had flown to the USA in a trip fully funded by external donations and activities organised by staff. That trip being a key moment in his personal decision to turn his life around and be positive in his approach to school.

We hadn't seen any signs of graffiti in school at all for a year, then some started to appear in the toilets. Having noted the Tag and taken a photo of it, the same was seen on a pupil's exercise book. He refused to acknowledge it was all of his doing, but the evidence was pretty clear cut. At the time British Transport Police were engaged with schools in trying to identify such tags on bus-es, trains and along rail side. As a result of this boy's indiscretion the school received a reward, the boy a fine and the word spread. Never again any graffiti found in school proving the old saying 'There are many ways of skinning a cat!'

The work produced by the pupils was often exemplar and went towards accrediting their progress in attainment. As some would try and destroy it ... either because they weren't completely at peace with being held up as an achieving learner, or they felt it wasn't very good ... the staff would literally snatch it away. It would be placed in their work folders and sometimes displayed on the walls in classrooms or corridors. Again, to save it from being ripped down these display boards were framed and covered with as good an armoured equivalent plastic as we could buy. Only then would they all sign a truce about damaging their own efforts.

On a very sad afternoon one of the seven-year-olds who had been displaying mental health issues saw a Teaching Assistant replacing work behind such covering. He was reported as saying "Oh I know they know where I live, but I didn't know they knew where I went to school!" He then picked up a piece of the wooden frame and struck the Teaching Assistant across the head splitting her face open from mouth to lower jaw. She was hospitalised and never really fully recovered from the physical scars and mental trauma. The boy was admitted to the Psychiatric wing of the School in the adjacent Hospital. Here assessments revealed he had been seeing monsters and the TA had been mistaken for one. He spent months there and was trialled on various drugs and programmes. At the end of this, I recall being appalled that the LEA repackaged his case files to try and secure a place for him at a similar school to mine in a neighbouring LEA. I phoned the school in question both for their sake and the long-term prospects of this poor boy. It was important to be open and honest with them.

In this case I never found out what happened next. Another lesson here for me in the smoke and mirrors used by some LEAs ...

much of which I was still to experience.

The Director of Children's Services (DCS) was mightily pleased with the HMI outcome for our school. His gamble in appointing me while on a secret visit from the Gulf had paid off ... as had been strongly suggested by HMI and OFSTED colleagues. He acknowledged my tongue in cheek remark that it was rare for a DCS to welcome a call from the Head of an EBD School as it could so often be to announce some sort of school disaster. His enthusiasm transmitted to the staff and it restored some faith in the LEA. Interestingly, the Inspector and all others with an opinion were not seen again for the following year. We were convinced that they were happier staying away ... and we were in agreement with them.

The challenges in EBD Special Schools and Pupil Referral Units had always been huge and the responsibility on leaders in them a real tight rope to walk. There was a saying going around that there were two types of such Head ... those that were suspended and those that were soon to be. Such was the feeling of isolation for them in trying to raise and maintain standards in these settings. In recognition of this a joint National College for School Leadership (NCSL) and London Challenge scheme was put together to work with such school leaders across London Boroughs. My name had been put forward and I went on to be trained as Consultant Leader with seven other colleagues from similar high-performing settings. The training was thorough and no expense was spared in funding our work.

I found myself in PRUs and Special Schools across six London Boroughs. The emphasis being on developing Leadership capacity that could be sustained when we stepped away. It meant for the next year that I was out for a day a week coaching and delivering training to school leaders and their staff teams. Without a doubt all I worked with were committed to their settings and pupils. They wanted to improve and be able to continue just so into the future. In some cases, the results were pretty quick and in one school the key changers were then cherry picked by another school with great contract offers. This required starting all over again before the school in question slipped back into a poor OFSTED category.

Such schools needed to have someone from outside for the Headteacher's to relate to and have as a critical friend and mentor. The fact was that every school would benefit from having such a link with another school leader colleague. It works ... for both parties. When given such a chance these headteachers in London needed no encouragement and took the offer without hesitation.

I recall in one North London setting arriving off the tube, and when walking to the nearby PRU feeling very self-conscious. The area was poor in its housing, with obvious other signs of social deprivation and many youths huddled on street corners. In the context of where I was going, no big deal, but I didn't wear my suit and carry an obvious laptop bag on my next visit. The Head commented on my more suitable camouflage thereafter.

One of the schools I worked with had recently appointed a new Headteacher. A dynamic sportsman and great motivator who needed a 'disciple from another land' to assist in training his staff team. We worked very well together and with me providing a 'professional echo' to his mantra, things really turned around quickly. We were later both invited to visit the USA by the British Council with eight other Heads from Special Education across London. Our trip saw us visit schools and Correctional Facilities with mental health education provision in Maryland. While there, our friendship grew.

During the visit we were allocated to a setting and I ended up in an Elementary School run by a charming Principal called Keith. He was an ex-military man who had taken his qualifications to become a School Principal, which is a non-teaching administrative role. The five days I spent visiting his school and meeting with him and his family were splendid. Since that time in 2004 we have written two or three times a year and become good friends. His school had a sixty per cent. Hispanic pupil population and served a mixed area of both poverty and affluence. It was a joy to visit and no effort was spared by him in making every pupil and teacher feel important and valued in his school.

When visiting the correctional facility, I was struck by the robust and jolly nature of the Afro-American Principal. We spent an hour sharing ideas, experiences, practices and philosophy on working with those challenged by their mental health and subsequent behaviours. Her knowledge and insight were tremendous and it was like being in a high-speed intensive Professional Development session. Later I was sat in a maths lesson with fifteen-year-olds being taught algebra way beyond any previous experience of mine. In the class were students with significant issues some of whom had committed serious crimes. I felt intimidated and anxious in their presence ... not by their personal life stories and the possibility of violence suddenly occurring ... it was more a fear of being asked a question about the maths! One boy who sat next to me was very polite and engaging. He punctuated everything he said with the title 'Sir'. As we got talking, he alluded to his troubled mental health and the difficulty it presented to him. He mentioned that this was a family trait and that it was more prevalent in the most intelligent members, going back in time adding that a grandparent had been one of the scientists working on the Oppenheimer Project making the atomic bomb in WW2. He added that he was due for his weekly review with his Psychiatrist saying, "I hope he doesn't mess with my meds as they are really working at present and I feel great ... Sir!"

When I got back to the Principal's Office she was intrigued with my findings and over a coffee we furthered our sharing of practice. When the taxi arrived to return me to our hotel, she stunned me with the offer of a position with her as Vice Principal. She added, "You see Kim I am known by all here as a 'Bad Ass' and I think that we could make this place even better together!" I said I was flattered and would think about it. Tempting as it was, my own school and the Consultant Leader role were providing me with enough – so I declined.

A month after returning to the UK I was back into the school with the Head I'd been to the USA with. He looked grey and tired when greeting me at the door. He died from cancer the following week. At his funeral I found out from his wife that his father had also died the very same day. His son being in hospital and just about hanging on for him to arrive he had rushed in his car to be at his bedside. On the way he had a heart attack and died at the wheel of his car. The sadness and sense of loss in the room was immense. Family, friends, colleagues and pupils from his school were all there filling the pews, aisle and entrance to the church. One of his young son's reading part of the eulogy with such pride and composure, his words completely undid the emotions of all gathered to say goodbye. He was a good man, much loved father and great leader of his school, and the loss was evident in everyone's faces. His ex-wife and second wife sat side by side holding on to each other, spoke loudly of him.

The trip to the US, work in other schools and loss of a friend were all nudged to one side when back in school. I had an interview with an Irish family for their seven-year-old to be offered a place in our Primary Class. He arrived with father and social worker, all looking a touch apprehensive. I heard the long story of his disruptive behaviour and its impact on numerous schools. He clearly ticked all the boxes of our entrance criteria and when I mistakenly asked him if he would like to join us, he leapt up onto my desk and shouted at me, "I'm not coming to your f***ing school!" I looked past him at his father and said reassuringly, "Don't worry … we love a challenge!"

The following week he started and all became immediately aware of his presence each and every day. He quickly settled into a routine which mostly went this way:

Morning arrival while Breakfast Club was on, when greeted he would reply, "F★★★ Off!"

First Lesson he would arrive at my office with a piece of work completed. He would be as proud as any child and glow with a sense of achievement. When asked what the whole 'F★★★ Off' thing was about at the start of the day he would reply, "Oh yeah … sorry it's nothing I'm just moody first thing!" At break time he would hit someone in his class and swear at the teacher intervening. Before lunch he'd be back with another piece of his good work … and so the day would go on.

His rationale for it all being that he was being asked to come to school rather than be a free roaming gypsy learning from the land. When called in to see me, his father would laugh at this explanation saying that his son lived in a council house and had never even seen a caravan and been on the road. His father would also refuse to see the Deputy Head responsible for Pastoral issues saying, "Jesus … the man is from Dublin … you just can't feckin' trust such people!" My Deputy for all his wit and charm accepted the insult as a worthy excuse to let me meet his countryman.

One morning I was called to the Primary Classroom to find the little Irish boy stood hunched up with his fists clenched and his face strained in pent up anger. On the floor in front of him lay a classmate looking rather dazed. The teacher and TA quickly recounted that the boys had argued and the result was one had punched the other. It was no normal punch though as evidently it was an upper cut which was delivered with such force it lifted the recipient off his feet. I turned to our little Irish Star and said, "What have I told you about hitting others boys?" He replied, "Sir ... I've told you before ... you deal with things your way ... but leave me to deal with them mine!" Not a shred of sorrow, guilt or concern for his classmate at all. Equally so, the matter was concluded in his mind and as such teaching and learning should continue. His sense of justice being very clear and although in need of some modification, he was admired for his ability to move on.

The complexity involved in trying to unravel the minds of our pupils was a challenge our Therapists didn't shirk from. Their hard work valued as indeed was the opportunity to review cases with them and generally catch up. One of their team, the only male, was due to see me one day for such a meeting. He didn't arrive, and my secretary tracked him down in his office. When she came to me, she said I had best go and see him there. On doing so, he relayed to me his childhood trauma of school and fear of the Headteacher. Ever since that day he had been unable to step into any office of a School Leader. It felt as though the Therapist was now receiving therapy as we talked through his experiences and sought resolution. It was not a long search as we agreed to convene a meeting the following week. It would be in his office and he would provide home-made biscuits baked with his daughter. When the day came, he was true to his word and we spent a couple of hours reviewing his case load and discussing strategies to be worked through with staff. The tea and biscuits adding to the moment particularly as there was a note from his young daughter hoping I would enjoy her baking.

Our meeting highlighted the challenges of two quite different pupils in the school. One had been involved with gangland crime in the town and as a result had been sent to the Young Offenders at Feltham. In school he had been a pretty quiet individual who would settle to his work and rarely pose any physical challenges. The therapy sessions had focused on his sense of loss for an ab-sent father and how that had been instrumental in his anger towards just about all other males. Now inside, the concern was that his mental health had crashed, and he was seen as being a suicide risk. The therapist was continuing his contact to maintain support. We agreed this was right as he already spent a day a week at a London Prison with inmates. As such it was obvious that he was well-equipped for this case load.

The second pupil was the son of one of our Parent Governors who was also a suicide risk, and because of his recent mood swings causing a great deal of concern in class. It was clear that his medication for depression was also having an impact on that prescribed for his ADHD. If he wasn't found in floods of tears threatening self-harm, then he was completely animated and wild in manner. A quick referral to the Psychiatrist managing his case seemed to encourage some joined up thinking about his medications, and slowly but surely the change helped some balance to be restored. He was then back to his mostly charming self in class and his father was so relieved the next time we met. I often saw him thereafter energetically waving to me from his black cab taxi in the town.

We also got onto the topic of some staff wanting to develop the use of 'No' and 'Do not' in their everyday language. A topic we had discussed many times as a staff and made inroads ensuring that the like of 'Do not Run' was replaced with 'Please Walk' … not a behavioural revolution at all.

The conkers were falling from the four laden trees at the front of school and the pupils had taken to throwing them at each other and back at the school building. Staff were rightly concerned and had slipped into great users of "Don't …". It was easy to resolve and didn't require lumberjacks being brought in to cut down each fifty-foot tree. I purchased a length of tough string and using a screwdriver to punch a hole through the conkers set up each boy with a start point to play this age-old game. Simple rules were taught to the boys and quite a few staff resulting in competitions each break and lunch time. Winning conkers and owners celebrated in Friday's reward assembly. No more throwing .... and losing conker pieces were scooped up by their sad owners after each defeat. Problem solved ... children taught how to play and enjoy. Staff often re-living their own childhood exploits and having the bonus of an additional fun moment with their classes.

Sometimes the solutions are not obvious ... I do believe though that they don't have to be very complicated.

This therapist ended up being one of several staff I have met over the years who found my office the cause of an edginess in their otherwise professional calm and confident character. It wasn't how it was set up or very often how I used it ... it was mostly too much of a reminder of a dark moment from their own schooling. Imagine if they knew of the tales of my childhood visits to a Headteacher's study!

Not all Parents and Carers were as engaging with the school as the likes of the Taxi Driver Parent Governor. There were some who seemed to feel it vital to show their own brand of odd, abusive and aggressive behaviours. It was as if they felt it was a badge of honour requiring full venting of an array of irrational outbursts or display of inappropriate intimacy. As pupil behavioural outcomes began to improve, they would often express total embarrassment at the lack of control shown by their family elders.

During the clampdown on swearing a grandfather came in to school and began making racist remarks about the Afro-Caribbean and African heritage pupils. His language and references to them 'needing to go back to their own country' that day saw me fly out of my office to challenge him. He was adamant that he had fought in the war to enable such free speech. I corrected him saying that he had fought ... if indeed he had ... it was for equality and freedom from oppression ... and my own grandfather had often spoken of 'the need for man to own his words' ... and how we should 'beware of the racist tyrant'. It stopped him in his tracks. Luckily the passing sixteen-year-olds had just missed his outburst as they would have stood shoulder to shoulder with me ... and undoubtedly been tempted to 'give him a slap' or more.

I sent the offending grandfather from the premises telling him that he was unwelcome in our rich multicultural school community if that was his default behaviour. Naturally on getting home he grew in conviction again and constructed a letter of complaint about me. I responded with the detail of our encounter and gave notice of him being banned from the site. He never appeared again, and his grandson came to see me to apologise for ... as he put it, "The old fool doesn't think when he opens his mouth sir ... I'm sorry about his behaviour and will speak to him about it!" Now, if HMI had been in that day, she would have referenced such a notable moment in the school's progress.

Two other occurrences were rather indelicate in the position they placed staff. One was when the Social Work team were doing a home visit. The mother appeared at an upstairs window in a state of semi-undress, to speak with staff at the door below. It became obvious that the man close behind her was not there to speak to the staff as well ... as he was continuing in the sex act irrespective of the conversation that continued. It seemed a cue for the staff to invite the mother in to school for a coffee at a more convenient time ... and they left. The postscript to this being that when she did turn up for the chat, she straight away apologised for the situation saying, "It's only when my son is at school that we get the chance for any uninterrupted sex!" Evidently the staff kept a straight face and resisted saying they were sorry for arriving at such an inconvenient time.

The other also involved a mother who was at the 'hatch' to the General Office talking to my PA. The conversation had developed to the mother describing the pain of having had her breasts pierced and rings placed there ... the conversation was in full flow just as I walked into the office. At this point the mother pulled out her breasts and dropped both onto the half-door counter to show the artistry of her piercings. My PA rose to her feet and spun around with her arms raised to cover my eyes ... which wanted to look anywhere and everywhere other than towards the proud mother.

As this parent was in for her son's Annual Review of his SEN Statement and the Authority had already apologised for absence, it was clear to my PA that I might not be safe in the meeting with nobody else present. As such, an unsuspecting teacher was caught in the corridor and ushered into my office to guard me from any other revelations of tattoos and piercings. Fortunately, the teacher was the boy's tutor and made a great contribution to the review meeting completely unaware of what had happened beforehand.

My PA ... with her Irish humour and usual mischief ... would always ask after subsequent reviews if my knowledge of parents had been enhanced by any such similar random act. Her raised eyebrows and stare suggesting that anything I had to say may be challenged in detail. Fortunately, no such revelations occurred.

I saw these events as unique in helping me to realise that my staff and wider team would know the 'local issues' very well. It was important thereafter to remember they were the 'wise ones' and could give me a special insight into the local community ... and probably keep me away from similar difficult situations.

The second year ended with us having successfully worked through Investors in People which really opened up the complete understanding of every member of staff in how the school worked and each other's responsibilities. To achieve the standard also proved that coming out of Special Measures had been done with and not to the staff as the feedback comments from the IiP assessor were very complimentary about working practices and the school as a happy and supportive workplace. Both Deputies played a key role in this and enjoyed the opportunity of further developing day to day routines. A noticeable impact being an increased sense of ownership and pride in the school by all staff.

This year was quite something for my newer Deputy as he had been accepted onto the FastTrack Leadership Programme and was seen as the potential first one to make it through to Headship. Another learning curve for me being photo-shoots and filming for its publicity. In seminars as both his mentor and tutor it was interesting to engage with such confident twenty-year-olds being fashioned for headship within a target space of three years by peers not much older. I reflected that being out of mainstream for a couple of years the influx in talented new and young practitioners was such that my Deputy was part of a star-studded and most welcome intake in the profession.

Within the following year he secured a position as a Primary Head in the LEA and left to take up post. To my amusement he would often refer to 'Having done a Kim' in some sort of situation as a school leader. It seems as throughout his time with me he had learned all manner of leadership tactics to meet all types of situations. He was honest enough to say that in his final interview with the Chair of Governors, hosted at our school, he had borrowed my office. The tidy and well-ordered working environment having impressed his soon to be Chair ... and being so much better than his chaotic office with its mysterious system of losing all manner of items, yet inspiring so much positive change.

My own situation at the school was now up for review longer term. With a change in Chair of Governors and DCS at the LEA a resolution was sought quickly. The one-year temporary contract had been extended annually and now something permanent was sought. It seemed promising to me as I was still very much enjoying my role and all implicit in it. It was more than two years since a pupil had inadvertently punched me in the face … only because the boy he wanted to hit had ducked when stood next to me. My parentage was now established as authentic and remained unquestioned in any verbal outburst. If I was told to 'F★★★ Off' then 'Sir' was added and it was said in an inviting manner as if it was a journey I should enjoy. Even parents and carers were supporting our 'Zero tolerance to swearing' which was mostly working and once backed up by a parent coming into school to remonstrate with her offending son, by screaming "What have I told you about f★★★ing swearing? Now, apologise!"

No longer was it the case that pupils left us and graduated to HMYOI Feltham as a matter of course, as workplace and FE College were now the regular next step. In fact, one of our previous Year Elevens had been nominated Student of the Year at the local Further Education College. In short it was all good and quite a bit to wax lyrical about should I apply … for my current job.

The interview took place in rooms attached to a hotel in the borough. As I walked from my car to attend, I noted numerous familiar faces running by in red tracksuits. It was the Liverpool football team who were due to play Crystal Palace that night. They looked more tense than I felt, and indeed whatever the result of that game, I won my match. The interview was very thorough with my Chair of Governors, the DCS from the LEA and the Taxi Driver Governor on the interview Panel. When offered the position on a permanent basis, the new experience was to be thanked for all I'd done in making the school great, rather than for all I would have promised to do in a brand-new job.

My work in evaluating our progress continued with a series of lesson observations to identify teaching strengths and any possible training needs for the following year. In a Science lesson I was impressed by the young female teacher in her delivery of sex education and the reproduction of humans. Many a teacher having winced at the thought of the topic having to be taught and in the case of teaching it to EBD boys they would have thrown a sicky. Not this Canadian lady with her confident 'can do' attitude. The key moment in the lesson being when one boy exclaimed, "Oh how disgusting ... if that's how you become pregnant, I'm never having sex!" When recounted in staff briefing the following morning there were several who said that this statement would ... if true ... be good for future peace and order and the greater good of mankind in the years to follow.

On a personal note, my marriage had suffered from my absence working in the Gulf and London while home was still on the Yorkshire Coast. Undoubtedly, I had rebuilt my professional self and now had an improved sense of place in my work. Sadly, and with much regret, my ability to be a distant husband undid my personal life and increasingly I felt detached. It came to a head when one morning I woke up and realised I just didn't fit any more. What happened next was my fault and I had nobody to help me unravel the mess I was both in, and causing. At that moment in my life, I had nobody to turn to for guidance.

At the same time a job caught my eye in the TES one Friday and I put together an application. My default on how to cope was seemingly to change job and let the new challenge consume me.

I was offered an interview in the South East for a large Secondary Special School to start in the September. The opportunity to work with children primarily with learning difficulties and autism being well within my ability ... so I went into the two-day process with confidence. The Governors and Local Authority were a pleasant panel and for the first time in twenty plus years looking for a new Head. Out of experience and to a degree rather out of touch of more up to date developments in SEN, they were not difficult to impress.

What came across was that they were looking for someone nice to continue the unquestionable good work of the current incumbent. What they ended up with was a choice between two candidates. One was someone nice who had framed their pitch exactly as the panel wanted. The other was me who recognised the school was a sleeping giant and wanted to wake it up, raise standards and professional competencies and go on to make it a centre of excellence in the South East. The Governors deliberated for several hours afterwards and phoned me that evening, as I got up out of the barber's chair, to offer me the position. Without hesitation I accepted.

The following Monday I had a Staff Meeting with all the current team and went through the arrangements for activities ahead. After feedback from other ongoing projects, I announced my news. I watched colleagues who had become friends crumble in front of me as the full meaning of my words registered. You often hear of silence being deafening and indeed it was at this moment. As the staff left the meeting there wasn't a word spoken. A couple gave me a hug but couldn't find the words to say anything. I left the room and found one of my social work team in the corridor besides himself in tears.

What had I done? The shock and upset was enormous … I just wanted the ground to open up and swallow me at that very moment. It was after all only a matter of months since I had accepted leading them into the future.

That mood prevailed for a number of weeks and it translated into a similar impact on some of our pupils. Fortunately, a training day was due, and the focus was changed to a variety of team building events at a Scouting Centre in the countryside. A day of many activities on all sorts of outdoor apparatus requiring quick thinking, body balance and buckets full of humour. It all brought us back together … and the barbeque and beer at the end of it saw us recounting many tales of woes and hilarity from the past three years … and the day we had just spent together.

None causing more laughter than the last activity which saw a TA and myself climbing telegraph poles while harnessed to ropes held by staff colleagues. On reaching the top we each had to exchange a tennis ball taken up in our pockets from beneath our chin to the other person's. Her ball was first to be passed, without success … then came my turn. As we almost completed this most intimate of a high acrobatic manoeuvre, those holding my rope just let it slip enough for me to drop and my face to be enveloped in her bust. The laughter was deafening and evidently my face the richest red ever witnessed by anyone. My apology accepted, the TA was then surrounded by her giggling colleagues.

The year ended with me bidding a great team of staff a very fond farewell. The memories we had made having changed so many of our lives. We had laughed and cried together as more than work colleagues, and all been the richer for the experience.

That key ingredient of a working relationship bonding colleagues had been forged with steely determination … which had held strong. It was valued by all. Such a foundation had made our sense of purpose determined and helped me immeasurably in my leading role.

My remaining Deputy had lasted the course and was the stronger for it. His loyalty and devotion to me immense. His commitment to our pupils … the boys we had been trying to turn into much better young men … this was unquestioned and indeed it was what every single day we spent together had been all about.

Our school had indeed risen from the ashes with its almost full original staff team. The whole community was together again in its desire and ability to provide the best for some of the most complex boys in South East London … and lets be honest, they were some of the most deserving too.

Part Four

A Bigger Stage for Successful Leadership

The journey to this point as a school leader had been about building, repairing and renovating schools to ensure they provided a great workplace for the adults and a shrine of opportunities for the pupils.

Creating in all staff a real sense of ownership in their school had been important and integral to it improving in the quality of education provided. The staff knowing that whatever their role whether it be cleaner, teacher, admin. assistant, teaching assistant, therapist or caretaker they were valued and respected for their performance of role. Part Three would have shown you how eventually that had won through and the pupils were more successful in their personal and academic development.

In all cases the words of Henry Adams rang true:

"They know enough those who know how to learn."

To move to my fourth school leadership role was to take on a new challenge. The staff who were genuinely happy in the performance of their school were unwittingly fooled by their acceptance of mediocrity because it was comfortable and unchallenged. They were compounded in this belief by the poor performance of an OFSTED team who had avoided the reality and necessity of an honest judgement.

If the art of teaching is a great way to keep learning, then those previously leading had not taught their team much at all of the ways of the educational world ... that had so passed them by.

It was Graham Cooke who said:

"Mediocrity is always invisible until passion shows up and exposes it."

This was the new challenge ... for although OFSTED may have said they were 'Good' the truth was they were 'Not Good Enough'. So the route forward required an acknowledgement that although perfection may not be attainable, if we were to chase it we could catch excellence. My task was clear. Taking a school team with you when many cannot recognise 'that the height of mediocrity is still low' will cause difficulties and in Part Four you will see how this was quite simply 'Oh so true!'

It took for me to take a chance ... take a risk ... find that passion in my key players ... rekindle it ... and then get them to love the pursuit of better ways and better days.

Here you will see how changing people as well as their minds ended up being the best strategy. Helped incredibly so by a mentor of great skill, experience and insight. I had known that a lot of people had gone further than they thought because someone else thought they could. This man was such a star and much welcomed for all his time. He engineered thinking so it wasn't just a case of 'Who can be your mentor ... but also who can you mentor'. That empowerment meant that all I wished for was achieved because a man from another land appeared and spoke the same words. The difference being in his gift of ensuring that nobody initially knew how to say 'No' ... and in time we had both helped them such that they only knew how to ask, 'What is next for me to do?'

New teams evolved and then they too grew new leaders who became the most able of all I had the pleasure to work with in my career. The next chapter will take you through that part of the journey and then a further chapter will finish with the realisation of greater things than Excellence in Everything. This achieved despite the inadequacies of a Local Authority still haemorrhaging its quality individuals and losing sight of its responsibility to school leaders.

The stepping out of a school ... by now an academy ... to take on the responsibility of a national representative role beckoned. It would mean being on a stage where effective change in policy and practice meant duelling with Ministers and Education Officials. This was an enthralling period and one where many years with behaviourally challenged boys was to prove of great use in sustaining my patience and resolve to assist them with their own learning and knowledge shortfall.

In this latter part of my journey the realisation of an Outstanding Grade meant a trio of such successes with each of my three English Headships. None so sweet as this with the most brilliant of students and a staff who were magicians.

As was said to me at the end of my time:

"The students may in time forget what you said ... but they will never forget how you made them feel."

You will see in this part of my book that there was a right time in my career when I knew it is time to hang up my 'teaching gown' ... be it real or imaginary.

When that time came ... it was as clear as day ...

I knew I was done ... and it was time to let go.

Chapter 14

From Muddleway to Great Ways

The OFSTED Report received the previous year indicated a good school yet when you went into the detail you couldn't help but question whether that was accurate. All the indications were it was less than, and if anything it was coasting along almost oblivious to the changing educational landscape taking place around it. The Council in its wisdom or otherwise had decided that mainstream schools were the responsibility of the Education Directorate, Special Schools were in Social Care and the Pupil Referral Units were in Youth Justice. This rather presupposed that those students in PRUs were destined for a future in the criminal justice system and both they and Special Schools were beyond the skillset of Education Officials. This may have contributed to the school I was about to take over having been in a backwater where the lead of Social Care and her team had little experience and even less support from her contemporaries in Education. Anyway, it was my new challenge, and all said and done, in much better shape than the start point of my previous school.

Faced by over a hundred and twenty staff from teaching, teaching assistant, admin., therapy and site teams sat in the large hall awaiting my presence and introduction, I was game to launch in with my take on where we were and my vision moving forward. The bottom line for me being that 'Life in our school was not just anything … it was a great opportunity to do something very special'. I noted the achievements of the Summer examinations and specific phrases in the OFSTED Report highlighting best practice. Smiles rippled through the gathering. I noted the absence statistics for staff and posed questions as to why they were so high and what must the impact be on those left to pick up the pieces. This was met by numerous nodding heads and an attempt to generate clapping. I told them who I was and what my experience had been. This being greeted with more vigorous nodding on hearing it was my fourth 'Headship'. I explained how I would get to know them as practitioners by taking time to watch them perform their skills. A few squirmed. I then added that I would get to know them as individuals to understand them better as my team. Smiles returned to the squirming few. Then I concluded with a vision of our school aiming for the highest accolade of delivering the very best for our students and being a happy place to work in every day. The irony in the last phrase registering smiles with those wanting to clap earlier. On finishing with the line "Now I am one of you and pleased to be so". I was greeted with surprising loud applause from all and then several walked towards me to shake my hand.

Ice broken, hearts warmed, backs slapped, and imagination challenged, I left the full staff to meet with my Leadership Team.

My Deputy had been on the staff a long time. Well thought of and clearly a good practitioner he had been interviewed for the Headteacher's position with me. The three Senior Teachers had differing responsibilities. The one leading the Autistic Provision totally committed to her team and students but had a sense of frustration and doubt about her abilities. The one responsible for the Post Sixteen Provision seemed tired and equally doubtful about herself. The third and most competent, engaging and forward-looking was soon to retire and had responsibility for Pastoral issues. She was alive with ideas and the notion of improvement. I sensed my arrival had lit up her hopes for the future, once departed. The final member of the team was the Business Manager who was jolly and hard-working with already a depth of understanding as to where the school was in all aspects. As individuals they clearly had something to offer in maintaining standards ...

the problem being this was not enough. My challenge with them was to find a pathway towards agreeing the School's actual health without being seen as over keen to rubbish all that had gone before. If I had five minutes with them collectively to do an honest share, then I knew it could pay dividends.

It took about a month to watch every teacher supported by their TA teach a lesson and then talk over their style of teaching, last training course, aspirations for the future, challenges and ideas of possible solutions, and what they wanted from me. I also met with each of the TAs for a short time covering the same topics and had the opportunity to hear more of them as people, as they tended to be less guarded than the teachers. The picture evolving was they believed they had more to offer but organisationally it had not been captured and realised in the past. The time seemed right after this to open up the debate with my Senior Leadership Team (SLT) and be honest about their school ... now our school.

The moment was enhanced by a rare meeting hosted by the LEA and run by the Assistant Director for Education. Yet this meeting was only for Special Schools. We were introduced to a Consultant who was to be offered as a School Improvement Partner (SIP). Confused a touch by the lead being taken by the very person who was not responsible for our schools ... but should have been ... I persevered. The SIP on offer had real experience in Special as a Headteacher, LEA Inspector/Adviser and Lead OFSTED Inspector. What was there not to like or want? For me it was a case of 'Yes please ... when can you start?' The same for two others but not the third. It was at this meeting I realised that the notion of a collective of Special School Heads supportive of each other and friendly in manner ... was just not the case. The word that came to mind was 'Dysfunctional'. It was too early in my time in the LEA to try and impact on that.

When the SIP came to the school, our discussion throughout was on the understanding there was to be totally open and honest dialogue with no tiptoeing around the difficult topics. It worked … we were on the same page. Our agreement being the OFSTED report was wrong but kind. The school was coasting and the Head's departure must be seized as an opportunity to move things on even if it meant moving the staff on to achieve it. To get the SLT members on-side and to open them up to being honest the SIP gave them the opportunity to outline the strengths and weaknesses of their areas of responsibility and come to a judgement about it in OFSTED grade terms. The result of this being every one of the team believed the school was at best no more than 'Satisfactory'.

When we reconvened their previous sheepishness had disappeared as if they'd cleansed themselves in confession with the SIP masquerading as the village priest. We established that what we now knew was our start point and the next step was to formulate a plan to move the school forward. They were relieved that there was no blame attached, for it was now time for solutions. In addition, they warmed to my requirement of replacing the term 'Weakness' with 'Area for Development'. A change prevailed with half-full being seen as the same but better than half-empty and so it started to seep into their language.

The word was out in the staff room and corridors of school. The Head was going to make changes and was confident about making them. He was to be assisted by a SIP who was a canny fellow who would ensure it all happened. This canny fellow, Peter, became a close friend, confidant and respected mentor. Each of us in school leadership need such a person … now I had one, I meant to make the most of it.

What followed was the requirement of them all going back into their teams and evaluating all practice and identifying areas for improvement. At the same time, I commenced a full review of the quality of teaching and learning by observing every one of the sixty teachers. Middle Leaders were asked to support SLT and also evaluate their departments and year groups. All this information to be available for the next SIP Visit and be used to draw up a School Development Plan (SDP) for the Governors to agree. The school was alive with its own health check and search for solutions. Well, most of it was. For there is nothing like a challenge to root out the lazy, shirkers and time wasters. In that I don't mean those that are not fulfilling their roles … if it is a case of 'cannot' rather than 'will not'. For in them there would be a need to invest time, coaching and support to improve. The 'will not' may need a firmer hand of encouragement. A former Primary Head was then available to do periodic coaching with the Middle Leaders and develop their minds to a level of motivation and belief that they should and could move things forward. It was successful with most of them and in the main they bought into as a refreshing change to former ways.

As the week of the SIP's next visit approached a number of events unfolded which helped me to better understand the culture both in school and across the LEA.

A meeting of the Special Heads was convened with only three of the four of us present and nobody from the LEA. I heard of the rivalry between the schools and how the acronym of three had caused the meeting to become BAD (each letter being the initial of the schools). The problem being that it should have been BARD and the 'A' Head was absent and the 'R' Head present … and very keen to be included. Cutting to the quick I suggested that being inclusive in our meetings must surely be a prerequisite for having a collective voice and strategy. In no time we were now BARD despite our absent colleague … or maybe even in spite of her. The 'R' was pleased and grateful but this was not enough for me for now and the two PRUs needed to be part of our group. Here sensing a touch of 'Our colleague 'A' really won't be happy at this' I continued with the request and, over diplomatic jammy dodgers and custard cream biscuits, it was agreed that the suggestion be pursued. Before the next meeting I had contacted the

LEA and requested the Director attend by invitation to the inaugural meeting of all Specialist SEN Provision to be hosted by one of the PRUs. My time in EBD once again called on 'to fix that which first needs breaking … so it works better!'

The next meeting was a success and the challenge of a new acronym although not resolved in 'Any Other Business' with digestive biscuits, was seen as unimportant as now the Sector had a real voice and forum. It had fully captured the attention of the Director and impressed her. She welcomed all of this and it seemed clear that she saw her Special Provision as an ally to be nurtured and developed further. Perhaps not unexpected 'A' arrived late and was fairly subdued throughout. The saying 'Sometimes the best thing to say is nothing at all' alive in my mind as I left the meeting with a broad and cheeky smile.

The second event was being invited to speak at the Secondary Head's Meeting. A group of about fifteen very serious individuals from two camps … selective Grammar Schools and non-selective Secondary. Some of them quite competitive in all they did but mostly a decent lot who didn't consider themselves elitist compared with their Primary peers. My predecessor had never attended their meetings nor really did any of my peers from Special with secondary pupils. Two of the Grammar School Heads vied for the place of number one school in the authority and really only had the width of a main road between them. The Head of one always late to a meeting and making a very obvious dramatic attention-seeking entrance. I noticed this but her contemporaries had clearly got so used to it they didn't even blink. At my first meeting I was asked to give a presentation on 'Me and My School' so I gave them my best performance. It was amusing to note one of the Heads didn't know what ASD referred to, but did say she recalled seeing the letters on a minibus delivering children to her school. I took the opportunity to explain the condition of Autism to those gathered … but she didn't seem convinced and probably went off later to check on the acronyms of local bus companies.

As a first time in their midst, it seemed to raise their awareness, interest and understanding of Special Education. At the end I was thanked and one Head from a non-selective school leant across the table and said loudly, "Thanks ... that was great ... but what the F★★★ are you doing working in this LEA?"

The third event added to a sense of muddled arrangements within the LEA. With all the work ongoing in school I had received a call from the Senior Education Officer (SEO) requesting my analysis of school performance, known as the Self Evaluation Form (SEF). He claimed he wanted this so he could carry out a review of my school's performance. This somewhat surprised me as once again here I was with Education being involved in Special Schools. To add to the confusion the Senior Social Worker (SSW), as my Line Manager in our confusing structure, had previously phoned to say she would like to visit me and catch up on how things were going.

I replied to the SEO that if OFSTED were coming, they would only receive my SEF a day before and manage accordingly. He wasn't initially happy with this saying that my Link Inspector should already be in possession of a copy. This claim short lived when I explained that in nearly three months nobody from Education had been to see me and if I really had a Link Inspector, he must have forgotten about me or got lost in traffic some months earlier. This forthright response did the trick and ended the conversation. It also provided time for our ongoing review to update our SEF. The current copy being the invalid document that had been good enough for OFSTED's last inspection.

When the SSW visited it was actually her second attempt. The first thwarted by her own directive to request viewing of any Council employee's CRB (Criminal Record Check Document). My receptionist had challenged her for this on her first visit and as she had forgotten it, a problem occurred. Swallowing her pride, the SSW had retreated graciously and returned the following day with it in her hand. In our meeting we discussed the odd structure set up splitting schools across three Directorates and then the progress we were making since my arrival. Satisfied and enjoying her visit she left to return to the Council Offices. Her embarrassment at not having had her CRB the first time somewhat diminished with the joy of knowing 'One of her Heads had put the SEO in his place'.

The fourth event was with my Governing Body. The first time I had met all of them as only three had been involved in my interview in the Spring. Preparation for this causing a bit of a stir with my Business Manager as she had previously written the Head's report for him. She was stunned that I should and would write it. When I jokingly replied that the clue was in the title, she explained that she had always written the report. I let her read mine once completed and she never questioned my responsibility thereafter. The meeting lasted almost three hours with School Business rattled through efficiently due to my prompts. A couple of the Governors challenged by the speed and thoroughness of explanations.

Unfolding before me I could see another deficit in the organisation of Governance and the need for their tree to be shaken to allow dead-wood to fall away. The majority of the Board were female with two men adding to the quorate. Although well-meaning they didn't collectively add much to the school's journey. The two men included a local businessman who was an ex-parent and great advocate for the school. He had been on my interview panel and gave me reason for hope in sense prevailing. The other was a local politician with a keen eye for detail and a keener one for mischief. The Chair and Vice Chair were good friends with each other and great fans of the previous Head and his style. The extensive update I provided and the promise of a new SEF and SDP pleased them. It was also obvious that my differing style made them all sit up and left some rather shell-shocked when compared with their normal 'gentle pedestrian chat'. That is apart from one who brought her dog into the meeting and let it sit under the table. She grumbled a bit throughout the meeting about things irrelevant to those being discussed. At one such moment with her Governor peers somewhat dumbfounded at a random and unconnected comment, her dog farted loudly under the table and the aroma began to envelop the room. Although this removed the need to engage her obscure question it almost caused the frailer governors to pass out.

One outcome from the meeting was that the Chair wished to meet with me each Wednesday morning. This catch up was welcome but too regular. It allowed her to keep her finger on the pulse but she would then spend an equal amount of time sipping her coffee and bemoaning her husband or seeking advice about her grandchild. As nice a lady as she was, it was clear that for the school and governors to take the much-needed leap forward, then her time as Chair had to be reviewed.

All the lesson observations were completed and revealed a mix of standards with the overall just about being Good. Quality in the Autistic Provision and Post Sixteen being less good although within their ranks there were some outstanding practitioners. The biggest surprise for me being that so many staff claimed they had never been observed before and nearly every member of staff said they had not received such a thorough and constructive feedback. The first time the documented claims in the SEF and OFSTED report were seen to be the mistruths the SIP and I had suspected.

The Head of English who performed a brilliant lesson with Year Eleven students ably supported by a very experienced TA being a case in point. Nervous before, claiming she hadn't slept, she took my breath away with a lesson so well delivered it received rave reviews from me in the feedback. It was then that she said that was the first time she had been properly monitored in the many years she had been in post. There were others likewise. Some with points to consider so as to improve, argued at first then recognised the evidence they had been provided with in the feedback. Where such staff were unhappy, they agreed to be seen again. Where the outcome was the same, they then conceded that there were changes to be made so as to improve. Better than this was the case of one of the ASD teachers who responded to my suggestions and as a result the lesson was excellent. Her response being conciliatory and thereafter her performance very much better.

The key throughout this process being that all judgements made were a start point on what was needed to improve to Good or Outstanding. Once this was realised the majority of teachers and their TAs recognised the process as carrying coaching support and further training to assist personal performance. They also accepted that their annual Performance Management would involve self-review and identification of tasks to further their confidence and competencies as a member of staff. Another revelation for me being that there had not been such a formal process for teachers at all in preceding years. This was quite an eye-opening moment and it furthered questions about Leadership and Management including Governance.

The self-reviews by Subject Leads and Pastoral Year Heads identified pockets of good practice as well as gaps in its continuity. The majority of this team keen to reveal all as they had a thirst for improvement. The SLT were a little more circumspect and troubled by the task. I believe they realised that in carrying out the process and sitting down with their middle leaders that their own performances were suspect. This was ultimately to result in three of them retiring. The one beam of professional competent light was the Senior Teacher who had already announced her departure for retirement on the Isle of Wight. Our review of Pastoral and the need for therapeutic staffing support was music to my ears. She was a believer and I had just come from a setting where it was successful. I promised her that my intentions were to build that provision up. Sadly, before the year was out, she died from cancer and with many staff I attended her funeral. Snatched away before she had time to enjoy retirement, I was able to tell her family that her wishes had been realised and she would undoubtedly be smiling down on her old school.

When the SIP returned, we had the basis for moving the school forward and in time this resulted in the appointment of new school leaders to take up positions running the ASD Provision, Post Sixteen, Pastoral Care and Academic Curriculum. We had also appointed half a dozen new teachers all from mainstream with an energy for their subject and breadth of teaching experience more than suitable to engage those with learning difficulties.

The SIP and I set about the SEF and the SDP. The Governors ended up being very pleased, albeit needing a glossary (as you may too!) for the cloudburst of acronyms as they signed off both documents in their next meeting ... which was in a more rarified atmosphere as one of them had to take their dog to the vet.

Two days before the review of my provision by the SEO and one of his Inspector Team for Primary (a cohort we did not have!) I emailed the SEF for him to see. On the day they sat on a stage behind a desk while I sat on a chair somewhat below them in the large hall. I'm not sure if that was because they felt safer there or it was a status statement. They read through key points of my SEF and relayed areas they felt I should now consider as next steps. I thanked them for their time and for reading my own conclusions back to me just in case I may have forgotten them. I was then told a written report would be sent within days. Bemused by this performance I pondered as to how such an excellent Director of Children's Services could have the like in senior positions. Then I remembered that her problem was the one I was addressing anyway in my school.

When the report arrived, it was full of typo mistakes and factual inaccuracies. I managed to find a red pen and set about making corrections on it. When the SEO came in to review his review of my review, I passed his corrected report back to him. He visibly winced and his head dropped. I thanked him for his time and the interesting sequence of events we had shared. I suggested that if the report could be made good then it would probably be well received by my Chair of Governors and the Director. It was returned two days later and neither him nor any of his team reappeared by accident or design for the next eighteen months.

So, the word was now out more widely that things were changing in our school. I felt further inspired and sure it was right not to be intimidated by the LEA. This experience helped confirm my confidence and resilience when dealing with them. After all, it was not so long since the words of the HMI had made that very profound comment about such as their ability in my previous LEA. It was now the case that in both the Council Offices and my own staff room they all knew that the journey to improvement was well underway and changes to staffing would undoubtedly ensure success. Fundamental to this was the appointment of four new faces on SLT.

The new Deputy Head was a Geographer from the non-selective secondary school nearby. He was a confident practitioner and able to lead by example in developing the curriculum through his breadth of knowledge and outstanding teaching. His office always looked like he had been burgled and his shirt tail was always hanging out. Neither indicative of his true organisational skills. He had a gift in his ease of relationships with staff and students. As a replacement for the previous tired post-holder he was a breath of fresh air and inspired all he came into contract with. He relished the opportunity this promotion had afforded him.

The new Pastoral Lead was a mathematician and Joint Head of the Sixth Form from the very same adjacent non-selective school. He was a quiet and thoughtful practitioner who shared the excitement implicit in developing his team to include a social work and therapeutic dimension. His office much more organised and indicative of his eye for detail and measured approach to all tasks. Also keen to make inroads into his role and improve both behaviours and attendance, he was very pleased to have been appointed as an Assistant Head.

The new lead of the Post Sixteen Provision had previously been the Deputy there. From first sight of her in action it was clear that she would benefit from coaching and through success in the Leading from the Middle Course, it was a no brainer in appointing her to transform the provision. On appointment the off-site section of school became a vibrant and more productive place for the sixteen- to nineteen-year-olds. Her energy levels suggested Duracell batteries were part of her make up as she never tired on appointment as an Assistant Head. Her office was organised down to a precision measured in millimetres. The mischief of the Deputy and Assistant Head Pastoral being such that they would subtlety adjust the layout after each visit just to lighten her sharp focus and amuse themselves.

The new lead of Autistic Provision was the teacher who had questioned the validity of my judgements when I first monitored her teach. She had then gone on to implement each of my suggestions and perform at an incredibly high standard. The outcome being I had evidently gone from foe to friend very quickly. Recognising her quality and potential, the same route through the Leading from the Middle Course saw her as the best candidate for taking on this provision. She was appointed as Assistant Head and although she believed she was not totally worthy of the position her early performances proved she was more than capable.

We all need a team around us to be able to better lead and manage our staff to greater things. Their skill set and confidence in role is something to be nurtured ... their performance as practitioners in the classroom underpins the impact. I now knew that in such a school it was vital to set about creating and growing their like in my team ... knowing that in good time they would add so much to the direction of our school setting.

With this great team around me supported by the Business Manager we were able to concentrate our thoughts on a staged approach to achieving the end goal of improved performance. Underpinning this was their sense of 'let us enjoy the hard work and be successful'.

After a meeting where we had focussed on this, I received the sad news that the Deputy from my previous school had died. I felt shattered by the news. At the end of a tough day at school where he had been involved in some disagreements with my successor he had been driving home and had what seemed to have been a stroke. He then had a heart attack and died in hospital shortly afterwards.

I received a call from his family asking if I would say the eulogy at his funeral. I had not performed such a task before but felt it an honour and on being told it is what he would have wanted, I agreed. The Chapel at the Crematorium was full of family, friends and staff from school. One of those present being my Assistant Head for Post Sixteen who had known him for years. I spoke of his value as a working colleague, mentioning the need to lock him away during HMI visits. Included were references to his love of Middlesbrough FC and anything to do with Yorkshire, his home county. I finished with these words:

"Wherever Terry is now, he will know that we miss him and will never forget him. He was a very good man, not a selfish bone in his body for he always put other folk before himself. I hope that wherever he is there is Black Sheep or Theakston's on draft, Borough are winning their games and he can keep a watchful and caring eye on his family and many friends. If you get the chance and it is your way, do as I did last Saturday when passing the Cathedral ... pop in ... light a candle ... and say: 'Now then Terry lad ... 'ow's it going?' I just sense he will surely have something to say."

Ever since that day, whenever I have been in a church, I have lit a candle for him and enquired as to how he is. His commitment to the pupils and colleagues an example of what I hold dear ... and I am sure all do ... when it shines in their presence.

With all the emotion of that service in my mind and a heavy heart beating in my chest we received notification that OFSTED were coming. As I drove into school to find out the news a green woodpecker flew gracefully up the drive, in front of my car.

The inspection was run by an HMI and he was joined by three others including a trainee HMI on observation. There wasn't time for the staff to freak out and lose the plot. In the time up until then we had noted that the school was literally buzzing. To know they were now due to be with us was fine. It was time to perform. My relationship with the Lead HMI was perfect. He didn't require a hand grenade to influence him at all, even though it was available in my desk's bottom drawer. We spoke about all he was finding out and cross referenced every judgement. Already we had been told by one of his team that they wished they could work with us and questioned if there were any vacancies. All the SLT were fielding their responsibility meetings confidently and things looked to be going exceptionally well. Then news broke of two lessons being poor.

One was a Supply Teacher who knew us well and the other was one of our un-qualified teachers we were taking through to qualification. The supply teacher's response to being told she would be seen again was, "Well ... look ... this is more important to you than it is to me so I will not be doing anything different." That was not acceptable and straight away she was told 'Goodbye!' The following day the Assistant Head for ASD took her lesson and performed to her usual brilliant standard. The preparation for this being done late into the previous night and seeing her almost locked into school after ten p.m. when all other staff had drifted away after the long day. Such a brilliant example of someone who was a problem solver and full of dedication to the school. It is so important to know these people and step aside for them at such times … because as stars, they truly burn bright.

In the morning as I sat with the HMI, we knew that the Inspection criteria was such that these two lessons precluded us from getting Outstanding as our judgement. The fact that he had a trainee HMI with him meant he felt he could not dismiss the lessons even though all others were Good and many Outstanding. Try as I may to beg a different view … he held firm. In our conversation I explained how we had given blood, sweat and tears to the task of raising standards and the staff had responded, not all happily or willingly. If Good was to be our judgement then he was implored to drown his report in superlatives to celebrate the effort of all and resultant standard. I explained that if he didn't, then there would be some of the original staff who would say, "We were good then we bust our backs and we are still good!" I made it clear that we couldn't afford this and it would set us back.

It takes for a 'good Inspector' to make the best job of an inspection outcome. I knew that it was important not to leave them to do so alone. They will of course lead their team … and with them I had the confidence and nous to jointly lead the overall inspection. Time had taught me to settle for no less. Arguably, the Trainee HMI would have seen such an omission of the two lessons as worthy and an opportunity for professional discretion. But there it was … by the letter.

When he fed back to Governors and LEA they were stunned that Outstanding was not the result as all language and separate judgements seemed to indicate, up until the final pronouncement, that overall Outstanding was indeed our prize. As for the staff they were too when I fed back to them later. We were all shattered by this. Those two lessons had truly cost us our prize … and cry as we may, we just had to move on.

In the term that followed there were discontent voices in the Subject Leader team and none more so than from three particular key subjects. Here the individuals had been long serving with the previous Head and had continually remained convinced that the School was Good or better at the last OFSTED. As such, in keeping with my fears, they voiced open discontent with all they had been expected to do, which they described as having done 'no more than to move us to the same place'. This actually transferred into hostility from one of the three and he took it upon himself to spread that amongst staff prepared to listen.

There were undoubtedly still some staff who disliked having to plan, teach and assess children in a collegiate way ensuring progress, no matter how small, was achieved. This individual then became the focus for rumblings at any opportunity and open refusal to carry out performance of his role. No matter who approached him from the Leadership Team he was hell bent on confrontation. It all coming to a head when he was spoken to by myself with the Assistant Head for Post Sixteen present. Despite all avenues tried from requests for compliance and offers of coaching if it was difficult for him to achieve his role and understand any direct reference to the requirement of Teacher's Pay and Conditions. As our attempt to reconcile the situation came to a close, we all got up to leave my office and in earshot of my AHT he challenged me to step outside and have a fight. His mind now so focussed I could see his fists clenched and face tighten. He stood there for a moment then turned and rushed away leaving the two of us trying to fathom what had just happened.

Yes … you actually read that a teacher wanted to fight with me rather than respond to professional improvement requests. The question now being how should I respond to this and still win the day on the challenges I faced with some of my staff?

Our LEA Human Resources Adviser was contacted and advised he be suspended without prejudice and for an investigation into his conduct to be commissioned. The result being he was given a final warning regarding his conduct thereby showing this type of behaviour was not uncommon. Other staff by now could see that listening to him and being easily influenced was an error of their own judgement. The air in school calmed and the other two subject leaders resumed a more engaging and purposeful approach to further developments within their respective subjects.

My personal reflection remained one of shock at someone being so oppositional, belligerent and aggressive. I had experienced it in many pupils in EBD settings and managed to influence them in accepting a need for change. But this was a teacher. He had responsibilities to his students, department team and profession yet seemingly he didn't care for any. More importantly his wife and children depended on him as a breadwinner and on a principle of unwillingness to change he had thrown all to the wind. I was truly baffled.

Over four centuries earlier John Heywood had quoted, 'There are none so blind as those who cannot see' and 'There are none so deaf as those who cannot hear.' The anger this man was directing towards me seemed to have such an origin.

This whole episode resulted in a number of other staff leaving as they either retired or found posts elsewhere. Without exception all of them had been aspiring for consistent Good and often dipped below that mark. As such there was no real loss, but there was great gain. The feedback being received from Middle Leaders was that nobody should try and convince them to stay as their personal departmental challenges would be enhanced if SLT accepted the 'not so grave loss'.

Once again, our reputation secured quality staff replacements from mainstream schools. Each and every one better than good teaching practitioners, with great subject knowledge and a determination to raise standards not just in their own classroom but across the whole school. Their knowledge and understanding of learning difficulties considerable and their desire to learn more about such SEN including Autism never-ending. This influx of disciples turned the staff mood further towards 'OFSTED were wrong and when they come next time, we will show them' as a mantra.

The head of subject who had been the recalcitrant individual decided to raise his banner once again and try to subvert the progress being made. His TA could not hold her tongue any longer and her loyalty evaporated as she angered at his open laziness to lead the department and perform all aspects of his role. She coughed to planning his work, marking it, leading tutorial sessions and preparing his assemblies. She added evidence to all of this which was duly presented to him in a formal meeting. He came across as completely unmoved, with his Union representative in attendance ... who privately admitted she was confounded by his lack of professionalism. After several further meetings with fully agreed targets including coaching support, he finally chose to show his true colours. He openly admitted he would not carry out the full performance of his role or engage in any supportive practices. Under advice from his Union rep. he threw in the towel and resigned. The detail of this long performance was leaked to the staff by his department colleagues who until this point had been long suffering in his charge.

As a Leadership Team this was a defining moment and one eagerly taken in both hands. The injection of positivity that followed resulted in a number of them receiving National Accreditation for their subjects indicating competencies in practice and outcomes that warranted such recognition. This desire to achieve such accolades not seen as badge-collecting but clear evidence of consistent excellent practice throughout every day of every week of the year. As one proud Subject Head put it, "This is a great statement to put in front of OFSTED the next time they dare to enter our school!" This immediately spread amongst others and such 'accreditation fever' was seen as genuine proof of great practice ... and became the norm year on year.

The exam results in Years Eleven and each of our three Post Sixteen year groups had doubled each year to that point with increased grades in Entry Level and more subjects looking to build upon this to achieve GCSEs. Projections for this particular year once again showing the potential for richer pupil outcomes. In a staff meeting it was acknowledged that if OFSTED had come that particular week then the staff would have blown them away with quality. It truly seemed that the barrel was empty of bad apples and those that remained were shining as bright as the staff stars recently joined.

As things always seem to happen ... then we were shattered by news. A newly appointed Head of a Core Subject had been running a Department Meeting and one of her team admitted to cheating in the external exam process. Straight away the need to share this revelation with myself and the Deputy Head responsible for curriculum and exams started a serious chain of events. The exam board was notified and the member of staff suspended, then interviewed. The exam board investigated the matter and thankfully found all other practices subject to the highest compliance and integrity. Our reputation therefore unblemished and the massive inroads into student exam success not questioned. The teacher was surprised at the fuss and somewhere between naivety and professional stupidity admitted to having told her students the answers ... adding "I don't know why I bothered because they still got it wrong!" Her resignation before the need for dismissal causing a few others on the staff to concede that it was probably the right time to leave too.

Subsequent adverts in the TES resulted in our mail being overwhelmed with applications. The challenge of shortlisting and interviewing giving senior and middle leaders new learning opportunities which they readily accepted and enjoyed. Once again, the resultant appointments securing further quality staff to our ranks. The buzz created by my energised staff had drawn such as these candidates to us. I did not underestimate how my team talked in the wider community of education and how their own success and enjoyment in post had become a great advert for our school.

The curriculum opportunities being afforded students with a wide-ranging scope of academic and vocational subjects with increasing accreditation at sixteen and beyond caused Secondary Headteacher's to comment "Your school is like a normal Secondary!" Quite what a 'normal secondary' was actually left me short in a quick reply. The real point being that our school had become a 'Can Do' place.

My emphasis on a three-pronged approach to education had initially left many scratching their scalps but now they could see it realised and acknowledge the philosophy was indeed real living practice.

The first principle being to develop an academic curriculum which provided each student with the skills to access learning, and then go on to achieve their potential. This may mean revising exactly what their potential was as their ability was unlocked by the very best teaching from a quality and professional staff. The curriculum had to have a breadth so it enabled all students to achieve both academic and vocational opportunities. All teaching and learning had to be exciting and enjoyable. It had to open up new horizons to our students that challenged their imagination and inspired them as individuals.

The second principle being to develop a pastoral curriculum which provided each student with personal social skills to be honest and truthful in their actions; show friendliness, care and understanding to others; accept differences in race, religion and sexual orientation; develop resilience for all challenges they meet; achieve happiness and fulfilment in their life; and, succeed without it ever being at the cost of others.

The third principle being to ensure successful transfer of their academic and social learning to the setting outside school. This required practical off-site opportunities for transferring these skills. The intention being that by the time they left, they had shown competencies that enabled them to be included in social, recreational, sporting, work and travel settings. This end-goal being to ensure all they had learned could be used in the wider world and the students had not been institutionalised.

To be truly successful we had to build in them a sense of gaining their rightful place in society with a desire to confidently seek out future life opportunities. Our progress over the years to this point was such it was all making sense to the staff and they had a sense of ownership and investment in their school. A good time to change the school motto to 'No Ceiling to their Learning'.

Can you see now why I took you through my school and college days in this journey? That trek and all I had begun to see, understand and want for the future was to shape what I was trying to create for each and every one of my students … and have my staff as full shareholders in its daily workings. Taking that 'pause moment' helped me to stop and remember Miss K. and others … then go on to influence and shape those around me.

When anxious Year Six parents and carers came to view us, the new school motto captured their imagination and mostly changed their aspirations for their child. Worries about leaving the smaller and more sheltered Primary School SEN environments or those in our Primary Feeder Special School mostly evaporated at the presentations received about our ethos and the references from our OFSTED Report. Indeed, what was there about a 'Second to None Pastoral Programme' and 'Excellent Teaching Curriculum' with 'Leaders relentlessly in pursuit of Outstanding Practices' not to like? For sure though the piece de resistance was the performance of students in our Lower School in Years Seven and Eight. They talked about the school with joy in their voices and pride oozing from their facial expressions. Had they been selling Time Shares in our school they would have regularly more than excelled at reaching their sales targets.

The students I had worked with and had the pleasure to teach over the years in my previous schools were undoubtedly truly amazing in a variety of ways. So many learning journeys for them and me. Yet, from the very start it was capped by those I had the responsibility both for and to in this school.

My first Friday at the school involved a visit to the Post Sixteen Provision as some were taking part in a regular sailing activity. At the old quarry lake near the coast a bustle of activity was taking place around the boathouse of an Outdoor Pursuits Centre. There, numerous students were putting on their life jackets and going through the safety procedures. I joined them and was soon with three in a sailing boat on the lake. One skippering at the tiller and two others managing the sails. As we tacked back and forward across the water our 'skipper' said to me "Don't worry sir, you'll get used to us!" This reassuring and encouraging remark coming from a seventeen-year-old with complex learning difficulties. As we sailed, the other two crew then engaged me in conversation about where I had come from and why I wanted to run their school. When we moored after an exciting sail together, two of the three shook my hand and the other, a student with Downs, gave me a hug. It seemed clear to me that I had passed my aquatic interview and been duly accepted.

On returning to the off-site provision, I was greeted with a fresh cup of tea and a crowd of expectant faces looking for a moment of my time. Stood at the back of them was my wise sailing 'Skipper' smiling and holding his thumbs up. Each and every visit was just so thereafter. The staff were a touch reserved initially and it took sitting in the staff room with a coffee and piece of cake chatting to them to ease their manner. One of the TAs, a gregarious Italian man, asked politely, "What do we call you?" When I replied that my Christian name would be fine, he said, "We can't do that ... you are the Headteacher!" The rest of the staff looked towards me mouths open and cake at the ready. My response was, "Yes, that is my job but my name is Kim" and then they all smiled before eating their cake.

Not long into the first term I established a very active and forthright group of students together as a School Council. They appreciated being given the voice and often managed to ask pretty searching questions about school rules and uniform – both being key to their thinking early on. We moved quickly on to issues around making the recreational areas within school more welcoming and comfortable and they began to realise that their views were important. This prompted one of the best unscripted moments when the Children's Commissioner visited. Having asked a series of questions and then sat back to receive their replies the Commissioner noted every word. The students showed some confidence in their responses and one in particular stole the moment. He slapped the palm of his hand on the table top and said crisply, "Look ... we just want to be treated the same as everybody else!" This caused all others to open up and talk about the challenges of disability and the often lack of understanding of others when they were out and about in the community. Undoubtedly the Children's Commissioner and aides left with a great deal to think about, and a student to remember.

This issue of being treated well and not being prejudiced against, was a vein running through future meetings and brought to a particular head by a sorry incident involving mainstream students. Nearby to our school was the adjoining campus area of two non-selective schools, one for boys and the other for girls. The girls accessed their playing field by walking past some of our classrooms and on one occasion took to banging on the windows. This startled the staff and students in a Food Technology lesson and was worsened by insulting remarks directed at the students related to their ability. That same week some of the students from the boys' school chose to stone the minibuses as they left our site. The drivers and escorts didn't stop to remonstrate with the offending stone throwers. Their concern was with our shocked and terrified students. Calls made to both schools requesting action against the students and indeed staff who had been close by eventually resulted in these anti-social behaviours ceasing. However, I had not expected to see a line of five police officers and PCSOs spaced along the roadside to ensure an end to the stoning.

The students anger in our next School Council meeting was expressed calmly by most present. They were troubled though by not understanding why these supposed 'normal children' should act so. It was beyond their understanding that they deserved to be treated in that way. That meeting focussed on the reality of Hate Crime and the ignorance of others related to our school and students. The learning was rich and consequently the anger and confusion somewhat subsided. As they left the room one turned and said "You know sir, we need to help them with their problems!" There it was. So, who really had a disability ...? Not my students!

At an event in the Cathedral, I found myself in complete admiration of students receiving their awards at a Duke of Edinburgh Scheme ceremony. The packed parents, families and staff full of pride, as students from across all Secondary phases were announced and applauded. This was my first such event and sat near the altar with other Headteachers I had a great view of proceedings in the front row. As my students queued up to receive their awards they waved and smiled. From behind me the well respected and senior member of the LEA's Headteachers reached forward and tapped me on the shoulder. He was the Head of the Boy's Grammar in the town that always outshone all others in most things. He enquired, "Kim, why are you sat in front of me?" I quickly replied with a chuckle, "Because I'm more important than you and have many more students here today receiving awards!" He smiled at the put down and sunk back in his chair. It was true, of course, as we had twice as many there at that time.

This type of celebration became common for us with successes achieved in further Subject Awards and Accreditation for developments made in our curriculum. The staff always quick to put students front and centre, and when done so they never disappointed. The word spread and one of our School Council was then invited to be a Youth Parliament Member and chosen to speak with Councillors in their Chamber. He set about explaining the benefits of specialist education in a Special School setting compared with his own previous mainstream experience. He then went on to berate a couple of Councillors about funding and told them they should take time to visit our school to have their eyes opened. His complete performance being his own words without any preparation or support from anyone. The first thing I heard of it was when at a meeting and the Portfolio Holder for Education came across to tell me the tale. He could not contain himself and laughed about seeing his senior colleagues sat bolt upright with their shoulder-blades firmly pressed against their chairs. Such was the conviction in our student that they had to take a tea and toilet break before continuing with their Council business.

To achieve the three principles implicit in our education model it was necessary to expand the boundaries of all that we did and where we did it. This involved developing international links with schools elsewhere in the world with the help of the British Council. In the first instance I continued the link from my previous London school with Maryland in the USA and the students exchanged letters. For most of ours this was the very first time they had received anything through the post except a birthday card. To write about themselves, their families and school, and add photos was exciting. Yet the exchange was in the universal tongue of English so we looked for additional opportunities. We taught French to all in Years Seven to Nine and some took it forward to Entry Level examination. The problem being we couldn't find a link school in France.

Then came the opportunity for me to travel to China with one hundred selected headteachers from England. We flew to Beijing and were hosted by Hanban, the equivalent there of our British Council. The aim being to build links with China through their schools and maybe even teach Mandarin Chinese in our schools. With an open mind and a fair degree of excitement I set off. My SLT wondering, 'Oh my goodness … what will he have us doing after this?'

Beijing was an eye opener with so many people and such order wherever we went. Tiananmen Square, the Forbidden City and the Great Wall all visited. Everywhere we went crowds of people stood to watch us. We may have been the tourists but we were increasingly on show. In an attempt to engage with some Chinese locals we encouraged them to join us for a photo. Immediately a young soldier rushed over to remonstrate with us, as we were on the Square where such things evidently should not happen. At this point we became aware of a plain clothes 'minder' who was with us and he calmed the situation.

After various prestige events with officials from the Chinese Education Ministry we all flew to different parts of China to meet the Headteachers of the schools proposed for our link. The eight of us from the LEA flew to Guangdong and then drove to the city of Foshan. Here I was to enjoy three days with the staff and students at Qicong Special School. The school was for students aged four to eighteen with learning difficulties, hearing impairment and autism. Once again, we all drew crowds wherever we went. In my school I was constantly shaking hands and having staff and students bow before me. Everyone terribly excited at my presence.

I made Chinese dumplings in a catering lesson, a paper cut house in an art lesson and had my hair trimmed in a hairdressing class. Every engagement with children resulting in great excitement and honest gratitude. When having my haircut, the student and teacher were keen to dye my hair black as was customary for all adults I had met. I declined saying it had cost me a fortune to go grey so I'd best stick with it. The caretaker came off the yard where he had been sweeping up leaves to have his haircut and roots dyed before returning happily to his work. This was used to try and convince me further but I held firm much to the disappointment of the students.

We enjoyed several meals with our hosts and learned so much via the interpreters about their school system. Throughout everyone we met was so welcoming and genuinely grateful for our presence. The time ending with each of us signing a Memorandum of Understanding drawn up with our respective Link Headteacher. This being a commitment to develop our school partnerships to the benefit of both school communities. The event filmed live on the City T.V. Station. From this my intention was to do more than have a loose link with a school some six thousand miles away. My SLT were waiting for the news.

On return, plans were put in place to appoint a Chinese Mandarin teacher, secure a Language Assistant from our partner school and commence teaching the language from the September start of year. And so, it happened. In time the subject taught to all in Years Seven to Nine and offered as an exam subject in Years Ten to Thirteen. The students loved it and none more so than one boy from our ASD Provision. He achieved a C Grade at GCSE and took part in the HSBC sponsored Chinese Mandarin Speaking Competition at Canary Wharf. His performance stunning all that saw him and resulting in him being feted by a Chinese delegation to the LEA later that year.

The link with the school developed such that on three occasions four staff and eight students visited Qicong School and spent a week there. As a once in a lifetime experience, it certainly stretched the boundaries of their imagination and expectation for future travel. It also showed an increasing positive impact on their social skill development. On the second visit to China one of the fourteen-year-olds sent a message back to us in England saying, "I have met the students with a hearing loss. They are wonderful but have made me sad. I wish I could give one of my ears to one of them so they could hear again!"

Each time a trip took place, all monies were generated by fundraising and I did my bit several Saturdays packing shopping for customers in a local supermarket. The confidence in our students was immense upon return and their attitude to their studies and each other changed for the positive. The staff likewise as they had been ambassadors for our school and delivered training to our Chinese counterparts on current methodology with pupils on the autistic spectrum.

Over six years we had five Language Assistants join us from our partner school in Foshan. All away from their families September to May and living either with a member of staff as a tenant, or in rented accommodation alone. With one of them I recall being horrified to hear that in his flat one morning he had a visitor in his kitchen as he ate breakfast. It was a rat. When I spoke with him to say how embarrassed I was that such a thing should happen he replied, "Do not worry … in China sometimes there are three!" He seemed relatively happy that the odds of him meeting such vermin had been reduced.

One great moment in reviewing the impact of this new language on our curriculum was when I monitored a lesson with a Post Sixteen exam class. The Teacher and her Mandarin Chinese Assistant had set them up in groups in a role play activity in a restaurant. They had to refer to a menu either as a couple out for a meal or the waiter. All language was in Mandarin without exception and the teacher was looking very pleased with the performance of her lesson. Then an error occurred with a couple in their order to the waiter and all three fell about laughing. Their amusement furthered in Mandarin with some giggles, then it was all corrected ... again in fluent Mandarin. At this point the only English spoken was between the teacher and her assistant. "Did you hear that?" they said in unison. In the feedback we unpicked the lesson and jointly marvelled at where the teaching had brought them in their confidence and application. This was a story shared on my last visit to the school in China a few years ago. By this time the Language assistant was back in China at our partner school and bathed in the praise of her peers as the story was told in a staff meeting.

At a Parent Meeting I was asked to explain why we taught Chinese when so many of our students struggled with their English. My reply captured the essence of this story and the fact that the students enjoyed learning another language and indeed it had helped improve their own mother tongue. The parent nodded acceptingly and said, "Zaijian Mr Johnson" (Goodbye) and walked off with a grin.

We also taught Polish, making it the third language on a carousel of languages taught in Years Seven to Nine. It was taught by the AHT responsible for ASD Provision as it was her heritage language. She was supported by a TA also from Poland who was training to become a Therapist. It was quite common to walk along a corridor and be greeted with any of the following 'Bonjour' ... 'Dzien Dobry' ... 'Zaoshang Hao' ... or 'Now then'. The latter greeting in keeping with an emphasis on increased student knowledge and understanding of Yorkshireness.

The International opportunities were increased with the success of two bids for Comenius funding from the European Union. One was with schools from Spain, Portugal, Turkey, Estonia and

Italy looking at learning styles and teaching approaches. Forty students and sixteen staff enjoying a week in each country over a two-year period. Each visit seeing our students either staying in a hotel or with a student and family from the host country. To see our students marvel at a hotel room and endless amounts of food bigger and better than anything they had ever experienced before was a sight to behold. As for the reality of being in a foreign country ... their senses were being taken to a completely new level.

Likewise with schools from Finland, Turkey and Portugal where we created a Youth Parliament convened in a parliamentary setting in each country. This further exemplified the ever-growing confidence and ability of our students matched against their European peers, all of whom were from mainstream settings.

The Youth Parliament presentation put together by our delegation in Portugal focussed on accessibility of students with a physical disability. They told the true story of one of their fellow students in a wheelchair capturing every moment of his acceptance in our school and the adjustments they had made to ensure it was an inclusive setting. The four of us, as staff, were touched by the love for this student expressed in the telling of the tale. In the same project one of our ASD Year Elevens ran the Parliamentary debate in the Finnish Council Chambers and was just oozing with confidence as she literally conducted the gathering like an orchestra of views.

After each trip the students would tell their stories illustrated with some great photos. The tales of buying a Fez in a Turkish Bazaar, reciting poetry in the ruins of a Roman Amphitheatre in Spain, trying to stand upright on a very windy Atlantic beach in Portugal and ordering a real pizza in Italian in Sardinia – just a few examples of memories that brightened up their lives and will live with them to be told for evermore.

Certainly, one of the most touching moments being in Sardinia when we were on a walk to see a bird sanctuary. One of our Year Twelve students with a physical disability that periodically prevented him from walking distances asked if he could sit it out. I agreed to stay with him while all others carried on. Then one of our girls in Year Eight asked if she could hold back too. Both students having come through the care system started to talk openly about their life journey and the heartbreak often experienced. Then referencing their current situation, the boy said "All through my life I had never felt that anybody really loved me until now. The family that has adopted me are different. They do love me ... I can see it and I feel it!" His eyes glistened with emotion and he added, "I have a mum and dad now ... real parents and I love them too!" His head dipped and he cried and smiled as he did. The girl did too and hugged him. Such openness and a heart-touching confidence in his ability to tell this story. I told him how I was both pleased for him and in admiration of him.

When he left at the end of Year Fourteen he threw his arms around me and said, "Thanks Sir. You have helped make me who I am." Off he went to College a brilliant example of what we were trying to do for all in our charge. When I share his words in talking about schools and education with those I am with, they are all in agreement and say, "No matter how much money you may earn ... or may not ... that tale is worth its weight in gold to have been said to you." Indeed, it was and still remains.

The value of stopping every now and again to spend time with those in my school ... whatever their age ... was so important. To hear their personal stories and appreciation of what we had created in their school ... or still needed to ... was to keep my mind focussed on making our school fit them. It was important to make time for these moments as often as I could.

When on the final trip to Portugal, I received a phone call from school to tell me that OFSTED had been in contact to say they would be returning to inspect us only eight months after their previous visit. At first, I thought it to be an envious leg-pull as we were bathed in sunshine and the trip was going so well. But it was not. I spent the afternoon finalising my update to the SEF and then emailed it off to the Lead Inspector and told him I would be flying back early the following day to be with him and my staff by lunchtime. Early the next day my wonderful PA Gill had a taxi organised to get me to Lisbon three hours away. My flight was on time and another taxi picked me up at Heathrow. My staff breathed a sigh of relief. While they may twitch about OFSTED they felt the Inspection team would definitely twitch more if I was back to take the lead.

The Inspection was no more than a collection of poor practice and unprecedented stupidity by the team. I speak well of them if you are shocked by so blunt a statement. The lead inspector seemed more willing to crack silly jokes, avoid detailed and well evidenced conversations, read the SEF so he could cross-check it with what was being seen and rein in a rogue colleague. I was staggered to find out that in a GCSE Geography class where the teacher was continuing with a topic on Longshore Drift, he was graded as Unsatisfactory. The rationale being that "these autistic students didn't need to know about longshore drift as it was not going to be of any value to them in their future lives!" The teacher was broken ... as his lesson standard was consistently Good or better. A totally outrageous and shameful incident.

When it came to the feedback on the second day, there were lots of examples of the school provision having been Outstanding, but the final judgement was that we were Good. The whole staff were angry as indeed I was, and my new Chair of Governors. It was clear that the team had been taken up the garden path by the lead inspector and the rogue colleague, who was actually a serving head of an ASD School. As for us we had bust a proverbial gut and all the signs were there for Outstanding to have been the best fit. But there it was.

When the draft report was received it had over one hundred factual inaccuracies and other errors. The vast majority of which were upheld. This amounted to as close as could be to a rewrite. However, the poor and extremely convoluted complaints procedure practiced by OFSTED meant we in the end had to just accept Good. The lack of independent adjudication revealing another flaw in this system of accountability. Our trust and confidence in the system completely disappeared after this. All that had been experienced before with HMIs lost to this poorly lead team and their inability to see what was happening daily in our great school. As one parent wrote into me ... "Don't worry Mr Johnson, you are much better than they judged. They should have gone to Specsavers!"

Meantime, one remaining bad apple was found to have been dormant in the barrel. Suddenly choosing to show her true colours and speak up for the Head of Subject who she claimed to have enjoyed working with. He had been gone months by now and all had seemed refreshingly positive in our school. Then her colleagues on our superb TA staff could take no more of her. She was delivered to me with TAs saying that 'her annoyance with me was for having got rid of her friend ... a super teacher' and how she also 'wished me a long and painful death from cancer' was all too much for them to listen to anymore. Her colleagues wanted her long gone and as quickly as possible. Playing the situation calmly and not rising to the awful remark, I commissioned an independent investigation. It didn't take long for my Governors to realise her time had come and the evidence was enough to have her dismissed. As it turned out she resigned and on her final day staff turned their backs on her rather than say goodbye. As one put it "God above ... she is so full of poison ... if she bit herself it might be fatal!"

Throughout the early years at the school, the LEA decided it needed to review its SEN Strategic Plan and call together Headteacher practitioners. At the start the Special Schools and PRUs were still absent from the Education Directorate, but nevertheless invited to contribute to their own future. It seemed a genuine attempt to look at what was available in the LEA compared with what was needed at the time and in the future. Heads were asked to volunteer for specific groups and as I had spent the best part of fourteen years in EBD day and residential schools, I opted to join that group.

The depth of research and detail of our final recommendations seemed to be very credible and certainly recognised that the growing exclusion rate in the Authority warranted a new school being built. It was passed up to another committee which was supposed to prioritise recommendations and produce a final paper for the LEA Officers and Elected Members. Somewhere in that trail it got lost and was never responded to for many years to come. It took for Free Schools to come along before anything happened and then mismanagement by the LEA caused that to stall once opened.

None of this came as a surprise and the final decisions about SEN Provision hardly changed the status quo. The LEA was in a constant time of change and senior officers lacked the SEN experience to make any difference at all. There was an Inspector with responsibility for SEN by this time but her workload precluded any sustainable impact. Having said that we worked very well in partnership and she would often seek an escape from the Council Offices to save her sanity and savour the coffee at my school.

The Council had the ability to create and change organisational structures with the intention of improving services. One such attempt being to have integrated teams (ITs) across the six towns. Each IT would have two of the towns. The acronym made up of the first letter of each town followed by 'IT'. How simple and clear. In true authority style the towns were grouped 'G' and 'R'; 'C' and 'R'; and finally 'S' and 'H'. It was only when presenting this to a mass gathering of heads that the LEA Officer heard her own words, "We have GRIT, CRIT and errr ... oh yes SHIT!" It just about said it all really and being in the CRIT area I cannot possibly add anything to say what things were like in the SHIT area.

When at a meeting in London I found myself with the Chair of the Education Select Committee at Westminster. When we had finished the usual round of table introductions he turned back to me and said, "Oh Kim I don't think you could surprise me about your LEA ... I know a great deal about them!" I replied quickly, "Well then we need to talk some ... as you need to catch up on their latest muddles!" In future discussions with him it was evident there wasn't much I could add to his extensive knowledge, however the detail I added left him shaking his head.

That both amused me and bothered me. If the incompetencies were so well known then why hadn't there been interventions. Privately, the briefing I received from others was that the marginal constituencies were held by three Tories and the Council was just so too. If the truth was really out, then the political outfall for Government would be huge. How that served the children and young people in the Authority was lost on me ... but then that was the reality for now.

During this earlier time our school had been promised a complete rebuild in the Building Schools for the Future Project Scheme (BSF) and the excitement within school was tremendous. At the time my eldest son was project managing such special and mainstream school builds in the East Midlands. I was ever hopeful that his already proven skills would be brought to bear on ours once the planning was complete. He had shared with me some designs and a real insight into successful project completion. I was clear in my mind as to what ours could look like after listening to him. Our project seemed to be unstoppable and funding was allocated. Once it was known that our Post Sixteen Provision had to move back to our campus because it was in the middle of a site due to be demolished, the LEA was rather forced to inject some renewed energy. Then the BSF promise disappeared and we were left wondering what was going to happen.

The adjacent Primary School was marked for closure so I began to pose questions of the LEA to hand that site over to us so we could develop it into our Lower School for Years Seven to Nine and open up a space otherwise for the returning Years Twelve to Fourteen. Perfectly simple and a logical solution which would effectively save the LEA a seven-figure amount. Naturally that was all too simple and the Council deemed the site best used to build housing. Once we pointed out that could only be done on the footprint of the current school buildings, they paused for a rethink. In that time, we pulled in our MP to add a bit of weight and serious questioning on behalf of our case. Politics being what it is that was effective and with her help the Council conceded and handed over the site.

Not long after this the LEA came to ask me to bid for extending our Provision to include additional places for Primary pupils aged four to eleven with complex Autism. We were successful and then from out of the blue they announced they had the funds to extend our provision even further with a significant building programme lasting a year. Our full community absolutely thrilled with the news, and in good time the upgraded and new facilities were provided. This took our numbers to over three hundred aged four to nineteen. The chain reaction of successfully playing poker with the LEA ... knowing the aces up our sleeve were political ... was a great coup for us. We had called their bluff and eventually they'd come back with much more than we had asked for.

Two years previously our much-liked and respected MP had been given honorary status as a member of our School Council. How things just work for you when you have someone so much a fan of your school ... with their School Council Membership Certificate proudly displayed in Portcullis House. In truth her admiration for our work was genuine, and months later she brought Brian May, the guitarist from Queen, into visit us. He played guitar with a few of our students, one of whom sang amazingly a song he knew 'fairly well'. Our Music teacher on keyboards wearing his noticeably aged 'Queen in Concert' T-shirt.

Brian May did a few radio interviews while with us and finished by saying he thought our school was 'incredible'. That quote was later used in our Parent and Carer questionnaire. Many of the questions were 'OFSTED said we were ... What do you think?' One being quite different and asked 'Brian May said we were incredible. Do you agree?' Every reply said 'Yes' with one additional comment being 'If Brian May said you are incredible it must be true ... as he is a god.'

There it was, redemption for us as a School. The temptation was there to have Brian May's quote on an OFSTED style banner for our front gate. Please be reassured we did not ... but Brian's judgement replaced that of the miserably inadequate OFSTED Team and the staff had a smile ... or was it a smirk?

When picking my moment to fight back against the system I had chosen my friends wisely and educated them well. In Politics the best way of winning the day is probably to have a politician on your side. Someone who needs no encouragement to wax lyrical of your staff and students ... that someone doing it with honesty ... and thereby help you progress.

Working in this school there were some very happy occasions created by staff. These had occurred throughout even the challenging times. Undoubtedly the characters in the staff team were always going to ensure that was the case. None more so than one of the Year Heads, a very cheery Black-Countryman from Wolverhampton. I first met him in earnest at the retirement party held for the outgoing headteacher. Here he had been fairly well oiled on his favourite nectar and took to playing an impromptu session on his guitar. Then he burst into a song inspired by my presence which included in the words, "... and his replacement was to be Kim ... and we didn't know at first whether he was a she or a him!" This caused a fair degree of hilarity in the small group I was sat with in a corner of the room. I found it funny too.

The next time we met was on my first day in post when he appeared at the door looking quite nervous. He wanted to apologise and kept saying, "I'm so sorry boss ... I don't know what came over me!" The relief in him quite something, when I replied that it wasn't a problem and that I'd laughed about it with friends and family during the summer. Over the next few years, he was a man of humour taking the ouch out of conversations in the staff room and always trying to encourage colleagues to lighten their mood. His professional performance as a teacher of French and Head of Year being exemplary in all aspects. The students adored him and the staff often just shook their heads in disbelief when he made some sort of risqué remark ... which never actually offended anyone. His health took a dip and he was hospitalised for tests which revealed cancer. When three of us visited him from SLT, we ended up being asked to leave him to rest as we had livened him up so much the laughter could be heard beyond his private room. I saw him again one evening after school and was mistaken for a Consultant as I walked through the hospital to his ward. He said he would prefer me as his Consultant as he felt sure I'd change the prognosis.

The hospital allowed him out over a weekend and two of us from SLT met up with him in a Sussex coastal town. He had wanted to play in a gig there even though he was clearly in pain. His performance quite inspirational and really causing the pub to bounce to the musical atmosphere. I noted him outside having an 'alternative' smoke ... to ease the pain. He was keen for me not to know he was being 'a bad boy' but what was there to say? He knew what the future held and every single day was precious, so whatever it took to get him through was fine by me.

On returning to hospital, he started to worsen, and I visited him again one evening. He was keen for a more lawful smoke this time and I took him outside in a wheelchair to the garden area. Here he sat chatting with me reflecting on all he'd done at school. We shared some laughs and then with a cigarette in his mouth he pointed at the sky and said "Look at that beautiful sunset!" I replied, "Bloody hell Jim ... you are really ill ... the sun is setting over this town and you really think it is beautiful!" He laughed loudly and held my hand tightly. He died shortly afterwards. When I broke the news to staff at the end of the day my voice faltered as we had all lost more than a valued colleague ... we had lost a dear friend. The staff room was never quite the same thereafter. The sense of loss was immense.

The staff working with our borderline Severe Learning Difficulty (SLD) students were totally committed to their classes. We had one such class in our Upper and Lower Schools and both stole the hearts of the rest of the school when it came to their turn to present an assembly, or in the Christingle event. Their lower ability didn't stop them from throwing themselves into every performance. It may have been off-key singing or erratic and jumbled lines, but it did not matter. It had once been the case that they would have not attempted anything and been happier shying away. The staff had changed this with a magical spell in their teaching which ensured increased confidence and 'give it a go' enthusiasm. Their best performances being to sign to songs in unison with the staff. Invariably this would challenge many to keep a dry eye.

When invited to go to local stables with them, their transformation into excited and even more confident helpers and riders was an eye opener. The staff there all experienced in the marvellous 'Riding for the Disabled Scheme'. They talked enthusiastically of how they looked forward to our Programme One students and staff being with them. I took the opportunity one morning to spend a full session in their company. The laughter and often serious faces on these wonderful students as they engaged in every activity and then told the true story of their learning experience was touching to hear. It was indeed ... just as I wanted to see each and every day from all my students.

When talking with headteacher colleagues I encouraged them to immerse themselves in their own student's learning. How good it was then to hear them also say how helpful it had been to do exactly the same and be able to gauge the impact and outcomes of their provision.

The teacher who developed Land Studies and Forestry was another who in a very modest way made no fuss about his work and the huge impact it had on students. To see him lead a class towards our woodland all dressed in overalls wearing red safety hats with earphones while pushing wheelbarrows with chain saws and other equipment was a sight indeed. They cleared pathways and made an open-air classroom with tree stump seats and benches where he spun tales of the wonder of woodland and completely captivated them. This vocational work inspiring students to take on other tasks where they cut the grass in the quad and tended the garden areas. Eventually two of them having paid part-time jobs with the site team and another became the Assistant Caretaker ... a role he performed with great skill and pride. Our grounds always looked splendid indeed.

The teacher raised funds to get a timber classroom installed in the quad at the centre of the school and fitted it out with artefacts and teaching materials that would have made the local Wildlife Trust green with envy. The opening ceremony for this saw us invite the Director of Children's Services and Council's Portfolio Holder for Education. Both attended, cut the ribbon and unveiled a plaque recognising their role on the day. It all seemed over the top to one of our governors until I explained that as the classroom had electricity it was a building and not a shed. If we wanted it sanctioned as a building then we would have had to apply for planning permission which we had not. As such, to have two important local dignitaries perform the ceremony meant I was satisfied nobody would say anything as they had been culpable in the act. My Governor looked at me in amazement and before she was able to say anything, I said, "Do not worry ... let's not get bogged down with red tape!" Not a word one way or another was said by anyone. The Councillor actually bought some vegetables from our allotment and went home happy with them knowing the publicity in the paper would serve him well. Land Studies and Forestry went from strength to strength in this room and soon another was added without any formal event to sanction its reality as a building.

The quality of Art in the school was beyond belief following the appointment of another teacher from the Black Country. Her accent and laughter livened up the classroom as she inspired everyone entering. Completely immersed in her love of all things art and able to conjure up interest, expression and quality in her student's work with total ease – it was a classroom that drew me to pop in most days. When observed, every lesson was deemed to be at worst outstanding and at best in need of a new OFSTED framework descriptor. A key achievement being when she took over a gallery in town and displayed students' work. The subsequent accolades from local artists and lecturers at the University Art School were well deserved. Her infectious manner as a tutor equally impactful on the Year Elevens. I told her once that she was completely bonkers and without doubt the best Art Teacher that I had ever met and had the pleasure to work with. She saw both comments as huge positives and was only upset with me when I wouldn't relax enough to accommodate a quite firm hug from her.

So many others on the staff having their own box of tricks, fingertip spells and words of charm to draw from the students the very best of outcomes. In a five-year period the Year Eleven and Post Sixteen exam results leapt up from around two hundred student pass grades to over one thousand. In addition, students were leaving to go to College of Further Education, Agricultural College and Work placements in greater numbers. Testament to a collegiate spirit amongst the staff to raise standards and make the school a centre of excellence.

It was at such a point that our link with the LEA came to an end on a daily basis when the staff decided as a whole team, that to become an Academy was better for us in seeking our own future going forward. It was an easy decision for us all to make as the LEA seemed bereft of any ability to help shape our future development and provide any positive guidance. So, it proved a great move as we became known for the quality of what we did as an academy and began to deliver support and training beyond the boundaries of the LEA and take on work in the South East and abroad, related to SEN in mainstream and special schools. These included projects funded by Academy chains, British Council and the Department for Education. My Chair of Governors at this point remarked, "So where are OFSTED when there's a chance they might get the judgement right?"

By this time, we were on our third Chair of Governors with the latest also chairing a well-respected Academy chain in the South East. He had replaced a very canny ex-Education Officer who had been with us for two years and proved a great ally for me in taking on staff difficulties and knowing how to play a winning hand with the LEA. The Governing Body had also improved greatly with more local and business expertise and less of the friends of friend's friends which had blighted progress and intellectual debates in meetings. No more dogs under the table or protracted discussions about families for me to contend with. The once puzzled look on my SIP when doing my own performance management soon relieved too. He had been asked once if I was pressing for improvement too much when he had expressed my relentless pursuit of Outstanding practice as a rich compliment. A Governor then asked if I was working the staff too hard. His retort was polite and simple.

The latter equating to her understanding of what was expected of a Headteacher, albeit I was now a Principal.

My SLT had changed over this time too with arrivals from mainstream Grammars, a successful Comprehensive School and an internal promotion. My charismatic Deputy had secured a Headship and been replaced by an equally industrious and high performing teacher who had found a way of fitting twenty-seven hours into a day when moving the pace of change on in school as well as running her family. The Assistant Head of Post Sixteen had retired to live in the East Midlands. A sad loss to me of someone so loyal and hard-working. Yet it was the best thing for her and her husband. She had been replaced by a quality practitioner teacher from a Grammar School who had previously worked in Prisons and now took on the Assistant Head post for the Upper School. The third change being the appointment of the most energetic excitable individual formerly teaching P.E. to become the Assistant Head of the Lower School.

Finally, my Business Manager had retired and after we had part sponsored her assistant through professional exams the investment paid off when she was promoted as successor. This being a great appointment and once in post the changes to admin. and site staff teams were transformational, and her impact on the upkeep and building programmes became key to our site being a much better place to work in.

It was a joy to work with them and let them play out their roles so effectively as high performing colleagues leading on all manner of academy improvement matters. Without a doubt they were the very best Leadership Team of all I had worked with and I could not have wished for any better. Something I told them readily … and from time to time gently reminded them of sustaining should their focus dip. My weekly hour-long meeting with each of them being my way of keeping abreast of their work, offering advice and direction, holding them to account of tasks in hand, establishing any coaching needs and gaining an insight into their well-being. These 'KIT' [Keep in Touch] Sessions used and valued on both sides and key to sustaining that drive to continued success. Used by them with their own teams within the academy their value proven in moving us forward together. This is simple and yet sometimes so easily overlooked.

The question 'Do you know what is actually going on in your school/academy?' can be a challenging one and I believed it required for such regular and well thought out contact. To be followed up with immersion in lessons, break times and so on enabled me to feel and see what I had heard in those meetings. If my door was 'always open' it was because I had gone out into the building ... not just so I could receive visitors.

After having worked for my professional association locally and then represented two LEAs in the South East as a National Executive member with lead roles on SEN, I had been encouraged to stand as a National Officer with the prospect of becoming National Vice President. I talked through the role and responsibility with my SLT and received warm encouragement to give it my best try. A month later the National Executive were faced with an outstanding Head of a Primary School in the East Midlands and myself to choose from. Following our respective speeches, the voting took place, and my mandate was secured with nearly two thirds of the vote. My team were pleased for me and knew that following my Vice-Presidential Year, I would be away as National President on a full time sabbatical. Their humour rich at the thought that a leading figure in education was soon to be their Principal, the Harley Davidson riding biker with an eagle tattoo on his arm following his sixtieth birthday.

That personal detail was not yet fully shared with my National Executive colleagues and was parked for the time being. It would undoubtedly cause a stir and a sense of disbelief as many of them had not seen me in that light ... as of yet.

The fact remained that as far as my SLT were concerned, I believed they were ready to step up for that challenge and spent the subsequent year adding coaching and delegated additional opportunity to ensure they could do just that. It gave me time to step back and watch them perform at the top of their game and in time my new Deputy, and now Vice Principal for Curriculum, was appointed as Interim Principal to take charge for my year away.

During the latter part of the Spring Term, I looked back at the milestones and the death of my Wolverhampton Head of Year and 'Champion of Wit' was first in my mind. I wondered what he would have had to say about the changes that had been achieved and the position I was due to take up. Then other losses of staff were remembered too. The very first being the Speech Therapist who had died of cancer. She had always giggled when I said 'last, grass, past, mast and class' with my northern accent. Her words so clipped and precise as she would have me believe. Yet she was originally from Scarborough, seen by my family as their home town. I had visited her in hospital at the request of her husband and daughter to find her in a coma and close to death. We talked at her bedside to each other and her with the knowledge she could probably hear as that sense is reputed to be the last to go. Her husband teased me saying "So Kim, when will you learn to speak properly and say 'clarse' and 'grarse' rather than your northern 'class' and 'grass'? You know we took ages to get her (pointing at his wife) to speak properly and she then made a living from it!" As he spoke, I'm sure his wife smiled. She died an hour later.

There was also the sad death of a quite mercurial therapist, again from cancer. He had made a massive impact in helping to replicate the Pastoral Provision to that at my previous school. When I attended his funeral, I realised sometimes we really only know a little bit about our staff and what they both do and how they live. At the church people were invited to stand up and tell a story of their life with him. To hear so much variety, much of it mischievous fun, was wonderful. As each friend stood up it almost became a competition to tell the wildest tale. It was capped by the telling of his top ten pop hit in the Dutch charts, decades before. I had never been present at an occasion where so much respect, admiration and love had been expressed for a single person.

Finally, there was the very sad loss of a Teaching Assistant who had succumbed to a drink problem. Despite my best efforts and those of numerous others we lost him to this sickness and he was found dead in a city nearby. His death had been a lonely affair, and it rippled through the staff reminding us all of how important it was to go the extra yard for all in our school family.

These five, characters in their own right, were all good people. As far as colleagues and many pupils were concerned, they had all been much valued and were subsequently missed in many ways. When our Speech Therapist died, her husband wanted a memento of some sort to be ever present in school. After much deliberation we agreed on a chair carved by the famous 'Mouseman' Carpenter from North Yorkshire. A wonderful legacy of her life with his 'signature' of a carved mouse on the arm. The seat was placed in one of the indoor open areas and was for a student in difficulty to go to if seeking help. It was often used and greatly appreciated by those challenged by their disability and seeking how to find a way through life.

All of these staff losses further focusing my mind on staff well-being and in particular the need to look after my key players ... my SLT. I knew it paid to invest time in looking out for the issues which impacted on my staff and consequently had put in place 'well-being' moments in our routine. It paid in this setting and when we introduced a performance management target on the topic all staff saw the value and worked as hard on that as they did on all others. The important postscript being whatever was achieved on this specific target was dutifully celebrated as a 'pass' ... with encouragement to do even better the following year.

I also reflected that in the period I was to be away that I may meet some difficult politicians and advisers at the Department for Education, but would they pose as big a mental challenge as one or two of my parents? One that particularly came to mind was the mother and sole parent of a very troubled and complex ASD student. Prior to her son's arrival with us she had been Chair of the Curriculum Committee on his School's Governing Body. On that basis any issues related to her son were portrayed as shortcomings in our educational offer substantiated by her alleged wealth of experience. While she had been acknowledged as making a fair point on a couple of occasions, it was by no means the norm. My Leadership Team would step aside very quickly and bow to my years of experience when such as a meeting with her was scheduled. They would even make me an extra strong coffee suggesting it would 'help me stay awake should she go off on one and get boring'.

After being routed several times by me her new approach had been to bring a tape recorder in to record all meetings. When asked why, she had replied it was useful to be able to extract both her words and mine later if she needed to challenge further or complain. When asked if she had watched reruns of T.V. Programmes such as Morse, The Bill and so on she confirmed she had. At that, I said that she must know then that her tapes were inadmissible ... as there should be one for her to take away and one for me so as to make sure there was no skulduggery. Having her on the back-foot I would then confirm that despite that omission I was happy for her to proceed. With glee on her face, she would turn on the tape as we commenced ... whereupon I would state the time, date and name those persons present. Where no verbal answers were given by her or her son to challenges made or questions asked I would state, "For the benefit of the tape I can confirm Mrs X (or Student X) nodded their head in recognition" and so on throughout the meeting. My colleague from SLT sat with me barely speaking and just about resisted laughing. Needless to say, this brought an end to her practice as it was all too much for her ... evidently.

When her son left, she thanked me for my tolerance and patience ... I just about resisted saying that she hadn't been that bad really!

At around this time Gervase Phinn was speaking at a local church in order to help raise funds for the Vicar's charity abroad. We had the brief opportunity to talk before he started and again in the interval. He was, as ever, genuinely interested in what I had been up to since the last time we had talked, which was at the Stephen Joseph Theatre in Scarborough. How refreshing it was to hear him speak well of a time when working in that particular LEA had been such a pleasant experience with so many supportive colleagues to hand. He showed genuine interest in the story bubbling up inside me and I was encouraged by his support. "Just write to me," he said and then went into the second half of his spell-binding talk to all those sat so attentively in the pews.

During this he caused a bit of a stir by making a direct reference to me and then pointed me out from his lofty position in the pulpit. All gathered, some being my neighbours from the street nearby, turned to see who this fellow was being referenced so warmly. I know I glowed ... both a tad embarrassed and indeed somewhat with pride. It is not often that one is commended so publicly for being a school leader. I have reminded several of my Chairs of Governors that it is okay for them to do likewise ... and said I will do the same for them when such situations arise. In doing so the challenge was once 'Let's see who makes the other smile the most broadly!'

That role was about to be added to even further as I had another cap to wear in our busy world of education.

My Vice-Presidential Year saw me out on numerous occasions at additional meetings and activities than previously had been the case. Seen as a 'prepare and learn' year it was enjoyable and often requiring being away for several days at a time. My contact with SLT remained timetabled in and the weekly 'KIT' sessions with them enabled me to keep my finger on the pulse and encourage them all to fly more freely in their roles.

Lower School was becoming the trendsetter for activities involving Parent and Carer engagement. The Assistant Principal continuing in her excitable vein and taking all her Tutor Team and students with her. As a result, the opportunities I had to monitor lessons, do learning walks at any time of the day and engage with staff and students revealed an energy and desire in every aspect of the provision. It was undoubtedly her peak time with her team, and her peers on SLT were often in awe of her relentless drive and long 'Next Week I will do ...' List. Upper School likewise, and the College placements and Work Experiences really took off. To see students race back in with tales to tell of hairdressing, engineering, mucking out the stables, learning to drive a car and meeting other students indicated that many were enjoying being with us so much that leaving in the summer may be an enormous wrench.

The ASD provision was continually inspired by their Assistant Principal and Pastoral Lead. Both Primary and Secondary phases having accepted some more challenging behaviours but never fully overstretched or out of ideas. That is not to say that there weren't any tough moments and the need for quick thinking to keep this jewel in our provision on task in its delivery of the most marvellous educational experience.

The presence of the younger ones in Primary gave this aspect of our provision a real sense of family. It also helped in a calming way to see their fresh-faced grins lapping up the experience afforded them. The confidence in these staff permeating across all others from Lower and Upper so when they taught such students they did so with greater confidence. These 'magicians' also found themselves more widely used in supporting our Outreach team in local Primary and Secondary Schools in the LEA and as far away as Portsmouth. Their knowledge and understanding of autism now being seen more than exemplar but also a regional resource. So much for the lead AP not believing in herself. She had become a magnet for practitioners wanting to improve.

Having established herself with the Subject Leaders to increase the breadth of our curriculum offer and its accreditation at examination level as well as by subject awards, the Vice Principal Curriculum had updated our assessment practices. Working with our SIP the process now assimilated our old 'P' Scale and National Curriculum assessment continuum into our own fully expanded adaptation of both. Small steps in student progress now more easily captured and evidenced. She then joined the Vice Principal Pastoral in working on measuring Social Skill and Behavioural Progress. Our overall evidence base for Student Progress now quite ground-breaking.

The VP Pastoral always had a keen eye for development of the Medical, Therapy and Counselling roles of his Team and the Parent and Carer Partnership duo. The work he established fully meeting the needs of our students and their Parents and Carers. It cost us close to two hundred thousand pounds per annum, which should have really been funded by Health and Social Care. The benefit for us being they were our staff team and they mostly prevented our complex students being absent to attend appointments off-site. So pleased was he with its impact I felt sure he would dream each night of HMI telling him the Provision was 'Second to None' ... as indeed he had two inspections previously. When reviewing that provision with him, I could see that the initial promise made in my first term was now fully realised.

Finally, the School Business Manager was fast becoming another star in our midst. Further courses and qualifications seeing her feted for advice both locally and nationally ... and accruing income streams to add to our overstretched coffers. We soon had solar panels on the roof generating electricity which we sold back to the grid and she was busy developing contacts for funding and construction of a much-needed sports hall. Her admin. team, led by my brilliant attention to detail PA, and the site team, ensured that the staff always had everything they needed to deliver education to the students. She was known for her 'I do not take prisoners approach' but her bite was harmless as every butterfly entering her office could testify to. Actually, it was only such as a butterfly that could stop her mid-sentence and cause her to run away. I told her several times that if one of the Senior Team was absent then we would only struggle a bit if it was for any length of time ... however, if she was away, the well-oiled machine she had engineered would stall pretty quickly. Fortunately, she was not a great fan of 'being ill' and one of her favourite lines was often 'Get over it!'

As that academic year ended and the new one started the academy community was preparing itself for change and a new leader for the year ahead. In my mind the Governors were confident in the preparation and the SIP was booked in for further coaching and development sessions. In short ... what was there not to be confident about in leaving the 'shop' to this worthy and hard-working team?

As the day approached for my departure, some of the students with autism struggled with the sense of this significant change in their structured learning environment. None more so than a Year Thirteen who had taken six years to look me in the eyes and speak to me. Now his greeting warm and the brightest of smiles extended to his deployment of a split-second fist bump with me when saying 'Good morning'. He was concerned about what was going to happen to my office and who was going to say 'Hello' to him each day. His body twitching as he spoke suggesting that he wanted to launch at me and surprise me with a hug. My words reassured him and he walked away muttering "See him soon ... see him soon!"

My last weekly 'KIT' meetings with my SLT saw me hand over more responsibility to them as they highlighted their aspirations and personal targets for the year ahead. They needed no reassurance ... just the opportunity ... their enthusiasm and confidence clearly showing that they would be fine.

Their smiles telling all ... and that they had something planned for my last day and this year-long absence that was to follow.

It wasn't some clever philosopher who told me, "What we create needs time to flower," it was a Year Thirteen when working in one of our greenhouses. She added, "You just have to let it do its own thing now sir!"

Those words equally applied to my team ... and they were about to start the realisation of their excellent 'growing time' to run the academy in my absence.

Chapter 15

The Head of Heads in a Game of Minds

Having a place on the Headteacher's Association National Executive was an interesting insight into trade union representation as well as their advice, training and policy development. With around fifty members and the Headquarter's staff, our four meetings each year had given me the opportunity to appreciate the workings of the organisation and its influence. Most of the members of Executive at the time being Primary Heads with a few from Special and Secondary Schools. Men outnumbered the women and at times the consensus of the 'middle ground' was that it resembled a bit of a 'Boy's Club' in some of its approaches. Perhaps a touch unfair, nevertheless the testosterone often seemed overactive and a few did little to dismiss such a jibe. Certainly, the Primary centric approach of its business had the potential to sideline the other two.

The General Secretary looked to wrestle with that and actively encouraged change, working hard with both sectors. His eloquent and much respected approach to all business signifying from the start that he was going to modernise the organisation and increase its credibility and influence. This helped by the seemingly gifted and intuitive manner he deployed on meeting, greeting and engaging with all within the world of education. At my start on the Executive, it was not difficult to admire him and pay absolute attention to him when in full flow. On more than one occasion I sensed in him a little frustration when trying to politely drag some Headteacher members up to a more modern and credible position in our meetings. As time passed, I heard the DfE openly admit he was 'trusted and sought after'. As indeed did members who also described him as respected, knowledgeable and persuasive in his tactics when engaging all other partners in the busy and ever-changing world of education. As the months and years passed it was obvious that his visionary style would ensure that our key issues would be delivered ... as indeed they were.

I had come to be on the National Executive after the representative for the South East resigned following disagreement over some policy issues. He was a loss to them with his background in Secondary and his current leadership role running a mixed Grammar School. When attending my first ever National Conference on the South Coast he approached me and encouraged me to take over from him. This was then added to by an elderly and long serving ex-head bringing me a coffee with a smile then trapping me in a corner while she added her views. This two-pronged approach clearly coordinated and for their part well executed ... as I agreed. With the recalcitrant subject leader and his mutinous ways now resolved back at school it definitely seemed an opportunity worth grasping ... even if just for a change.

My involvement in the Association first started on my return from Germany when I took up the Deputy's post in the Residential Special School. During that time my early engagement had been very low key with no specific active role. Then the Head and Deputy from the school where my wife was working encouraged me to go to the Special Head's Conference organised by the Association. Meeting with other school leaders from the EBD sector was too good an opportunity to miss, having just become the Head myself. The professional debate and advice updates were very engaging and empowered my thinking as to how to manage both my staff and the LEA.

There were a few interesting moments highlighting that some of those attending liked to play hard, as they felt it was only right after working hard. Not unexpectedly, they tended to be from the very same type of provision as myself. Their conduct suggesting strongly that there was more than a degree of truth in the belief that if you worked with children with behavioural problems long enough then you were likely to take on some of their attributes. At the end of the first day their consumption of alcohol was such that in the black-tie dinner their revelry was over the top. Our keynote speaker, the then esteemed and long-serving General Secretary, was in full flow relating political challenges with the Government, when a noise erupted. It was on a table nearby to the one I was sat at with my colleagues. The table had about eight serving heads from residential EBD schools sat seemingly in their own little world or was it universe? The laughter and language such that all others present were both shocked at their behaviour and embarrassed for our numerous guests. Oblivious to their impact they continued and only stopped when the wine ran out and so did they ... to the bar.

The following morning, I went into breakfast having scanned the room so as to avoid any of these fellows. I went to sit at another table where a male headteacher and his wife were already having their breakfast. As I sat the wicker chair collapsed underneath me as a leg folded. In getting up I apologised to my breakfast companions saying, "Oh my goodness how embarrassing, I'm sorry about that ... you must think I'm one of those EBD Heads from last evening!" The man chuckled and replied, "It's okay, it wasn't your fault ... and by the way I am also a Head of an EBD School and I'm pretending to be otherwise so as to not be associated with them either!" We all laughed, then I explained that I was too.

Later that day a keynote speaker on education practice delivered an inspiring speech to rapturous applause. Eager to use the bathroom he then rushed off stage. The loudspeakers in the hall were then filled with the noise of him emptying his bladder in the urinal. The background to this being a reflection of two EBD Heads of their alcoholically damaged grey matter and resultant headaches. I was urged to rescue the keynote speaker and spare him any further blushes ... and protect the sensitivities of all others from our hungover colleagues. He had walked into the Gents still wearing his radio microphone switched on. I'm sure he referenced it in the future as an ice breaker when presenting at other conferences. Undoubtedly missing out the words of those stood near him at the urinals.

After that I got involved in the local branch of the Association covering the coastal area and part inland. The lead person being a Primary Head of immense height accentuated by his slim build. It was during this time that I became more aware of the representational role performed by him and regional officers. This being called for when I was taken ill and proving supportive in helping me leave with dignity. My time in the Gulf and then in London being fallow years for such engagement and only renewed when with Special Heads during the 'Acronym War' and the battles of BAD ... BARD ... or does it really matter? It was at this point I took on the Branch Secretary role.

The suggestion of the title being that organising meetings and taking the minutes was all that was required. But nothing could be further from the truth. I took over from the Grammar School Head who had been mildly upset with my superior view and seat at the D of E Awards Ceremony in the Cathedral. He claimed I was well suited to the role of representing members, arguing the toss with the LEA and thwarting the efforts of other teacher union representatives. Indeed, that became a focus as such work requirements rolled in from beleaguered members.

The LEA had not been noted for its Outstanding practices and this reflected on the quality of provision found in several schools. In an attempt to raise standards, various initiatives were put into practice by them with Headteachers being put under great stress. The heads in some cases bullied into practices with their staff causing them additional pressure. They then turned to their teacher unions claiming they were bullied. In turn they then complained to the LEA about bullying Headteachers. Overly keen Human Resource (HR) advisers too often missed the start point of this cycle and how the top-down approach had not worked. Subsequently they did not advise on change of strategy but just went for the Head. In some cases, such beleaguered colleagues lost their jobs and were broken by the experience. It came as no surprise to hear of developing mental health issues amongst some Primary Heads within the LEA. One summer the tragic news of a Head hanging herself at home in the garage in the South West was shocking news ... but sadly not a surprise.

In meetings with other Union representatives, it was pleasing to note a desire to try and find a positive and mutually beneficial outcome to such difficulties. Many such challenges being resolved in this way. However, two of the reps seemed pre-programmed with revolutionary guard behaviours akin to that deployed I recall at the long-gone British Leyland. Whatever the rationale for such Management and Union relations then it seemed outdated in these times. Yet, the two reps could make the use of the word 'Management' sound more abusive than being told to 'F★★★ Off!' by one of my former behaviourally-challenged pupils. With them there was often not much room for manoeuvre. I regularly wondered if the training they had been through required some sort of frontal lobotomy and use of drugs to induce aggression. When sharing this with colleagues the rather sick joke of 'Have you tried dropping Ritalin in their coffee?' although outrageous in suggestion it often seemed rather tempting.

In meetings directly with the Director of Children's Services (DCS) the conversations were positive in outcome. Issues related to her concerns about schools and their heads were often identical to our worries about LEA practice. The result being something that worked for both without resigning to mediocrity on anyone's part. This could be a challenge for some Headteacher colleagues and best exemplified by a Head whose school was in dire trouble due to poor test outcomes. Rather than talk about operational changes in Literacy and Numeracy to improve the quality of teaching and learning with her Year Six pupils she wanted to develop happiness within the school with a curriculum initiative. Being a big believer in such a strategy I commended her saying it would be a good way of improving things within her school at the same time as improving Literacy and Numeracy. To my surprise she pondered and then announced she was just going to do the 'happiness work'. At this point I had to be more robust in my supportive and coaching role fearing if she continued in this way, she would lose her job. So I said, "When OFSTED come next they will be pleased to see your children happy and smiling but if it isn't translating into or indeed because they are achieving better outcomes then you will probably fail your Inspection!" She was stunned by my suggestion and said she would think on the matter. Months later they failed their OFSTED, the children were not smiling much, the literacy and numeracy provision was cited as poor and the head criticised for lacking a focus on improving standards. She was dismissed by her Governors at the request of the LEA. This tale repeated in similar ways elsewhere.

In follow up discussions with colleagues it was clear that this particular headteacher had chosen her path despite support and advice on offer. Our concern being how many others were there in similar difficulties ... and how do we reach them?

The enjoyment in overturning challenges by some Governors who were 'wannabe Headteachers' was welcome. Two cases saw Chairs of Governors at a Secondary and Primary being removed for overstepping their role and trying to take over the operational performance of a Headteacher. It actually required having to embarrass them in meetings with the LEA by going through their full actions to show malpractice. This was then followed by a number of training sessions where the LEA were updating Chairs of Governors on performance of their role. The LEA trainer stated that 'As a Chair you should not believe your Headteacher when he/she presents their report in your next Governor's Meeting'. This information received from a number of Heads who had subsequently been in such a meeting and confirmed by two Chairs of Governors also present at the training. As an Association our good working relationship with the Director was such that I was able to send an email to her stating what had happened and added, "As such I have asked all Headteachers when delivering their Report in Governor's Meetings to place their left hand on the Bible (recent copy received from Michael Gove, the Secretary of State for Education) and say: I swear that the HT Report I am about to give is the truth, the whole truth and nothing but the truth so SEF (Self Evaluation Form) me God!"

To her credit immediate action was taken to remedy the situation ... and next time we met she said my email had been helpful and amusing in its direction to HT members.

When she left her role with us it was a sad loss to the LEA as her integrity and honest engagement 'for children and young people' was always excellent. Many Headteachers believed she had been let down by inept performances of the senior and middle managers in her team. My experience of such officers had been I could clearly see that there was some truth in that belief.

On joining the National Executive, I found it best at first to work out the dynamic of discussions and protocol for engaging. It seemed that certain voices were often prompted into making challenges, requiring technical clarification or just being mischievous in pre-arranged discussions. This bandit-style practice belying the fact we were all on the same side and while holding the General Secretary and his HQ staff to account was part of our governance role it wasn't particularly solution-focussed and indicative of the majority of experienced headteacher practitioners present.

It was really after a few Executive members came to an end of their tenure in office, that things began to change. Part of that undoubtedly due to many younger more open-minded members and indeed the fact many of them were female. Soon after, I was spurred into rebuking a statement made by a colleague in one open discussion about representation afforded to School Business Managers (SBMs) on Executive. The suggestion being that they didn't require separate representation and stating they were not 'school leaders'. I cited my SBM in her qualification, performance of role and credibility on my SLT as an example of what they were in all forward-looking schools. My colleague smarted somewhat at my words. His silence on the matter secured at our next National Conference when I proposed a successful motion for SBMs to have a member on National Executive. Part of my case being 'You cannot say welcome … pay your subs … and not give them a voice!' It worked and their influence subsequently increased and their performance in schools was significantly more valued.

How pleasing it was a few years later to open their Conference in the Midlands and state that 'SBMs were a key cog in the wheel of successful leadership teams'. My speech was welcomed. In it I had slightly embarrassed my own SBM who was sat in the front row when I turned to her and thanked her specifically for being our SLT's 'key cog'. Afterwards a number of her colleagues approached me saying they wished they were seen in the same light … showing there was still work to do on their status.

We moved around the country for our National Executive meetings in order to open some sessions up to local branches. It was disappointing that this was not always taken up by them. Probably more indicative of how busy members were in their own schools. Of all the locations we visited I found Cardiff, Bath and Belfast the best for both the accommodation and opportunity to explore in between meetings. It was usual to have an evening meal in a prestige setting and Stormont Castle stood out as quite spectacular.

Another was the Churchill War Rooms in London. Here we entertained the Press in the historic underground nerve centre from WW2. We were sat at large tables with Press members either side of each of us. Some I recognised as regular faces on the T.V.. When in conversation with one from a national newspaper she became quite intrigued by my Special School setting and our practice. Her questions seemed genuine and she was complimentary about my stories of students and staff. When she asked if she could do a story for the Sunday edition, I was very pleased at her question. Her follow up was astonishing as she asked, "Do your pupils look like they have got special needs? I'm sorry to ask but if they do then my Editor won't want a photo of them!" All others around our table paused mid-sentence and looked towards me. I replied, "Oh they are fine ... but some of the staff look a bit dodgy!" My ironic rebuke ensured that was the end of our conversation ... needless to say, no article was ever written.

Each Autumn at Executive we would vote in the next National Vice President after holding hustings. I had seen several very worthy colleagues on Executive be successful and after a year in post go on to be the Association's National President. My continued outspoken nature and alleged quick wit were deemed enough at an Executive Meeting in Wales to warrant colleagues from London to actively encourage me consider standing. We were in a bar one evening watching a pitiful England footballing performance when they started down this road. I was amused and flattered by their thoughts and engaged in a discussion with them in a more serious vein when England went two nil down.

During the summer I was approached again by two close colleagues and decided I would have a go. I remembered the words of three Executive members from two years earlier, over coffee. They were discussing who they were going to vote for and the notion of a Special Head was scoffed at. Surprising really as the hardest-working and singularly most knowledgeable person I was regularly meeting with at the time was an ex-Special Head and ex-National President. How limited their memories were and this opposition stuck with me as I prepared my speech for the hustings. I was up against a very capable female Head for whom I had a great deal of admiration and respect. If she was to win, I would have accepted that without question. If she won because the poor thought processes of those dinosaur-like outspoken former colleagues was prevalent, then I would be very disappointed. Having won with a two-thirds mandate I received the generous and genuine congratulations of my opponent.

I became Vice President at National Conference in Liverpool and so started a three-year period of being a National Officer of the most respected Association representing school Leaders in England, Wales, Northern Ireland, Isle of Man, Channel Islands and Service Children's Schools. The occasion was an eye opener up on the platform and in support of Tony 'my President' a Primary Head from Milton Keynes. The meal for Executive took place at Anfield, the home of Liverpool FC where I had first visited with two of my Uncles back in 1971. Photo shoots on pitch side saw President and Vice holding on to the Champions League Cup in a quite pretentious way with the famous Kop as a backdrop. That photo was shown a year later in a bar to a group of Red Scousers who were over to watch Barcelona play at home. It silenced them and their jealousy was such that my brother and I received free drinks and I had to airdrop the photo from my phone.

At conference the key matters of the moment were Academies, Assessment, Pay and Conditions and OFSTED. Subjects that proved dynamite in debate and strong motions were subsequently voted through shaping our policy and practice for the year ahead. In a meeting with the press, reference was made to OFSTED and its impact on schools. The phrase Maverick teachers came up and I spoke on the matter saying that, "The brave or perhaps the 'Mavericks' amongst us had been leading our schools with the confidence to take calculated risks for and on behalf of their learning community. That a maverick was someone prepared to innovate and lead their team without fear that OFSTED may not see it fitting the framework." I added that, "I believed that we had let OFSTED worry us and dominate our thoughts in a way that sometimes destroyed our confidence and limit our energy."

There was a brief thoughtful moment in the room when I spoke as such a maverick … it delayed their next question and made them think. It soon followed that the Chief HMI for schools was somewhat critical about 'maverick' heads. Interestingly, he too must have taken some time to think through those words and in a wise farewell speech on his retirement he was reported as saying more heads should be just so.

During the 'VP Year' I found myself in demand for various speaker sessions and other meetings and soon learnt how to perform to such audiences with guidance from our able General Secretary. The preparation for Presidency was quite thorough and the more I accepted, the more I was asked to do. At one event I was fortunate to once again meet the Chair of the Education Select Committee. It had been a while since I had last seen him. The most recent being when I spoke at a Westminster Forum event. I was on the second panel of speakers and in the coffee break stood at the back of the room taking in the majesty of its decor and thinking through what was about to follow. He approached me and smiled then stood alongside me with his back to the wall. He turned sideways and said, "Special Branch?" Surprised at his question I replied, "Sorry, what did you say?" He then responded with, "Are you Special Branch?" and he pointed at my lapel badge, adding "That's the badge they are wearing this week!" When I told him it was a Scarborough Football Club badge and I was one of the Speakers he would shortly be introducing he rocked with laughter. I met him again in the House of Commons the following year and spoke at another event he chaired at the Conservative Conference on School Leadership. He remembered thereafter that I had not taken up any offer from Special Branch despite that brief question as an eighteen-year-old when at University.

It was very pleasing to play a part in developing the relaunch of the Special Heads Conference which then had to be more inclusive in both its title and content to recognise Special Educational Needs Coordinators (SENCOs) in mainstream and those from Alternative Provisions and PRUs. This made absolute sense, but did cause a bit of a stir with one colleague on Executive who, despite the fact he had inclusivity running through his veins, could not cope with the change of title. The work on Autism with learned colleagues from Education, Research and Psychiatry another milestone at this time. The 'Big Shout' Conference and book publication acknowledging that girls had been an overlooked cohort within the Autistic Spectrum community was an extremely popular development ... with the Head and pupils from a Surrey Special School successfully raising the profile of girls with this condition. It had added specific value to the ongoing Neuroscience work that I had been championing with other SEND Committee Members and eminent Professors.

Further work with the Royal College of Speech and Language Therapists (RCSLT) in London also gave me the chance to progress my own professional development and take on a role in the 'Bercow Ten Years On' Review Group. The staff at their offices in London and other professionals on the group keen to amplify the issues of speech and language difficulties in schools and the need for further work with our association. It was at this point that I was struck by the lack of real commitment by some colleagues at our Headquarters to pick this issue up for the benefit of mainstream schools as well as special. In the end it felt like the challenge of furthering the great work of RCSLT was a burden they would rather pass on. It was a bit of a struggle to open a few minds and often the blocking was energetic in its ability to be unproductive.

My presence on this review group was clearly more valued by the RCSLT and I found myself at events in Westminster supporting their work and yet continuing to try and engage our Policy

Team. The fact that one in ten children have long-term language difficulty and around fifty per cent. of children starting school do so without the language they need for their learning, ended up being the tipping point for real engagement. From this, a working partnership began to thrive and the need for action research was agreed.

When at an event in the Speaker's Rooms I managed to talk with the Speaker himself. He had been the instigator of the initial report and was pleased to meet with me particularly as his son's early year's teacher had been my daughter, at that time a very successful Deputy in a London Primary with specialist provision. The event also having an ex-politician, former Secretary of State and T.V. dancing celebrity present who eloquently explained his skilful strategy for answering questions without stammering in his delivery. It was at this point that I reconsidered the cynical view that the reason politicians took questions in threes was so that they could be expansive in their answer, avoiding any of the three questions and broadening their reply so as to make a political speech. He explained that he was then given 'take up time' to think through how to reply without using certain letters at the start of words which would trigger his stammering. Whether completely true or not, it served well in him making a point which he then developed in a charming and empathetic way with a stammering Sixth Former giving a welcome address. A different side of him was there to be seen and one I hadn't really noted when he was in office.

There were some meetings at the Department for Education (DfE) which were curious in content and never really seemed to have any noticeable impact. One such being a SEND Expert Group where we were given papers we had to hand back at the end as they were not allowed to be taken from the room. At one point the secrecy was such I questioned a colleague whether we were in fact in the midst of MI5 policy-makers. The first two questions they were seeking answers to were: 'What do schools that offer really good support to all SEN pupils look like?' And: 'What are the barriers to schools being able and willing to offer this kind of support?' Aside from the fact I was amazed that such questions seemed to indicate a total lack of understanding on their part ... I was in my element in this session. I was able to talk about how I felt aspirational leadership impacted on such schools and develop the DfE officials on the sense of my school saying, 'There was no ceiling to the student's learning' and how we made sure that 'school fitted the child'. The real question remaining ... how much notice was actually taken of us as practitioners after we left the building?

When visiting OFSTED, I was always amused by their security being provided by ex-Gurkha soldiers. The very idea that their lives were in danger would be a tremendous surprise to the teaching ranks of English Schools. The Chief Inspector (HMCI) was a gruff character and when in his presence one always sensed that his HMI teams were guarded about all they said ... and probably needed to be so. To meet with their lead on SEN was much more open and as such the conversations helpful to us and him. Albeit, he would often say that he would deny anything if it was repeated outside the building. At first, I thought this was for real. As time passed, I was just not quite sure.

On one occasion when in a meeting chaired by HMCI with other union representatives present and several HMIs the agenda was worked through fairly quickly. There then followed a touch of mischief when HMCI pushed his national annual report across the table and growled, "Tell me ... why is it that schools in the North don't do as well as schools in the South?" There was a pause before anyone dared to speak and then he must have wondered what was happening because he said, "Oh I am sorry, is anyone here from the North?" At this point a Secondary Union rep put her hand up and he offered a half-hearted apology if he had upset her. I was sat at the end of the table and had my hand raised. When he looked towards me, I said, "Yes I am ... but it is okay ... I am down here doing missionary work!" All those facing HMCI turned and looked at me worryingly as if I was about to be taken away by the Gurkha guards. The HMIs behind him all had brave grins on their faces that they managed to restrain from turning into laughter ... and then lose when he turned to them. Afterwards the joke was that I would probably get the call saying my Academy was getting a quick inspection because I had gone back at him. The call never came ... and the green woodpecker was probably busy somewhere else anyway!

When I became National President at our Birmingham Conference my inaugural speech referenced SEND as a key agenda item for my year in office. It was welcomed and I heard no dinosaurs repeating 'We tried a SEN Head as our President and it didn't work' in the auditorium. Far from it, as the ever-increasing challenges presented in teaching children with a co-morbidity of needs was as much a mainstream issue as it was one for specialist provisions. Sitting in the hot seat I was pleased to be in post and about to totally launch myself into the role leaving my school behind. They had given me the most incredible send off and clearly spent a great deal of time and thought in making it a quite memorable day. It was so touching to hear from them all ... students, parents and carers, staff and governors ... how much they valued me, were going to miss me and how much success they wished me. Then I was gone.

A few days later, there I was in Birmingham with delegates from across England, Wales, Northern Ireland, Channel Islands and the Isle of Man. The huge room of the conference centre packed with them, guests and the press. Our 'speak out loud to the educational world moment' ready to go. My inauguration a formal part of proceedings was a key part of the event as I then took the chair to lead the conference proceedings.

It was customary for the incoming President to have a member of their school community introduce them and paint a portrait for Conference. My SLT and staff with Governors, students and their Parents and Carers had a different idea and put together a short film. It was based upon the classic T.V. Comedy 'Car Share' using a minibus driving up and down our long school drive. The conversations laced with humour of all sorts serving to tell the story of me their Head/Principal, now the Association's President. Sat in the front row of the auditorium were my parents, brothers, children and grandchildren. Periodically I would glance towards them to gauge how they felt about what was said about me and what I was saying in my speech. Two of my grandchildren were absolutely out cold … deep in sleep and obviously riveted by every single word.

One of the main topics at conference was the issue of schools being forced to become academies. My speech had been released to the press beforehand so National and Local press as well as radio stations and T.V. News were keen to pick up the item, not least of all as I was a serving Principal of an Academy. One national newspaper running the title 'Headteacher's union chief slams Government over academisation policy' stating I was going to express dismay over the government's education white paper. Indeed I was and did. Being able to say that they were not winning the argument on academies and that they had no answers for critics of their policies really warmed up conference and ensured news reporters both sharpened their pencils and cleaned their camera lenses. I used the phrase "To be or not to be, that is the question over academies" and I made the point that schools must be free to answer the question themselves and not be forced. It was important at the time to point out that the Conservative Party in Government was divided over the issue at council level where votes were key to them remaining in office. In addition, the fact that there was so much going on in Good and Outstanding Schools that was working without the need to be an academy. I added that "On a political note it was interesting that the philosophy of a free market and diversity in services … so often at the core of Tory policy … did not seem to apply at this time, in education."

I also picked up on the issue of Assessment and the DfE's changes to the Primary School process. The press labelled me as highly critical of controversial new assessments that had been introduced, and in some cases withdrawn through departmental error ... such as the one on spelling, punctuation and grammar known as SPAG. I posed the question in my speech, "Do we now have the 'Hokey Cokey' of assessment? You put your SPAG test in, you put your SPAG test out, you put it online and wait for the children to shout I know the answer ... what was the question?" Such was the debacle over publication errors. I added, "Schools and parents cannot face another year of assessment chaos. Now is the time to call for a better system on assessment ... one that works for parents, pupils and teachers, rather than one that just ticks boxes for bureaucrats and politicians." It was right to challenge, as serious mistakes had been made in the implementation of primary school assessments that year, including frequent changes as well as contradictory guidelines.

We all knew and accepted that testing had a role to play in the assessment of children but the poorly-designed tests and last-minute changes added no value to teaching. In addition, there was a tremendous belief that increasingly parents and teachers were agreeing that high-stakes statutory tests were making it harder to find out what children were actually learning, and how we could improve their learning. As I looked at my grandson, who was still awake, I said that I wanted him to enjoy the awe and wonder of discovery in his learning and not be taught how to take a test and then be tested on that.

I was interviewed on Sky News outside the Conference Centre immediately after this. My very first 'live' TV interview. If I had nerves then the cameraman was worse than me as his unit failed and they struggled to get it sorted again. There were other interviews on BBC and ITV as well as Local Radio. All the time our experienced Media and Publicity team providing great briefings and clues to expected questions. This was particularly useful the following morning when I appeared on the Radio Four Today Programme hosted by the 'slayer of politicians' John Humphries. He was intrigued with my stance on Academies particularly as I was running one. At the end of the interview experience he had captured two quotes from me … first of all as my former LEA was not fit for purpose in respect of SEN …'it wasn't a tough decision to become an academy so as to step away from them' … and, with reference to forcing schools to become an academy 'If it ain't broke, don't fix it!' By all accounts I had done well and come out having not been mauled by him.

Later that day the current Secretary of State visited and gave a speech and then took part in a Q. and A. session with the General Secretary and myself on the stage. In both she did well but in answering a question from delegates she got it all wrong and lost the support from the hall. As we came off stage, she offered me the opportunity to meet and asked her specialist adviser to set it up. It turned out to be a tough fortnight for her as earlier in that week she had to defend her Academisation Plans when appearing before the Education Select Committee. At the end of the following week, she dropped the plans and performed a U-turn. I was rushed to the Millbank Studios and appeared on Radio Five Live, BBC News and Sky News to respond to what was portrayed as a 'win for us'. When interviewed by the BBC I said, "We have been working very hard with government to try and get them to understand … with regards assessment, funding and the academy programme … that actually there isn't a one size fits all solution." This was my seventh such appearance in a week but as I had pointed out 'You are only as good as your last performance.' I was happy with that as the Sky interview went very well. Before we went on air, I had a brief talk on the academy issue with the newsreader so that ended up being a trial run for the real live questioning. We were both happy.

The amusing tale accompanying this visit to the studios was that in the BBC the lights were so bright I had perspiration on my forehead which the cameraman wanted me to dab away with a tissue … which I did not have. Whereas in Sky, I was taken into the makeup artist's room and all 'oranged-up' so I looked like I was an ex-Leicester, Barcelona and England goal scorer presenting Match of the Day! When I had finished that final interview, I was on my way out the studio door when I realised that I hadn't got my glasses. I popped back into the makeup room to see if I had mistakenly left them there at which point the artist said she thought I had placed them in my bag … and then said, "Kim, before you go … do you want your orange face returning to it's normal colour?" I had completely forgotten, so there was a relief to having been caught by her. I certainly would have turned a few curious heads on the train with the heavy make up on … so that was a narrow escape.

The U-Turn on 'Forced Academisation' had been due in the main to pressure from such as ourselves and backbenchers in Parliament lobbying the Government. While welcome as a tactical retreat it actually changed little in respect of some schools having the imposition of academy status because the Secretary of State retained the view that low performing schools would benefit from the process and this would help her realise the aspiration of a 'world class education system'. As many Local Authorities began to lose the capacity to support their schools due to funding cuts and the demise of many school improvement staff, the practical and political momentum behind academisation gathered pace. At this point many more school leaders began to take a long hard look at whether academisation could work for them.

I popped into school a week later and in front of a number of students and staff colleagues one of my new teachers for ASD students said out loud, "Oh sir … you were in my bedroom on Saturday!" All stopped in their tracks to engage their focus on her remarks and my eagerly expected response. Before I could say anything she quickly continued saying, "We were watching the News on Sky in our bedroom and there you were on the screen!" No scandal in that … so those gathered dispersed bar one of the Year Nine girls in our ASD provision who wanted to tell me I was now famous and as such she needed my autograph. So within ten days I had become a 'Union Leader' ... changed government policy ... and signed my first autograph as a celebrity in the world of autism ... the stuff of dreams eh! My theme for the year was 'Leading the Way' and the start suggested it was indeed to be just so.

The following week I spoke at a Conference of Newly Qualified Teachers, most of whom looked younger than my Year Twelves. They were enthusiastic and razor sharp in their understanding of the world they had entered. The room of about a hundred oozed with ideas and solutions to the problems current in education. It was a pleasure to be in their midst and an honour to share my experiences and thoughts with them. From there I was rushed to Heathrow and flew to the Arabian Gulf to present awards at a prestigious SEND Provision the following day. On returning two days later a series of meetings was followed by a flight to a Conference in Barcelona where my attendance as a guest had been requested. The miles I was traveling and the audiences I was expected to engage with were becoming more and more varied. In Barcelona I met many Professors and other professionals involved in healthy eating, all wishing to access our Association and its twenty-nine thousand members, their schools and pupils. It was interesting to see how the academics became challenged in their ability to engage in consistent intelligent conversation as the evening progressed and the wine availability diminished. On the return flight one of the dieticians was sat in front of me and after some discussion she took a leap of faith and decided an introduction to meet her mother would be a good idea. That certainly captured the attention of other passengers in our area of the plane.

Throughout my time as a National Officer and particularly in my Presidential Year I received many invitations to events at the Houses of Parliament. Although it was good to meet and network with a variety of other educational professionals on the terrace at either the House of Commons or House of Lords ... often with a refreshing drink ... to be present for launches of various initiatives and All-Party Parliamentary Groups (APPGs) was more business-like and interesting. There were months where being in Westminster was an every-week event and I felt rather at home when wandering the corridors seeking out the various committee rooms. Certainly, when chatting with MPs and Lords it was a far more relaxed affair as they were on their 'home turf'. In such moments the opportunity to search out views and identify the reasons for policy was always a lot easier.

A highlight in the year was to be invited to the Royal Garden Party at Buckingham Palace and see Her Majesty the Queen and Prince Philip at close quarters. While both looked their years, they were attentive to all they met and took their time when engaging in conversation. It was a lovely Summer's day and the gardens looked splendid with added atmosphere provided by military bands. I had heard much about the Royal Garden Party events and the rational for them. It was very pleasing to see so many present, all having contributed something significant to our society. Everyone looking very splendid in their finery and all enjoying the occasion as much as I was with my partner. Only a few weeks earlier I had actually been present inside for a special event hosted by the Prince of Wales. On that occasion the champagne had been flowing fast. The Garden Party was much more reserved and an occasion for more decorum.

When I was asked if I would like to take up the offer of a visit to the Isle of Man, I checked the diary and noted that the TT Races were taking place at the same time I was due to travel. Now I would have gone anyway as it was obvious that conversations were needed with their Education Department on salaries and terms of service. However, the chance to walk the pits and talk to riders who were then going to race around the just under thirty-eight mile track in around seventeen minutes at speeds in excess of an average of one hundred and thirty miles per hour was dream land for me.

The formal conversations with officers were completed and they were encouraged to sustain open talks with our Association's Branch officials. After this I had the chance to visit three schools and see a quality of buildings and a much more relaxed curriculum system very well taught by enthusiastic staff. I recalled having seen posters at arrivals basically asking visiting teachers to stay ... and I wondered what there was about this paradise of a place that was not a draw for the likes of those young teachers I had spoken to not so long ago.

On my last evening, I was invited to have supper with a Headteacher and guests where the road track was at the end of her drive. With a full stomach of fine food and a glass of wine in my hand I watched sidecars racing past on one of their practice sessions. The two Marshalls in the garden both volunteers were very chatty. In an extraordinary couple of hours, I found out that one of them was from my family town on the Yorkshire Coast, the other from the town where my academy was located ... and my host had started her schooling at the same Primary School I had in West Germany. Coincidences alive ... and lots of additional memories made in the conversations that resulted.

Other enjoyable parts of the year included the opportunity to meet members at Branch Meetings and Conferences in such as the South East, North West, East Riding, Devon, Buckinghamshire, Cornwall, London, Wales and the Home Counties. All committed School Leaders looking for updates and an insight into what was going on nationally. It also gave me the opportunity to emphasise the need to take note of, and respond to, the needs of all learners and point out that this really does mean looking to current research to inform future practice. At one such conference it was inspiring to introduce various workshops and see the keen delegates raring to go and hear the speakers explain how they could successfully explore ways of building school and academy teams around their children. It reminded me of the phrase that we had been pushing as an Association that 'Yes, we are Leaders ...

but let us not forget that we are still learners'. Wherever I went there was that thirst in all I met.

At many such events the question of Academies was very live and now the interest was shifting to whether there were benefits in stepping away from LEAs and joining in partnerships with other schools as academies. It was important to remind colleagues at this point that the Association had never been anti-academies per se. Its position was and remained against the forced process. The fact remained that there were Good and Outstanding Schools with excellent LEA structures, relationships and support in place, and such as these should not be compelled down the same route. There were still many Heads suspicious of the Academy process and in fact there was often a need with HQ staff to remind them to insert the term 'Academy' when writing advice and information papers. In addition, a few colleagues in National Executive literally saw red if there was mention of academies ... and grammar schools ... and they needed to be reminded that our Association had many active and valued members in both. That was a tough one for some but nevertheless we were representing a broad church and such Heads, Principals and Chief Executives were in our ranks.

In time the debate really moved on and many Heads were either already running academies and enjoying the fact, or proactively looking at the pros and cons of going down this route. I believe that this is where we had been successful in our impact on policy ... we had made it a choice for so many such as these. What soon followed was an eleven-page article in our Association's magazine 'Unpacking Academisation' which looked at the process and the principle. It examined the potential end goal, already seen by many members, of their inherent aspiration of trying to achieve and improve.

I soon found myself on the platform at a Conference speaking on the topic 'The Only Way is MATs (Multi-Academy Trusts)?' In my presentation I outlined our Association's journey and indeed the one I had taken with my own school community. Specific points made resonated with those in attendance particularly when referencing the belief that schools and/or academies needed to be at the heart of their cities, towns and villages. It was what they really wanted and needed to hear. For such a change wasn't to embrace the devil. In essence the process of becoming an academy was such that as leaders of learning we believed they must reflect and encourage the values and beliefs of such communities and retain their identity as centres of excellence lead by them as aspirational leaders transforming the lives of those in their charge. There was a notable relief in many as if their thinking and motivation had just been forgiven in confessional. The key message I enjoyed delivering was that we supported our members to make the right choice for themselves and would advise them accordingly ... and at the same time resist the 'no choice' model. My contribution to the conference being.

"The question was 'The Only Way is MATs?' ... My Answer is 'No!' ... it is one way ... and there are others."

The fact I was able to illustrate with my own experience undoubtedly helped. However, on hearing my own words 'Unashamedly, I say that in respect of SEND the local authority was not fit for purpose and failed consistently to show drive, ambition and future proofing of its specialist provisions' it reminded me of the sorry state of affairs that made our conversion a joy to achieve. In questions that followed I was able to talk about how my academy was thriving and how the whole staff team had embraced the change ... as an option to choose ... with aspiration in their mind. The result being that it had improved the quality of our academic and care curriculum and in turn realised better student outcomes.

Not long after the Association Policy Team produced a brilliant document for schools on the Academy process and new models of school and academy partnerships. The notion of 'Academy' being a choice not a crime fully exorcised from most doubters and indeed the very word no longer used with the vitriolic expression of a horrid swear word. The curl on the lip of some colleagues continuing its facial journey north towards becoming a refreshing smile ... even in London.

News of this was picked up by Local Councillors and referenced when I appeared at an Annual Conference for Local Government on an Education version of 'Question Time'. To hear one of the audience say, "Never mind all the bollocks being talked at present ... it is time for local people and local politicians to sit with their local educational experts in the profession and take charge of education for their own communities!" I couldn't resist replying "I would happily sit on any group if it was called the Removal of Bollocks from Education as the implicit castration of politics in education was such a temptation." A Director of Children's Services sat next to me on the stage, spluttered as she drank water, then half choked and laughed at my remark. Once again, the Maverick in me revealing itself.

As for such labels being attributed to me, two new ones quickly followed. I received an email from a colleague in the North West stating that I might want to reflect on my approach as it was attracting some criticism. He cited that there was growing concern that I was seen as being 'too enthusiastic in my role'. At first, I wasn't sure how to take it ... then without a flash of blinding light it was obvious that I should see being any sort of enthusiastic as a true compliment. If in talking up the profession and expressing the absolute joy of being a school leader I was seen as being over the top ... was I to stop? Absolutely not! For I believed then and still do now that the honour, excitement and challenge of school leadership was in being a 'change maker'. The very point I had once been cited as being 'maverick' about.

The next startling label was when in conversation with local LEA Senior Officers and questioning them on funding for Specialist

Provisions. It had become apparent that their funding formula had been worked out in detailed fashion on the back of a cigarette packet and needed unpicking to identify inequalities. When presenting their own policy statements and data back to them, as well as providing real time funding figures I was stunned by the Deputy Director saying, "Kim you are dangerous!" The explanation that followed amounted to my danger equating to my factual knowledge, ability to collect their own data and understand it, and then deliver all in a well-argued presentation.

It seemed that my statement, "I will fight tooth and nail to ensure you deploy your financial support to schools in a fair and equitable way" meant she could no longer cope. Her voice actually quavered when saying 'dangerous'. What was I to think and say, "Oh I do apologise for having the cognitive ability to see through your bad practices" ...? Should I have apologised for forgetting a learning disability implicit in this LEA manager? Then I remembered my student with a real disability banging the table and saying he wanted to be treated the same as everyone else. The outcome of this meeting was a further loss of faith in this particular LEA when purchasing places at local schools and academies. I believe the officer in question didn't have their interim position renewed soon after, but I'm not sure if the salary was part shared with specialist provisions as the first step in making good the numerous shortfalls in their funding. With her gone I didn't feel the need to go and show the four DBS certificates I had collected for different responsibilities so as to at least prove I was not a 'dangerous' criminal!

The stresses and strains of leading schools was very topical and thankfully greatly appreciated these days ....and seen as a priority. To meet with teams involved in mental health and rightly explore how to improve provision for children and young adults in our education system was very exciting. Their knowledge, experience and variety of practices offering so much to the profession. At the same time, to discuss opportunities available for staff, particularly school leaders, was something I was keen to explore. My own experiences not forgotten but mostly healed … prompted me to meet with many practitioners.

One particular opportunity opened up with a small consultancy developing tools for use in schools. They were keen to put something together for Headteachers in the area of Mindfulness. I was quite taken by a phrase used 'How to be a better version of yourself'. This meeting was closely followed by another in London with the potential of six hundred thousand pounds being accessed as a grant to develop Teacher Well-Being. The monies coming from an anonymous source was for funding research and development of innovative projects. What a great opportunity this seemed and I entered into preliminary conversations with my usual enthusiasm. Those present talked of 'Great Leaders making Great Schools' and understood that they needed to work with our Association to ensure Well-Being was a priority in schools with Headteachers leading the way. Ideas bubbled around the room as all manner of best practice in other public and private employment roles were talked through. The comment 'Teachers make the best of an ever changing and lower funded system where accountability and workload is excessive and impacts adversely on both the profession and those they teach' being so true of this time.

It never seemed to quite capture the mood with the then Policy lead staff at HQ and despite one of their team attending somewhere in discussions it was parked and forgotten as an initiative. They would shrug their shoulders and say workload dictated that some ideas and approaches could not be pursued. How ironic that at our Conferences we were regularly having James Hilton as a speaker. This ex-headteacher and now well-respected author was leading the way on the very topic and being feted by attendees. His books 'Leading from the Edge' and 'Ten Traits of Resilience' being a godsend to school leaders trying to survive in the job long term.

At the time I felt we had missed a trick as professional leaders, what a relief that he filled that space for so many. In his messaging he highlighted the importance of school leaders understanding how to lead with a 'positivity of purpose ... building trust, being decisive and taking better care of themselves physically and mentally'. With well-being and retention obvious and real growing concerns, it was essential that school leaders passed on this confidence and optimism to their staff members too. Being interviewed by him over numerous cups of coffee at a St Pancras Station cafe was very worthwhile. He gained my perspective and some examples of my own tested strategies for his book of the time and our lively discussions certainly helped us both to further expand our thoughts on 'looking after ourselves ... so we were better placed to look after all those we were to lead'.

A lot of people have a stereotypical view of Unions and Professional Associations seeing them as a dark art in confrontation, unrest and negativity. It was a battle sometimes to unlock such thinking and that was even the case within my own extended family and a circle of friends. The very fact that in Teaching these organisations supported profoundly important research and development initiatives into child development, psychology, leadership skill, academic curriculum and so on just wasn't seen or maybe was even ignored. The idea that it was a good job to do if you didn't want to work full time was still a jibe I had faced at family gatherings. Yet putting on a uniform and being given a truncheon or gun was seen as a real job for many years whenever the family came together. Encapsulated by my mother once asking me "When are you going to get a proper job Kim?" The art of decoding such straight-talking remarks a lifetime challenge for me and probably would have been likewise for many codebreakers at Bletchley Park. Seeing my inauguration as National President and speaking on TV posed the need for a change in attitude ... which remarkably still holds true. Thank you John Humphries for sealing it for me on Radio Four!

The issue of Primary Assessment continued to both anger and worry members and despite representations to the DfE and Secretary of State, no real headway seemed likely. Some quarters within the profession rattled their sabres threatening industrial action. It was decided that we would ballot our membership to gauge via an 'indicative ballot' their view on potential industrial action. The wonders of technology revealed that two thirds opened the email and read the message and only forty-four per cent. of them cast a vote. I was surprised that at something so crucial the figures were so low. I was corrected by our HQ staff who stated it was higher than most trade union benchmarks. The results showed that seventy-eight per cent. were in favour of continued negotiation and twenty-two per cent. were in favour of ceasing negotiation and proceeding immediately to action. There were various takes on this by Executive colleagues with the most militant, if I can call them that, being despairing while the moderates talked of a longer game needing to be played out. The fact remained that across all regions of England the pattern was the same with none of them returning less than seventy per cent. in favour of negotiation. As was said, "Yes ... that includes London!" ... which seemed to deeply disappoint one Primary Head Executive member from London.

It was not unexpected to hear the General Secretary say he was adamant that the way the ballot had been worded was neutral. Some, still grumbled clearly wanting confrontation. He went on to say, "We made no recommendation but did spell out clearly and factually the consequences of each choice. I am confident school leaders were able to make their own minds up on that basis". When with colleagues, I felt that this was surely enough to dampen the 'to the barricades call' of our red mist colleagues in our next meeting. The reflection afterwards of 'Does this mean we are content?' being fully explored and answered firmly with a resounding 'No!'. Personally, I saw this as a sober determination to secure the most gains for children rather than perhaps squander them in a failed protest. This being based on the fact we had overturned Assessment plans in the Government's manifesto which was a huge achievement for a Teaching Union. It was good to hear the plans then for us to continue with our negotiations and hear that top-level discussions had already secured signs of a move away from some elements of policy. The work continued ... and undoubtedly will roll on for some time every year.

I was given the opportunity to accompany the General Secretary and his Deputy to a meeting with an Education Minister. To my surprise I found our seating arrangements to have me very much front and centre, opposite the experienced Minister and MP. We were there to discuss the secure fit principle in Primary Assessment and put forward our argument that it was unfair to dyslexic pupils. It became clear that this topic had been tried and tested with him but he hadn't grasped the challenges for such a learning disability and had dismissed requests for a re-think. My role and experience being brought in to soften him up? Or maybe even to enlighten him? Whatever the thinking, I was galvanised into speaking when he said, "You will have to keep on teaching them until they get it and they make the required standard!"

At this point I could not remain in negotiation mode as a clear gap in his understanding was screaming out for help. So I spoke ... "Minister, excuse the non-academic language that is to follow but you need help here. I will put it in simple terms so you will understand. You see, their wiring is such that it does not really matter how many times you teach it they just may never get it. As their other assessments show their ability then accept that fact in overall terms."

He looked quite taken aback ... his Specialist Advisers (SPADS) looked at me intently ... and my learned HQ colleagues took a sharp intake of air and must have thought 'Oh no ... Kim is off on one!'

I continued, "In fact Minister, your comment does seem to equate in arrogance to the view that when speaking to say a Frenchman with no English ... if you kept on speaking in English raising your voice each time you repeated your words, then by the time you were shouting he would eventually understand!"

The room was silent and he looked back at me through his glasses quite intently. "Oh!" he said ... and paused again. Then he turned to his lead SPAD and said "Mmm, Kim is right, we need to look at that again don't we?" Immediately they replied, "Yes Minister!"

Aside from my mind flooding with images of Sir Humphrey Appleby in the sitcom 'Yes Minister' and wanting to giggle ... we took our leave thanking all for their time. Not long afterwards the discriminatory practice ended ... and rightly so. I was then able to add the tale to my speeches at various events and say, "You see ... having a Special Academy Principal as your President has helped the Government overcome its problematic learning disability about education in England!" As I have said throughout, I had always believed that having run two schools for boys with emotional and behavioural difficulties (by now branded SEMH) I was well versed in working with challenging individuals. Increasingly my naughty joke that many of the brightest went on to become Cabinet Ministers seemed to resonate as each day passed.

If that seems another harsh remark ... it was spurred on when one such blue tie parliamentarian was evidently reported as saying in a meeting that standards in education were not good enough and mediocrity was being allowed all too often. His plea was for improvement so more children were 'above average'. Undoubtedly, we may have tried to arrange for his own arithmetic or maths teacher to get him back to school at the next parliamentary recess.

The year continued with many other work streams where I was able to add a Leadership insight as a practitioner to debate in furthering policy and practice development. These included links with the Royal College of Psychiatry on Mental Health issues (where years earlier I had enjoyed a fine glass of wine with my lunch when attending a lecture) ... the VSO to try and encourage retiring school leaders to do a period of voluntary work abroad ... the British Council to further International Educational Links to benefit student learning and teaching expertise ... and, play an early part in the Leadership Foundation to explore new generation practice were all very enjoyable. However, working on projects related to Sex and Relationships Education (SRE) really caught my interest as it had been something that we had discussed many times in our SLT meetings about our own students.

I took part in a video shoot about SRE in a London studio. It took a whole day and the very thought proved too much to my mischievous staff who ended up being quite disappointed that I'd been in a sex video fully clothed. I received my lines the day before and on arriving at the studio semi-prepared was taken aback that they had been completely rewritten. Nevertheless, the shoot was successful, and I delivered the required serious words to camera despite overflying jets, a helicopter and the bin men. The crew were brilliant throughout and their patience admirable. The end result being used to promote a work scheme in secondary schools which was sponsored by a well-known brand of condoms. This fact furthering the amusement of my SLT who often asked if my work was being branded accordingly ... "You are safe with Kim as your President!"

I was then asked to speak at an event in a House of Commons Committee Room where their DO Resources were being launched. I was on the platform, the sole male, with various MPs and prominent figures in SRE. My role being to give a key address and certainly a School Leader perspective. I related my speech to our Academy setting where we included relationships and being a responsible citizen in our community as well as having regard and respect for others. I was able to reference the resources I had played a part in developing ... but that was really expected ... so my talk was from a personal perspective, as follows:

"As a twenty-four-year-old newly qualified teacher and indeed a number of years afterwards it was always a daunting moment being told you were to teach Personal Social and Health Education (PSHE) to include Sex Education and also have it included in your tutorial sessions. The challenge of facing sixteen- to eighteen- year-olds was considerable. I mention this not to relive the blushes of that time but to add context. First of all, the well-produced resources I have referenced are now available and at the time I was a young teacher they were not. The second point and relevant to my contribution is that of training. The staff in schools and academies have made it clear that they need proper training to be able to deliver quality teaching and learning activities in SRE. Students too are quite clear that they feel more comfortable and able to engage in discussion and open debate if the teaching performance is based on access to such quality delivery and resources. As students have increasingly identified school lessons as their main source of information about sex, it is clear there is a need to respond. In addition, they continue to report needing a broad range of information on sexuality, gender, family life, HIV prevention, pleasure, violence prevention, STIs, contraception, diversity, sexual rights and what is absolutely key ... 'relationships'. All this with an emphasis on the guarantees of respect, dignity, equality and opportunity."

As you can see, I had been well-prepared and the stimulus of endless unfinished debate within my Academy had played its part. I continued ... "Every child and young adult has the right to be informed. Information leads to confidence and strength of mind. Such will enable girls to say 'No I don't want that ... What I really like is this.' And if the girls have learned that they

341

have as much right to pleasure as boys then we might be moving towards a much healthier sex life for all young people ... all of whom we care so much for."

This undoubtedly resonated with all sat both beside and in front of me. I added, "I would end with this: In representing school leaders, the importance of statutory status for SRE and the need for quality teacher training is a priority for us. As a leader of a large Special Academy for students with complex learning needs and autism, I would add that the development of specific resources for those with such disabilities is a challenge too ... as they may unfortunately be at risk of being abused/offended or being offenders if the delivery is not sensitive and matched to their special educational needs."

My words having been spoken from my head and heart ... I then sat back in my chair. The response was tremendous and the debate and resolutions that followed exciting. At the conclusion I was approached by many to assist with their own work in this field. On walking back from Westminster to Victoria Station I had a tingle in me thinking that once shy twenty-four-year old squirming SRE teacher had just delivered such confident words in a Parliamentary setting. The changes that followed were good to observe from the side lines ... none better than to see SRE become RSE as I had always believed that the relationship was important before the sex!

It came as a significant surprise months later to find that our support and pursuance of the SRE work was put in doubt because the General Secretary, for whatever reason, felt it not a suitable focus. I was unclear as to why this decision was made and not least of all as we had an outstanding practitioner on our Policy team with former experience in a mainstream secondary. So what was the logic behind it? Once again, the initial impetus of sending a National Officer off to give credibility to our interest and involvement in new work was in danger of stalling. At this time the word that came to us in Executive was that work overload was such that new projects couldn't be picked up. This didn't make sense as two years of work time had already been invested in a 'matter of the moment' topic.

It would be fair to say that at this time I started to lose confidence in the way decisions were being made and wondered if HQ staff had perhaps lost sight of who they worked for, and on behalf of. That may have seemed harsh but I was not alone in wondering whether some frank discussions were needed. On the topic of RSE I decided that the best way forward would be for the General Secretary to face up to the two groups we were now working with in mainstream Secondary and Primary settings and tell them that our Association did not have the capacity to continue supporting the work for its members. Strangely enough that never happened ... but I received looks depicting the presence of bad thoughts for a while afterwards from a couple of HQ staff.

Rather confused by this experience my mood was lifted by a brief trip to Germany to stay with my youngest son in the Rhineland-Palatine region. A good catch-up with him and nice opportunity to see him at work, very happy and speaking fluent German. We travelled into a large nearby city to visit galleries and sit in a large square drinking alt bier. As a break from the Association and its now rather confusing processes it helped me reset my thinking and expectations of my role. It also made me think back to the many happy days of living in Germany when the family were growing up.

In the Autumn after visiting the site of a well-known Children's Charity in London I was captured by their passion and drive of those working there. Founded in 1739 by Thomas Coram to care for abandoned babies in what became known as the Foundling Hospital it had grown into a magnificent charitable organisation committed to improving the lives of the UK's most vulnerable children and young people. A link was established with our Association as their Education Department had resources related to behaviour, safety and learning which could impact positively on mental and physical well-being. I was invited to give a keynote speech at their annual conference in Warwickshire where I was amusingly introduced as the 'Headteacher of Headteachers'.

As time passed this saw me appointed to their board of trustees which included three other headteachers, one of whom who had been instrumental in developing the use of some of their resources. In particular I was interested in what they had to offer in respect of RSE to Primary Schools and how that may be adapted to Special School students. This engagement with them gathered pace and I soon became Chairman of the Trustees for the Education side of the charity. This saw me take over from the impressive Lord Russell of Liverpool. Rather amusingly my eldest son posed the question as to whether the noble title went with the position and if it was then hereditary. His humour only bettered by his aspiration.

The OFSTED issue remained an annual one of 'let's change the rules and criteria'. If we were to draw an analogy with football it would have been the equivalent to changes resulting in the pitch being triangular in shape, seven players on each team, a tubular ball and five referees. As for the Video Referee in the current football game ... that may have been something headteachers got a wayward Year Eleven to do with his mobile to assist the school in cancelling any fake dives, trips and penalty pleas from inspectors wishing to cry 'Special Measures'. That may all sound a bit daft but that's exactly where the whole inspection system was and it was not funny, as it was grinding down staff and eroding their joy in the job.

The Association came up with a brilliant alternative worked out with external Consultancy assistance which was based on Peer Review. The opportunity for an inspection then resulting in an action plan response with headteacher peers and a programme rightly termed 'Aspire' available to support improvement was not a revolutionary idea. Certainly, the prize was … Inspection and Support for improvement … rather than Inspection destroying a school and then the team walking away. Those of us who had been around the block in school leadership remembered what HMIs had originally done in supporting school improvement. Personally, I had good memories of such practitioners and as already referenced, it didn't really need a hand-grenade to get them into a positive frame of mind.

The title for this process was what made it noticed with a wry grin. We had the alternative to OFSTED it was INSTEAD … and it worked! Sadly, no Secretary of State (SoS) was ever fully brave enough to say it should be the new model … but then as they were changing as quickly as the seasons, that was not a surprise. With some policies coming directly from Number Ten and Cabinet … I'm sure that there had been some in the SoS position who had experienced frustration and a touch of being sidelined in respect of the authority they should have been allowed to bring to their job in the delivery of policy. I recalled the scurrilous joke about jobs people had, that often seemed a bit of a waste of time … such as the BMW factory workers who fitted indicators. One or two of the SoSs must have felt just so from time to time.

As my year drew towards its conclusion the illness of my dear friend and outstanding colleague on National Executive was tough for me and the rest of my colleagues. It was incredibly tough for him. He was Colm, our Vice President and due to become National President at the end of my tenure. A diagnosis of Motor Neurone Disease (MND) caused him to resign that position and increasingly find himself absent from leading his wonderful Special School in Belfast. This brilliant man ravaged by the illness sobbed in my arms when breaking the news to me. From that day forward his positivity in the face of such adversity remained an amazing example to us all of the power of resilience.

We had a National Executive meeting in Belfast and I arranged for him to be picked up from his school and brought to the hotel where we were meeting. What he didn't know was that the pickup had something quite special about it. He had been told 'Just make sure you are wearing a warm coat'.

When he arrived at the school all the staff and students were outside and numerous members of the Press. Then a cavalcade of Harley Davidson motorbikes from the Belfast Harley Owner's Group (HOG) Chapter arrived with a pulsating roar in the school car park. One of them a three-wheeler trike to carry him as passenger into Belfast city centre. Stood outside the hotel with the rest of Executive and many HQ staff we greeted his arrival and used the occasion as a photo shoot launch of the MND Charity as our own charity for the forthcoming year. He was like an excited little boy in a sweet shop ... sat astride the almost two-litre motorbike with his leather clad and bearded new-found friends as escort. The HOG members ... some having once been in Belfast Police, Schools and Civil Service but now retired ... were marvellous in their engagement and only too pleased to have added to the memorable day. As a Harley Davidson rider myself ... the only downside being I had to then chair the two days of meetings, when riding the roads of Northern Ireland would have been so much more enjoyable with him close by doubled up on the trike. A precious moment which I was not able to enjoy.

Colm remained a fighter throughout the years that followed, as this terrible disease took hold. With a smile he lived his life as fully as was possible ... and sadly passed away as I was finishing writing this book. A wonderful man ... a truly inspirational school leader ... and a dearly missed friend.

On return to England, I found out that OFSTED had announced they were due in to my academy. By this time, I had already announced my intention to retire from the Summer and thereby increased the roles and responsibilities of my team and secured the Interim Principal as my successor. There was an experienced HMI leading the team and a depth of SEN experience throughout all its members. How strange that once again as I drove in that green woodpecker flew straight up the drive, in front of my car.

Our engagement with the OFSTED team was secure and every conversation had and observation made was in partnership with one of us. It became increasingly clear that they were impressed and the students were at the top of their game in every way. Staff seemed calm and their performances like any other day. Previous experiences of OFSTED having hardened them to any sense of having to show off ... so they just did their normal thing ... magic!

The feedback from the HMI on the second day including the following:

"Staff are acutely aware of what the students can do and provide good challenge to deepen and extend knowledge ... It is astonishing to see students engage in a mature way when being taught such subjects as Sex and Relationships ... Students have a good awareness of disability and a tolerance of difference ... Students enjoy coming to school and their world has been opened ... Research work is seen as a key tool for improvement ... Staff have brought everything about this place to us with a passion ... There is excellent leadership by Senior and Middle Leaders ... You put the students at the heart of everything you do ... As a school you are enabling the students to chase their dreams."

This was a journey that had been started nearly twelve years earlier and finally been realised. The students and staff had finally been given the recognition they deserved.

When I announced the outcome to my full staff team, I was a very proud school leader. As they sat there taking in all the quotes, you could see their backs straighten and the little tear drops of joy start to well up in their eyes ... then I told them, "We said we would give OFSTED another chance ... they took it. We are now outstanding!"

My job almost done as their leader and likewise with the Association, I returned to the last six weeks of my Presidency. A few more important tasks to complete and thanks to be made.

One Hundred and twenty years earlier our Association was formed in Nottingham in a Primary School now part of the university. I was asked to attend the unveiling of a brass plaque to commemorate the occasion and celebrate with Executive and HQ staff also in attendance. I made reference to us representing twenty-nine thousand school leaders and how we were seen as the most solution-focussed and wisest challengers of education policy and practice. Adding that our position as a much-respected advocate was valued by our members and sought after by politicians. My closing remark being, "Today as in 1897 there remains much for us to do. Our pedigree established and unquestionable, and with that in mind it gives me great pleasure and pride to unveil this plaque commemorating our one hundred and twentieth year."

A week later I had the chance to speak to a large group of aspiring Middle Leaders in the South East. I was keen to meet with them and take up the invitation of sharing my experiences. For some time, I had been worried that emerging leaders were fewer in number. So the chance to express the joy of making a difference and the excitement and opportunity of being a change-maker was welcome. The irony of having four more months before my retirement not going unnoticed.

In discussion with them afterwards it was pleasing to hear their young voices talk up the profession and show excitement about the prospect of being Middle Leaders. They made me a promise that they would continue to aspire to great things and take their bright and creative ways into leadership. One added that he wanted to be a maverick and push the boundaries. How good it was to hear those words.

Another opportunity afforded me included speaking at a Prince's Teaching Institute event for School Leaders at Madingley Hall, Cambridge University. A prestigious organisation focused on disseminating best principles and practice in education. This came two years after being an attendee myself and leading on a piece of work on transition from Primary to Secondary provision. Those present wanted to be known for being enthusiastic with a touch or more of maverick in them to take risks and make their schools/academies exciting places for all. How my heart warmed to hear that expressed.

With my last remaining conference to open and speak at, I noted that the keynote speakers were well known for being notorious wranglers as campaigners, inspirational and outspoken promoters and provokers of change. And so they were in their various presentations. But, what also came across was their place as challengers of the educational parliamentary scene and their ability to impact on thinking. Each had tremendous credibility and influenced policy change. When I thanked them and closed the conference, I noted references made to them, by those that would or could not open their minds to change, as 'The Good, The Bad and the Ugly' ... for they were indeed compliments. In finishing, I added that I trusted that they would continue to display a 'refusal to be silenced'.

At the end of my Presidential Year I handed the mantle to a Primary Head for her to take things forward. My belief in our association mostly strengthened by the experience of my term in office because we were formidable in our work and ensured that each session was delivered with a purposeful challenge ...

in a solution-focussed approach ... with the resolute determination to 'lead the way' and take back control of education. We were respected by Ministers and the DfE and trusted for what we contributed. I was pleased to have been given the platform to play my part in that work.

There was a different feel about what some individuals in Executive and at HQ had brought into our forum with the departure of our prized General Secretary. Perhaps some were seeing an opportunity to introduce more political spin and feting single parties. I had always tried to ensure that we were neutral and open minded. It was right not to bring adversarial politics into our practices and I had avoided that personally albeit my own politics of the time were known.

I felt the writing had been on the wall (excuse the pun) when one leading member decided to circulate a tweet depicting the Prime Minister in a bad light. I contacted him saying, "Regarding a retweet of yours where you show the Prime Minister on a wall mural of the Ulster Freedom Fighters Second Battalion D-Company with the motto 'Strong & Stable'. I have to tell you that I am appalled that you have chosen to make such a statement inferring a relationship with a paramilitary group who were responsible for more than four hundred deaths ... the majority being Roman Catholic civilians killed at random. I am unable to fathom what motivated you to do this on Twitter where you openly badge yourself as one of our Association's National Figures."

I just had to point out that his motivation had clearly not taken into account that the UFF were a 'proscribed organisation' in the UK under the Terrorism Act 2000. I also queried whether this had been naivety on his behalf motivated by the Conservatives seeking a working majority in Government ... and if it was, then perhaps he needed to be reminded that a previous Labour Prime Minister had sought the same sort of 'propping up' relationship when in office. In my mind it was obvious he had not thought things through ... but he had posted something quite damaging to both himself and potentially our Association.

This was as an example of the real concern I had at some 'lone wolf behaviour' and attempts to politicise our work. An error indeed as whoever had been in Government in my time in teaching our response was often 'kick those in office' and 'fete those in opposition' ... to only find out when they came into office, we duly kicked them too. Some political growing up was needed by some of my peers and a realisation that such words as this tweet served to do nothing other than to damage our credibility as educationalists and lead players when engaging the DfE. Despite the protestations of some, this wasn't about freedom of speech ... this is what one of my EBD ex-pupils would have described as "A bit of a f★★★ up sir!"

On that note my time as President ended and my period of Immediate Past President and a National Officer with the Association was taken mostly in absentia. Sharing this with you I hope you have gained a sense of the 'behind the scenes' world of teaching and the importance of the safety net of representation. As a school leader it was important to never doubt that such insurance is of benefit ... for there are many banana skins awaiting your every footstep. Undoubtedly, there are a few 'naughty chimps' holding positions of responsibility within the system ... and we all need to be wary of them!

It was now time to go back to the day job ... and be with those that worked tirelessly as my staff team. I also looked forward to being with those that warmed my heart ... the very ones who had taught me so much about disability ... my students.

Chapter 16

The Return to say Good-bye

It was strange walking back into the academy and being with my Senior Team and staff once again for it seemed longer than a year since I'd been there full time. To be in the presence of my SLT, all excellent practitioners, and many other dear friends and colleagues on the staff was very welcome. My successor already in the groove of senior leadership and although now trying to fit thirty hours into her day, she was enjoying the role immensely.

I spent the first few days walking the corridors and entering every room. I found time to be out on each of the four playgrounds to chat with the students, and sat in the two dining rooms to share lunch with them. Each morning I greeted them as they arrived and each afternoon bid them a goodbye as they left for home. Every day I realised that after thirty-nine years all this was soon to come to an end. However, for the moment I was back in the environment where my traditional greeting and appreciated transaction of a hand-shake was eagerly sought by those from four to nineteen years of age. My absence had not detracted from the memory of my Harley Davidson motorbike needing a clean and polish. So the trickle of enquiring faces soon appeared ever hopeful of such an opportunity ... and to then be rewarded further by having a print-out of their photo taken when sat on it afterwards. On one such of these days I sat back in my office chair with a cup of tea and said to my PA that it was all very like being a visitor rather than the man in charge.

That feeling relieved briefly when I was given the opportunity to battle once more with the LEA. During the Summer before I left to take up the Presidency, they had decided to cut the amount of top up funding they provided to us in our direct budget. Their reason was that the students had made such great progress that they no longer needed that level of funding anymore. My response was that it was exactly that level of funding that had helped secure their progress … if it is removed then that improvement may stall or stop, and indeed our ability to remain Outstanding.

Once again, the logic and well-presented case confounded them. Knowing that I was retiring, the word on me now was that 'I was going to be even more dangerous!' In my own way I replied that before we go down that road it would have been great to hear them say 'Well done!' … and as that fell on stony ground, I left the Council offices to continue its weary drift towards further failure.

In the remaining weeks I received numerous tales from students, parents and carers, staff and governors (now Trustees). Although I had a very good salary to feed my hopefully long retirement, what I was to hear from them was better than gold to that silver.

When in lunch with my Year Fourteens I sat with a group I had seen come all the way through from Primary School. One of whom was a dear and quite remarkable boy in a wheelchair. Our first such student and one that had been a trailblazer for those with a similar disability. He had such humour and a slight mischief which had developed during his time with us. If my staff were to be believed … it was his endearing manner and evidently in part my fault. He was recounting his visit to the USA with his parents and admitted although under age he had been drinking a few beers with his father. He turned to me and said "Sir … have you ever noticed that the more you drink the more beautiful the girls look?" The nervous laughter from his table causing other students to look towards us to see what was happening. I told him I would share this confession with his dear mum the next time I saw her. His response was to just smile and in shaking my hand said, "It's okay ... I think she already knows!" The signs were obvious ... my word, how he had grown up and in the truest sense worked with his disability to become a 'quite normal developing young adult'. He did admit later the remark was rather sexist and apologised. Further proof indeed of his growing up.

A parent came in for an appointment and asked to see me. He reminded me that at the Year Eleven Exam Certificate Presentation Ceremony he had said the following ... "When my son was at Primary School he just could not engage ... would not learn ... he often hid under the table. Now my son has many certificates for his GCSEs, BTECs and Entry Level courses ... and he is talking of going on to College ... so since being at this school you have turned him around ... helped him reach his potential ... developed him into a more confident and happy young man ... there will never be enough words for us as a family to express our gratitude to you and your team. Please let me shake your hand." As he left and walked away, he turned and waved towards me.

A former student came in for a visit and appeared at my door with his ever-present beaming grin. Once at provision for those with behavioural difficulties he had been over time a regular visitor to my room as a result of a scrape or disagreement. I usually collected him from a classroom where he had upset the decorum of learning. I would send him on ahead to my room to ask my PA to make two cups of tea. One for me and one for him. After a few moments I would then amble slowly back to meet him sat at the large table in my office sipping his tea. On joining him I wouldn't speak ... as I drank my tea. When we were both finished, he would look up at me whereupon all I needed to say was, "So, here we are again ... do I need to say anything to you?" He would always reply "No sir, sorry ... I've done it again haven't I? I'll go back and apologise, then catch up on my work." At this he would return to class happier, focussed and calm.

Now at College he was keen to see me. He started to speak then faltered a bit before he regained his composure with a cough to clear his throat. Then he said, "When I came here nobody expected me to be able to stay out of trouble ... I did though, thanks to you ... Sir, you made a difference because you believed in me ... and now I do too!"

Then as he got up to leave the emotion in him was evident in his body which had started to tremble. He shook my hand, then on letting go gave me a quick hug and spun around and out of the office. Seconds later with that cheeky smile he popped his head back around the door and said, "While I am here ... please let me clean your Harley one last time?"

That young man's words about believing in himself struck home to me as it was the very place I was in too ... years earlier I had crumbled when working too hard and forgetting myself. This job, of all I had done since that time, had seen the completion of my rebuild.

There were many such rich moments not least of all in the conversations with staff who felt empowered and valued ... and at this time they also got a tad emotional. Such as one of my middle leaders who came to me to say, "We talked of creating a place where 'Excellence and Enjoyment' was at the heart of all we were going to do. I have treasured being part of that ... and now as for Excellence ... we are the very best ... and as for Enjoyment, the very point of our lives ... that is what we do every day. Thank you for giving me this job." His performance in all he did was obvious the first day I met him ... he was never going to walk out of the front door without a job ... and six years later he had actually become even better!

Another, a Teaching Assistant, said "I just cannot imagine you being retired ... you do know it is harder than you think!" She had been with me the whole journey and often reminded me perhaps I should stop breathing school.

In my last meeting with my Governors, I expressed my gratitude for the opportunity the position had afforded me and stated that they needed to guard my successor and keep her. It was important for them to remember that when I arrived, I had the experience of three school leadership roles ... this was her first. Our academy was now known from Maryland USA in the West, to Foshan China in the East, to Tampere Finland in the North and Soweto South Africa in the South, and as such it was important for them to continue supporting its growth and influence.

They knew this was right and I'm sure as they move forward it will be so vital for them to sustain that dimension. Undoubtedly, they may have been looking forward to a Principal who was less robust and relentless in the pursuit of excellence ... but did they really think that the new Lady of the Manor was any different? She was already a tough performer who was signed up to the mantra 'The difference with excellence is that it wants to improve constantly, whereas mediocrity wants recognition for doing its job'. Her high expectations were a perfect dovetail joint to my leadership style ... maybe her smile was just a touch nicer for them.

In our last SLT meeting together we laughed about the long and sometimes bumpy journey together. The fact that with my departure there were only two of the original sixty members of the teaching staff remaining from those present on my first day said a lot about exactly what it had taken. They knew that being a school leader could be a lonely place at times and a true test of one's resilience, and that going forward together they had to look out for each other. There was humour there too. Not least of all the memory of snow falling behind me one winter which

356

when they pointed it out, I just said, "Oh don't worry it won't settle!" But indeed it did and some of them slept in school that night because the drifts were so bad.

In the chatter, all of us citing examples of leading our staff team to create a wonderful learning community ... there was only one of them there who had been present for the whole period and able to give the context of the start point. They felt safer in knowing that there was nobody left wanting a fight by the front door, or wishing them a painful and lingering death. It seemed a safe belief. I told them to take care of themselves and to look to the future with confidence.

When the last day came it was filled with some spectacular celebrations, all led by the students. Each of the Upper, Lower, Primary and ASD sections putting on something very special to say their very own 'Goodbye'. None so dramatic as the one where the Lead ASD Teacher and a Year Three student appeared at my door with a spare scooter inviting me to their assembly. The long corridor and open spaces journeyed by me on this scooter at great speed ... to the cheer of others changing lessons on our campus.

Finally, having bid the students goodbye for the Summer holiday we all got together as a staff for a barbeque and drinks in the quad area bathed in sunshine. Speeches followed and what we all knew was that the life changing experiences we had shared had helped make our learning community 'outstanding'. These times were special to us all. We had given each other and our students so much ... and in all honesty gained so much back for ourselves too ... which was something very special.

My last words emphasised the confidence I had in them and in their abilities. I told them to remember they were all incredible people who should never underestimate their impact on our wonderful students. The mixture of emotions was immense. The

joy of having been together everlasting ... and then it was goodbye. Goodbye to them and goodbye to a career that had lasted
thirty-nine years.

That last OFSTED being the final realisation that my relentless
pursuit of excellence could be and had been achieved with this
brilliant school ... and I had avoided breaking myself in giving
it so much. That fact being testimony to those great colleagues
who were my much-valued inner circle and core of true and
supportive friends.

Conclusion

It is Over ... What Now?

I had heard that many people struggled not knowing quite what to do with all their time once retired. For those that had been School and Academy leaders this was often seen as a cliff edge where they went from being a very important person in the educational world to suddenly being ... a nobody.

This didn't worry me at all. Maybe naively, I actually just thought it a bit daft. After thirty-nine years of tightly organised term-time and many additional hours at weekends and non-term time (a.k.a. holidays) retirement was seen as 'a non-structured free-range life for me ... as soon as possible please'. No more Sunday night deep thinking about the week ahead. No more self-evaluation about my impact on one hundred and sixty adults and three hundred and ten students. No more meetings with Trustees, Councillors and confused LEA personnel. No more OFSTED ... will they get it right?

All this was now taken off my agenda. What was there to struggle with? What was there to miss?

I knew what my legacy was in all of the settings where I had worked ... for I had made contributions to the lives of pupils/students, parents/carers, staff and other colleagues in that very focussed educational world. I had taken many to a place evidently, they would never had dreamed of going. In a few cases this had neither been their intention nor preference ... yet it had worked and even the 'less than willing' had benefitted in some way.

When visiting Scarborough, I bumped into the very pupil who had tried to hang himself and I had rushed to visit in Critical Care ... then startled enough for him to show life signs. He had his wife and two young children with him and glowed with pride at being able to introduce them to me. Now in his late thirties he kept saying, "Mr Johnson Sir ..." at the start of every short story of what he had been doing in the intervening years. His excitement being because he remembered what he felt I had done for him and who he had consequently ... and eventually ... turned into. That meeting captured my deep thoughts once again. Certainly, the philosophical comment 'If you don't break a rule now and then ... nobody would know what they are for!' was straight back in my mind on seeing him. The difference now being that at the end of my career it was as much a statement of me as it was him ... and all the other pupils I had taught.

About a month after finishing as Principal it started to dawn on me ... it was the smiling faces of the students ... and the 'craic' with colleagues ... especially the future proofing Friday afternoon debates with my senior team ... and of course, those naughty hard working wonderful ladies in the academy's real nerve centre ... the main office.

Yet, there was so much I had neglected doing during my years of working and now I wanted the time to do whatever I could, as and when the mood grabbed me. This being so different from my working life that I actually joked 'I also want to discover boredom'!

That notion of not being able to cope when retired did not arise and has not since.

So indulge me, for some of those things have been ...

Fly-fishing for brown trout on crystal clear chalk stream-fed lakes in Sussex with an ex-colleague from the London EBD Special School. We have turned it into a competition each time we meet and fish for a trophy. It provides those important 'pause for thought' moments to take in the panorama of the country-side around me with its own hustle and bustle of wildlife working through their day. The catches are often very good ... although there are some days when there is a 'blank'. As my father would say, "That's to remind you why it is called fishing and not catching!" On the car journey back to London we always stop in Arundel for a meal and, during it, have many 'do you remember' moments giving rise to chuckles, sighs and maybe even the odd reflective profanity.

Watching Charlton Athletic FC try and win at the Valley with the groans often outweighing the cheers as I soak up the atmosphere generated by the crowd ... many of whom are quite elderly and clearly supporters since their own childhood. A friendly club and a safe ground enhanced by the most charming Afro-Caribbean steward in the West Lower Stand where I sit. His arm always available as support for elderly men and women to manage the steps to their seats. His smile on a par with any subsequent goal scorer ... and usually seen more often!

Riding on my Harley Davidson Fat Bob motorbike along the tree-lined lanes of South East England ... with the sun and wind in my face as I speed along, sat astride that purring 1868 cc engine. The opportunity to meet up with my dear friend of forty-six years and ride together, a real delight. Including visiting the Nags Head where all those years earlier we had supped a pint or three as students ... but now can only take a soft drink as we are 'riding out'. The very first revisit a humorous moment as we left the barman speechless when we said 'What have you done to the decor?' then admitting we hadn't been back since 1978.

Making that last minute decision to go to a top-class cricket match at the Oval with the brief journey being courtesy of the Mayor of London and my TfL Over Sixties Oyster card. Sitting there in the sun watching our curious game being played out before me. The joy of this being it really is an impulsive and unplanned day out. Novel beyond belief.

Engaging with the most charming staff and trustees in my charitable role in London. Knowing that it is truly about 'making a difference for children'. Marvelling at the professionalism of their work and being instrumental in their strategic plans as a Chairman.

Enjoying the rarity of having a glass of Malbec at a weekday lunchtime with my family and friends ... and our discussions being completed, mostly without reference to matters of current education.

Having my first ever flying lesson at Biggin Hill and taking the small plane high above Kent and Essex. The whole experience quite exhilarating ... being mesmerised when taxiing to take off by the magic of an iconic Spitfire on the apron as it also readied itself for a flight. A day with my head in the clouds ... real ones.

In addition to these fairly normal pleasures ... most of which I had denied myself full access to over the years ... there was the time to sit in the garden after busying myself there throughout the day. Those moments were often ones of reflection on it all ... and increasingly the words of a young Swedish student made me consider what sort of world I would be passing on to my children and grandchildren. Here that revolutionary spark started to smoulder with a tad more energy and the question began growing in my mind 'what could, and should I do?'

So what indeed was it that could mean that I may struggle and have no place or focus?

In working so hard, my family had come second far too many times and sometimes not even that close. A mistake. One that weighs heavily still and is mentioned as a cautionary note to all in School Leadership ... or similar roles.

The greatest opportunity for me is now about having the chance to catch up with my previously neglected three wonderful children and now six beautiful grandchildren, in East Anglia, Yorkshire and Scotland. Simple but important pleasures and the unrestricted time to bond without the interference of work and its endless calls. Such moments are taken and savoured with joy in my heart. Being a father is very special ... now the added role of Grandpa is that ... and much more.

Although 'work' is a four-letter word it had never been seen as being on a par with the outbursts and challenges of other parts of our rich language, many of which I had received over the years. Sure, there had been some tough moments and yet despite all that, I had weathered the storm.

The thing was that I recognised that my working life had been about my choice to work and live in that way ... because that's what I had literally allowed to be my way. Yet in doing so it had sometimes been such a hindrance to accessing and sustaining any 'real me' time.

This was laughable and ironic really as I had always pressed home a 'work to live' not a 'live to work' mantra to my staff team. There was no defining flash of lightning at this moment ... for this time of being retired was beginning to open up new adventures with excitement and fun top of the agenda.

The new now was all about living in a relaxed unstructured setting ... and being happy in both my head and heart. It was about taking the time to notice and take in the world around me each and every day.

No cliff edge … no being nobody. The truth being … I was now 'just me' with the chance to live new experiences and catch up on life. There was now just a little bit more of an urgency as my recent diagnosis of cancer had brought an increased sense of how precious life was … and how it was to be enjoyed and not wasted.

With all that I had been through on getting to that point there was so much I needed and wanted to write down … if for no other reason than to explain to those I had travelled the journey with … particularly those near and dear to me … as to what I had really been doing for all those years … and where it had started.

The End

EIN HERZ FÜR AUTOREN A HEART FOR AUTHORS À L'ÉCOUTE DES AUTEURS MIA KAPΔIA ΓIA ΣΥΓΓΡΑ
HJÄRTA FÖR FÖRFATTARE UN CORAZÓN POR LOS AUTORES YAZARLARIMIZA GÖNÜL VERELIM SZÍV
CUORE PER AUTORI ET HJERTE FOR FORFATTERE EEN HART VOOR SCHRIJVERS TEMOS OS AUTOF
SZERZŐINKÉRT SERCE DLA AUTORÓW EIN HERZ FÜR AUTOREN A HEART FOR AUTHORS À L'ÉCOUT
BCEЙ ДУШОЙ К АВТОРАМ ETT HJÄRTA FÖR FÖRFATTARE Á LA ESCUCHA DE LOS AUTORI
MIA KAPΔIA ΓIA ΣΥΓΓΡΑΦΕΙΣ UN CUORE PER AUTORI ET HJERTE FOR FORFATTERE EEN H.
SZERZŐINKÉRT SERCE DLA AUTORÓW EIN HERZ FÜR
VOOR SCHRIJVERS ACÃO BCEЙ ДУШОЙ К АВТОРАМ ETT HJÄRTA FÖR

The author

Kim Johnson attended day schools in Germany, UK
and Cyprus before becoming a boarder in the UK.
His childhood experiences planted the seed which
developed into an impressive career in education,
specialising in helping children with complex
needs. He held a wide variety of Head Teacher positions culminating in advising the government on
educational matters and ultimately becoming President of the National Association of Head Teachers.
He has three children and six grandchildren. He is
spending his retirement involved in charity work,
fishing and riding his Harley.

The publisher

*He who stops
getting better
stops being good.*

This is the motto of novum publishing, and our focus
is on finding new manuscripts, publishing them and
offering long-term support to the authors.
Our publishing house was founded in 1997, and since
then it has become THE expert for new authors and
has won numerous awards.

**Our editorial team will peruse each manuscript
within a few weeks free of charge and without
obligation.**

You will find more information about
novum publishing and our books on the internet:

w w w . n o v u m - p u b l i s h i n g . c o . u k